T0339996

"This book by Khan and Merritt is an important contribution to a complete (full) understanding of all factors that intervene in the phenomenon of migration and remittances. They cover a lot of important topics regarding migration that economists, because of their training, do not pay attention. The chapters include a lot of field work that Khan and Merritt have done during several years."

—**Dr. Jesus Cervantes**, Director, Statistics & Forum on Remittances in Latin America and the Caribbean Coordinator

"Khan and Merritt's book is an exciting contribution to our understanding of remittances. Remittances have grown in importance over the decades. Even as the flow of people has decreased in many countries, the flow of money has not. This book also helps explain why that is the case. They focus on two pairs of countries: Saudi Arabia-India and USA-Mexico, which have long been among the most important corridors for flow of money. This book is a great addition to the literature and a must read for anyone wanting to understand voluntary action, civil society in these contexts."

—**Dr. Shariq Siddiqui**, Assistant Professor of Philanthropic Studies Director, Muslim Philanthropy Initiative, Lilly Family School of Philanthropy Muslim Philanthropy Initiative

"Amidst the alarming discrepancy between the empirical and complex realities of migration and its perception by the general public, politicians, and policymakers, the publication of this book on remittances behavior based partly on migrants' own narratives is particularly timely. Writing beyond the usual lens of macroeconomic policy, governance, and security that reduce remittances to dehumanized and decontextualized flows of money, the authors tell a 'story of remittances' from below, that is, from the perspective of anonymous migrants who, through their remitting behavior, contribute to changing the socio-economic fabric of receiving communities. Readers will find in this book a sophisticated and nuanced examination of remittances and hopefully new avenues for future inquiries."

—**Dr. Hamza Safouane**, Postdoctoral Research Fellow at the Institute for Migration Research and Intercultural Studies (IMIS)—Osnabrück University, Germany

Remittances and International Development

This is a first of its kind book which examines the remittances in the two largest corridors in the World: India-Saudi Arabia and Mexico-U.S.A.

This book aims to treat remittances as an act of social norm involving individuals, nation-states, and diaspora communities. It treats remittances both as an act of individual obligation as well as a social fact that needs to be understood from the perspective of the actors, i.e., the givers and recipients. Using theories of motives of giving, policy analysis, international development, and international relations, the authors offer a compelling narrative of how and why remittances occur and the impacts on both the giver and recipient. The authors—both scholars of philanthropy and remittances—bring their shared perspective and understanding of this crucial phenomenon and delve deep into examining its impacts on community development and the relations between the nation-states. This book offers a sophisticated understanding of how vital remittances are to the world we live in.

The book sheds light on this important social reality and will be of value to researchers, academics, and students interested in remittances, as well as to practitioners working in the international development sector, NGO actors, and policy makers.

Sabith Khan is the Program Director (Master of Public Policy and Administration) and Assistant Professor in the School of Management, California Lutheran University, Thousand Oaks, CA, U.S.A.

Daisha M. Merritt is the Associate Department Chair of the Department of Management and Technology in the College of Business at Embry-Riddle Aeronautical University, Worldwide, U.S.A.

Routledge Studies in the Management of Voluntary
and Non-Profit Organizations
Series Editor: Stephen P. Osborne
University of Edinburgh, UK

Voluntary and non-profit organizations are playing an increasingly significant role, worldwide, in the provision and management of public services. Drawing together significant and ground breaking research, this series will be essential reading for students of public policy and management as well as the thinking manager. Topics covered include the management of innovation and change, financial management, performance evaluation and management and organizational development and project management.

Remittances and International Development
The Invisible Forces Shaping Community
Sabith Khan and Daisha M. Merritt

Also available from Routledge

Financial Management in the Voluntary Sector
New Challenges
Paul Palmer and Adrian Randall

Strategic Management for Nonprofit Organizations
Roger Courtney

Regulating Charities: The Inside Story
Edited by Myles McGregor-Lowndes and Bob Wyatt

Philanthropy in Practice
Pragmatism and the Impact of Philanthropic Action
Ekkehard Thümler

Transformational Leadership and Not for Profits and Social Enterprises
Edited by Ken Wiltshire, Asatha Malhorta, and Micheal Axelsen

Remittances and International Development
The Invisible Forces Shaping Community

Sabith Khan and Daisha M. Merritt

Routledge
Taylor & Francis Group
NEW YORK AND LONDON

First published 2021
by Routledge
605 Third Avenue, New York, NY 10017

and by Routledge
2 Park Square, Milton Park, Abingdon, Oxon OX14 4RN

First issued in paperback 2022

Routledge is an imprint of the Taylor & Francis Group, an informa business

Copyright © 2021 Taylor & Francis

The right of Sabith Khan and Daisha M. Merritt to be identified as authors of this work has been asserted by them in accordance with sections 77 and 78 of the Copyright, Designs and Patents Act 1988.

Publisher's Note
The publisher has gone to great lengths to ensure the quality of this reprint but points out that some imperfections in the original copies may be apparent.

British Library Cataloguing-in-Publication Data
A catalogue record for this book is available from the British Library

Library of Congress Cataloging-in-Publication Data
A catalog record for this book has been requested

ISBN: 978-0-367-52188-2 (pbk)
ISBN: 978-1-138-34441-9 (hbk)
ISBN: 978-0-429-43853-0 (ebk)

DOI: 10.4324/9780429438530

Typeset in Sabon
by Apex CoVantage, LLC

For my parents, who brought me into this world & showed me how to be charitable my uncle, Aṇwar Khan, the most generous remitter of money I have known my wife, Fabiola Lara, for her constant support and love
—Sabith Khan

To my family for coming along on this journey of life with me and to my mentors, without whose guidance I never would have been on this academic line of inquiry path I am today.
—Daisha M. Merritt

Contents

Figures

Photos

Graphs

Tables

Acknowledgments

There are far too many individuals who have helped shape this book, both in form and content. We would like to take the time to thank a few key individuals and institutions who have contributed in making this book a reality.

Sabith Khan

This book was in my mind even before I knew what the word 'remittance' meant. As someone growing up in India, during pre-liberalization India, I recall receiving calls from my uncle in the U.S. His long-distance phone calls, which were sometimes about the money that he sent to my relatives—through my mother—were the first education I received in the phenomenon of remittances. I grew up with the understanding of remittances as a family obligation, as something many people who had left 'home' did. As a migrant myself, I have experienced this over the years and have a much deeper understanding of this phenomenon. Family ties, social obligations, individual dreams—all these come together in this phenomenon called 'remittance' and makes it a fascinating lens to view the migrant experience.

* * * * * * * *

I would like to thank my graduate assistants Gagandeep Kaur, Reza Javadzadeh, Josiah Gonzales, and Darshika Jitendra Limbachiya for their help in conducting background research. Over a period of more than two years, they have at various points contributed in significant ways to furthering this research project.

A small grant from The Institute for Humane Studies, George Mason University in summer 2018 helped me attend a conference in Mexico. I subsequently conducted interviews during that trip.

Dr. Lon Otto at the Iowa Summer Writers Workshop and my fellow workshop participants taught me the importance of a good narrative.

Dr. Jesus Cervantes of CEMLA, Mexico City, Mexico has been a kind and welcoming figure, always ready to share insights on remittances to

Mexico. Through him, I met some other wonderful people who have been generous with their time and insights. The most significant one is Mr. Hugo Cuevas-Mohr, a veteran of the remittances business and the founder of International Money Transfer Conferences.

Dr. Rafael Reyes and his assistant Ms. Jiceel Luis from the Instituto Tecnologico de Oaxaca, Mexico were kind enough to introduce me to several individuals and helped with interviews in Oaxaca. Dr. Sylvia Alicia accompanied me on several interviews and I am grateful for her help. I would also like to acknowledge Yvonne Padilla for her insights and in connecting me with interviewees, many of whom were her colleagues.

Dr. Dhanu Raj of the Center for Public Policy and Research, Kochi, India helped us place the context of remittances in Kerala. Conversations with my childhood friend Dunston Noronha helped formulate and bring some clarity to the remittances and disaster relief phenomenon. Leaders of various Malayalee Associations in the U.S. were also generous with their time and insights.

Cal Lutheran University, my employer, deserves acknowledgment for the Faculty and Creative Works Grant (FRCW) that I received in 2018. This grant of $5000 helped me make trips to Mexico and India for data collection. My colleagues at Cal Lutheran have been very supportive during the writing of this book. Special thanks to Dr. Jamshid Damooei, who is a true teacher and mentor to many of us.

Thanks are due to my friends and co-researchers: Dr. Hamza Safouane who has helped me understand the complexities of migration in a much more nuanced manner. Dr. Andrew Schoeneman, who has been a collaborator on a few academic projects. Dr. Shariq Siddiqui, for his critical insights on the study of philanthropy and remittances. Dr. Ming Hu from Nanjing University for helping me think about civil society and related issues in Asia.

My friends in Mexico City: Paula Sánchez Mejorada Ibarra and Homero Garza Teran for their insights, conversations, and company. You have taught me a lot about your beautiful country and I am grateful.

As always, I am grateful to all my teachers—especially Dr. Mehrzad Boroujerdi and Dr. Joyce Rothschild from Virginia Tech and Dr. Peter Frumkin from UPenn, who remain mentors to this day.

Much gratitude to my own family: my brother Saif, my uncle Anwar Khan, my wife Fabiola Lara, and her parents, who have shared multiple stories spanning generations on how remittances have shaped their own lives and that of others around them.

Finally, I owe thanks to all the dozens of people around the world who spoke with me and shared their stories and insights on what remittances meant to them and their families, friends, communities.

Daisha M. Merritt

With the coming together of this manuscript and a reflection on the time and effort spent creating the words you are about to read, it is with the sincerest gratitude that I would like to thank my co-author for encouraging me to embark on this written endeavor and, truth be told, shepherding me along the way. Writing a book and one of this importance has always been a goal, though it was never idealized in my mind as such an undertaking as it has been. Dr. Khan has without a doubt been the driving force, the manager, and the networker of this endeavor.

I reiterate the above thanks to the amazing researchers, travelers, money followers, and do-gooders that have elevated this book to where it is today and furthermore have raised my internal knowledge and understanding of remittances.

And finally, thank you to my family who supported me on this journey and put up with my nighttime typing adventure. With love and thanks, you are my all-time supporters.

Foreword

Remittances are indeed a major reason for human migration in the later decades of the 20th century and the beginning of the 21st century. As humans, we have migrated since we began our existence, moving from Africa and spreading throughout the inhabitable lands of this planet Earth. When did our ancestors begin reaping the benefits of the riches they found in distant lands and begin to send valued items, maybe gold, precious stones, or coins, to their families back home?

As communication became easier, as value-transfer networks became trusted, as the knowledge of distant lands became inspiring and travel opened up, we began to see the movement of vast amounts of people from place to place. For cultural reasons, some people felt the need and obligation to send money home, to support the families back home, and whole economic structures gave rise to a remittance industry that has grown with regulations, technology protocols, with challenges and opportunities still evolving. Politics are impacting more and more the different ecosystems as migration fears and electoral populism discourses abound.

But why the need to send remittances? Why they are so resilient? What motivations are so interesting, complex, and intriguing? How do love, obligation, identity, and altruism drive remittances forward? These and dozens of questions need to be answered, discussed, researched and this book certainly has inspired me, well beyond my initial expectations.

Hugo Cuevas-Mohr

Director, International Money Transfer & Cross-border
Payments Conferences (IMTC), Miami, U.S.A.

1 Introduction

Purpose of the Book

"The amount of remittances sent back by migrants is three times the size of International development aid."
(Hudson Institute's Index of Global Philanthropy, 2016)

You must have heard this fact stated several times, from the World Bank or many of the think tanks such as the Hudson Institute, which produce research on remittances. This fact, which has become a lodestar for many who advocate individual action, is not intended to discourage international aid from the U.S. Despite the cuts to aid from the U.S. since the election of Mr. Trump, we remain, albeit with less influence, a major donor internationally. Americans have given over $400 billion in philanthropy to causes ranging from children's education, healthcare, post-disaster recovery, etc. Remittances sent by migrants support many of the economies that are recovering from a disaster or war. They are the lifeline that sustains families.

This book brings together some of the emerging ideas and debates in remittances from multiple perspectives. It is a synthesis of existing research as much as it is taking a step further in theorizing what remittances *mean* to the senders and receivers and also what impact they have on communities. We aim to offer a synthesis of existing theories of remittances and a clearer narrative of remittances. Given the overall scope, collection from various data sources, and rich discussion contained within this book, we believe that the reader will find the content fresh and valid, spurring further research and discourse on remittances.

While an ever increasing amount of quantitative data is being generated by the World Bank and its affiliates around the world, one can see that there is not a lot of theorizing about this phenomenon. There are few agencies or scholars who are asking how migrants, remittance senders, are making sense of this phenomenon and what long-term impact remittances have on their families, communities. In addition there is also not a lot of focus on the externalities of remittances—both positive and negative. As observers and participants in this phenomenon of remittances, we are intrigued by what all of this *means*—to the participants and their communities back home. We are also aware of scholarly analyses of some negative externalities of remittances, but wanted to delve deeper into the nuances of this phenomenon.

Serendipity and conversations with individuals working in this space has as much to do with this book as a deep interest in understanding migration and its impacts on remittances. We are both scholars of philanthropy and remittances. Our initial theorizing led to a paper which we have included in this book.

The Untold Story of Remittances

Existing scholarly work on the subject of remittances is not read widely. Policy-related documents are read by practitioners and scholars who study policy issues and often end up in some news reports. We believe that there is a need for both the practitioners-produced literature on remittances such as that emanating from the World Bank and think tanks (CEMLA in Mexico City, etc.) and existing academic research to help us understand this multifaceted phenomenon.

What we have attempted in this book is to tell a *more complete story* of remittances. While data from financial institutions and statistics may illuminate and point out the ups and downs of what is going on in terms of employment figures, remittances flow, and the like, the numbers are not able to capture the *why* of a phenomenon. We are particularly interested in why something happens—in the case of remittances—and for this, we have sought to build on the narratives. To achieve this, we referenced various forms of data including qualitative, observational, and quantitative. We have been agnostic as far as a particular leaning, in terms of methodology or the kind of data gathered.

As Steve Almond points out in his book *Bad Stories* (2018),

> stories are the basic unit of human consciousness. The stories we tell and the ones we absorb, are what allow us to pluck meaning from the rush of experience. Only through the patient interrogation of these stories can we begin to understand where we are and how we got here.
>
> (Almond, 2018, p. 6)

Almond goes on to explain that it is "hard to be a human being because humans have anxieties and unmet desires that we are trying to manage" (p. 6). He suggests that one way we do this is by telling stories that help us manage and endure our feelings, which tell us not to be ruled by our worst impulses. We are in other words, trying to tell *good* (and more comprehensive) stories of remittances.

The story of remittances, we believe, has not been told comprehensively. While annual reports from think tanks and similar agencies offer number crunching and an analysis of trends in remittances, they do not offer a comprehensive picture of the context of why remittances are the way they are. In other words, the narrative of remittances is incomplete. While we are not suggesting or implying that these existing stories of remittances are false by any means, we certainly argue that they are incomplete.

Our modest attempt has been to add to this narrative meaning the missing pieces, to synthesize the theories and data, toward making this narrative complete. We suggest that a more complex and nuanced narrative is needed to understand the phenomenon of remittances. Taking a longer view and using a multi-disciplinary lens is crucial for this complex narrative to emerge.

The State of Remittances: An Introduction

The World Bank offers fairly comprehensive data at the national level. However, this data only captures the estimates from known and official channels of remittances such as through banks, remittance transfer companies, etc. However, as many scholars have pointed out, this is not the complete picture. With a sector where 90% of the transactions take place in cash, it is hard to make a claim that this data would capture all, if not most of the remittances sent.

We approach any data source with some skepticism knowing these facts and while also being aware that the narrative of remittances is far more complex than what any one source can offer. This humility and awareness of the limitations of what data tells us is crucial for building a more comprehensive understanding (see Table 1.1).

The World Bank estimates show that remittances are on an upward trend, having reached over $500 billion USD (see Table 1.1). This increase

Table 1.1 Estimated remittances from the United States, 2010–2018 (Estimated, Billions of U.S. Dollars)

	2010	2011	2012	2013	2014	2015	2016	2017	2018
Mexico	21.69	23.17	22.81	22.59	24.00	24.32	28.10	30.02	34.70
China	11.40	13.31	13.07	15.15	15.85	16.25	15.41	16.14	14.52
India	9.37	10.86	11.96	11.11	11.19	10.96	10.66	11.71	12.73
Philippines	9.33	10.00	10.60	9.08	9.65	9.68	10.54	11.10	11.42
Vietnam	4.70	4.88	5.68	6.22	6.81	7.45	6.68	7.73	8.33
Guatemala	3.78	4.03	4.40	4.87	5.28	5.98	6.76	7.72	8.49
Nigeria	5.92	6.14	6.13	5.73	5.74	5.67	5.67	6.19	7.28
El Salvador	3.09	3.29	3.56	3.63	3.87	3.99	4.19	4.61	4.87
Dominican Republic	2.71	2.87	2.73	3.34	3.58	3.83	4.09	4.59	5.05
Honduras	2.30	2.50	2.58	2.74	2.94	3.26	3.37	3.77	4.06

can be linked to increased economic growth in the United States and also a rebound in infrastructure from Russia and some Gulf Nations (World Bank, 2019). To further emphasize the increased flow of remittances in low- to middle-income countries, money transfers have become the largest source of foreign monetary exchanges, surpassing foreign direct investment (with the exception of China).

Within the context of this book, we focus on the inflows of remittances. Our targeted discussion and analysis is offered using USD currency. And we discuss money transfers as whole dollars as well as a percentage of GDP. Given the domestic U.S.A. lensing, we offer data on United States remittance outflows. And from available 2017 data, the United States remains the largest contributor to remittances, recording $68 billion USD in remittance outflows. To further emphasize the amount of monies recorded that flow from the U.S.A., the next highest contributors are the United Arab Emirates and Saudi Arabia, at $44 billion USD and $36 billion USD, respectively. There seems to be a tie between economic growth, migration, multinational enterprises and ventures and remittance flows.

What Trends Are We Seeing Around the World?

There are some trends that stand out to us, as we look at the data emerging from the countries we examine (see Table 1.2). For one, there has been an increase, not decrease of remittances. In the case of Mexico, there has been an increase in remittances reaching Mexico, despite there being a fall in the number of migrants coming to the United States. Scholars and observers of Mexico point out that this could be due to the fact that the quantity of remittances have increased over the past few years, despite stricter enforcement of immigration laws and a general fear of migration among youth in Mexico, who are more likely to make the trek to the U.S.

Table 1.2 Ten largest remittance corridors, 2018

Sending Country	Receiving Country	Remittance Estimate ($billions)
United States	Mexico	34.7
United Arab Emirates	India	18.53
Hong Kong	China	16.34
United States	China	14.25
United States	India	12.74
Saudi Arabia	India	11.67
United States	Philippines	11.43
United States	Guatemala	8.49
United States	Vietnam	8.33
United States	Nigeria	7.27

Source: The World Bank, 2018 Bilateral Remittance Matrix

Remittances flowing into India have seen a significant rise over the last year. India is the top recipient of remittances worldwide, reaching over $78 billion USD in 2018 according to the World Bank. These monies come from a variety of diaspora Indian migrants, concentrated in the Gulf region, U.S.A., UK, and Canada. Interestingly, India received more than 50% of its total remittance from the Gulf region. Remittances play an integral role in the economy of India. Recent increases in remittances to India may also be linked to humanitarian aid, for example in the recent floods in the southern Indian state of Kerala, outpouring of disaster relief aid may account for some of the increase to remittance inflows in India.

Overall, remittances are on the rise and further predicted to increase steadily. However, public policy ventures and proposals also play an integral role in shaping the current state and future of remittances. The policy that surrounds the private transfers of money is not standardized nor are they limited to a single type of transaction or location of the transaction. Policy enactments have trends and tend to be politically bound in their foundation, use, and conception. We aim to further diagnose and deduce the implications that policy has on the nations of Mexico and India in relation to remittances.

Changing Policy Landscape

Remittances are largely an unregulated phenomenon. While there are banking laws and regulations that have made it harder for people to remit money through banks, there are newer forms and technologies of remittances such as blockchain that are completely changing the way that remittances are being sent.

A report by the Congressional Research Service (2019) titled *Remittances: Background and Issues for Congress* discusses the need for increasing regulation of remittances, which total over $56 billion from the U.S. This report indicates, "At the same time, additional regulatory requirements, such as consumer protection requirements included in the *Dodd-Frank Wall Street Consumer Protection Act*, may raise concerns about the compliance costs for remittance providers and consumers." It also admits that the receiving end of the remittances are countries with low or non-existent regulations, which may lead to misuse of funds and possible 'financing of terrorism.'

Pointing to existing norms of remittances, the report indicates that a major goal of existing policy on remittances is to "increase the attractiveness of regulated remittance systems to potential remittance customers, without regard to their legal status," meaning that even undocumented workers from Mexico and Central America are able to remit. Some members of Congress have asked for a crackdown on this phenomenon, the report mentions.

The CRS report points to the growing Indian, Chinese, and Philippine diaspora as being the cause of the dramatic increase of remittances in the past two decades.

> Between 2000 and 2014, remittances to developing countries in East Asia and Pacific increased by 370%, growing from $17 billion in 2000 to $79 billion in 2014. In South Asia, remittances increased by 571% over that time, growing from $17 billion in 2000 to $116 billion in 2014. Despite accounting for a much smaller amount of global remittances, flows to Sub-Saharan Africa increased by 608% from 2000 ($5 billion) to 2014 ($34 billion).
>
> (CRS, 2019)

As one can see, this significant amount of money has drawn the attention of both scholars and practitioners who seek to understand how this money is used and what target areas this money could be used towards. The significant jump in remittances could slow down depending on how the oil-rich economies of Middle Eastern nations perform in the years to come.

The discourse of 'financial inclusion' has become prevalent when it comes to remittances and financial institutions including banks that are looking at remittances as a way of bringing the unbanked into the banking and financial system (CRS, 2019). The CRS report also mentions how credit union participation has also been encouraged by the World Council of Credit Unions International Remittance Network.

As far as regulation of remittances is concerned, standards and norms set by the Financial Action Task Force (FATF) and the Bank for International Settlement (BIS) are usually followed. The focus of American federal laws is mainly to prevent money laundering and also combating financing of terrorism (CRS, 2019).

All of these policies and norms of regulations are emerging in contexts of increasing domestic polarization, increasing xenophobia among host countries towards foreigners (Almond, 2018). As Steve Almond points out, in the 1950s, just 10% of American voters had negative feelings towards the other political party. However, today, that number is at 90%. He further adds that those who hold "very unfavorable" views of the other party have gone up three times. This change in attitudes and polarization can be seen not just in the U.S. but is also reflected in movements such as Brexit, anti-immigration policies, and *Saudization*, *Emiratization*, and similar initiatives that have sought to replace foreign labor with domestic workers. These measures that have become government policy have the potential to dramatically change the status quo with regards to remittances.

There have been debates, for instance, on starting a remittance tax, which is similar to the one that exists in Oklahoma and across the country. This measure has been met with limited success. Mr. Donald J. Trump proposed such a measure recently, during his attempts at building the border wall with Mexico and suggested that the revenues that would derive from such a measure would help fund the building of the border wall (Trump, 2017). This plan was subsequently shelved, but even the fact that it was taken as a serious proposal shows that the government is aware of and wants to use the potential of remittances towards its own objectives such as the building of a wall on the U.S.-Mexico border.

Securitization of Remittances: The Dominant Discourse in Policy That Needs Change

In a post-9/11 world, there were several new regulations and changes to existing norms of money flows, mainly aimed at reducing money laundering and the financing of terrorism. As Edwina Thompson and other scholars have pointed out, this singular focus—of viewing flows of money that were not through formal channels—as somehow illegal and leading to bad outcomes has stymied the entire lens through which remittances are viewed.

Thompson argues that the traditional ways of sending money, doing business, based on individual trust—as in the case of the *hawaladars*—in some parts of the world is hard to replace. The fact that informal ways of sending money has existed for centuries and technology has only recently entered this landscape is important to bear in mind. There is no tabula rasa, or blank slate, when it comes to remittances. We agree with Thompson's assessment that societies develop their own norms of doing business and what infrastructure has existed for centuries, cannot be replaced in a year or even ten years.

In this book, we focus on delving deeper into the norms, values, and traditions which make migration possible. This is a point that Thompson emphasizes, rather than purely focusing on the dichotomous perspective of looking at remittances as a ritual, devoid of rationality (Thompson, 2011; Grabher & Stark, 1997).

In a 140-page report published in 2017, the Charity & Security Network, a Washington D.C.-based organization, pointed out several issues that U.S.-based nonprofits were facing in regards to accessing financial services in countries around the world. As the report points out, a few key points stand out:

- Two-thirds of U.S. nonprofits that work overseas face difficulties accessing financial services
- Delays in wire transfers impact more than 37% of nonprofits and these can be prolonged, sometimes over months

- More than one-third of the nonprofits have experienced increased fees and 26% have faced increased documentation requests

(Eckert, Guinane, & Hall, 2017)

The report highlights what is well known to scholars and observers of remittances in general—that the U.S. government and its agencies have taken the 'derisking' perspective and avoided or terminated relationships in contexts where there is a risk of running short of regulatory requirements. The report adds that there have been instances of lifesaving assistance being delayed or stopped due to inability to transfer funds to countries such as Somali and Syria and other conflict zones. "Banks under pressure to comply with AML/CFT regulatory expectations and sanctions have delayed or denied financial transfers and closed accounts complicating the delivery of aid" (p. v). The authors go on to add that nonprofits are treated as high-risk and are forced to use other non-transparent mechanisms as a result of the delays. These delays are particularly problematic given the scale of issues facing humanitarian aid agencies, with increased numbers of refugees and migrants fleeing to safety.

There is also call for greater leadership in policy-making, as this is seen as a gap that needs to be filled. The authors point out that inaction can be costly both for nonprofits as well as the recipients of this aid, often the most vulnerable people in the world.

The authors have a few recommendations that include a) launching a solutions-oriented stakeholder dialogue; b) updating the "bank examination manual and bank examiner training," to re-educate the bankers that NGOs are not by nature high risk; c) creating a special banking channel for humanitarian crises; d) instituting safe harbor protections—that would safeguard NGOs in case some of their money does end up in the wrong hands. This is crucial as compliance costs increase dramatically, as one does business in conflict and post-conflict zones.

The report also advocates use of non-formal alternatives such as Bitcoin, virtual currencies, mobile money, and similar technologically driven tools. This would make remittances faster, less expensive, and also—once there is regulation in place—safer.

The Role of Remittances in Development

We place the phenomenon of remittances in the realm of voluntary action. However, it is also an activity that is bound by tradition, family obligations, etc. in some cases; so it is not a purely 'voluntary action' for the common good or 'philanthropy,' as Payton and Moody would define it (Payton & Moody, 2008). Writing about the urge to help one's own family or friends or strangers in a different land, they ask: "How do we justify intervening philanthropically in another's country affairs to provide philanthropic assistance?" (p. 2). They offer a partial reason saying that organizations and philanthropists such as George Soros made it their business to help the weak and vulnerable but there were others who did so for political and economic reasons.

The questions they ask about meaning and mission of philanthropy are important, given the way in which modern life is structured. We need to ask the question "why do we exist?" to get to the heart of the meaning of philanthropy, they suggest.

We, similarly, argue that to get to the heart of remittances behavior, we need to probe beyond the notions of tradition, family obligations, community or national-level obligations to think of how people think of their roles and relationships, at a distance. We are as much interested in the praxis of remittances as in the way in which people conceptualize and talk about it. The practices of remittances are varied and different across national boundaries and each nation-state has sought to increase its flow, or restrict it, depending on the macroeconomic policies of the sending and receiving country.

Individual Choice, Collective Obligations?

Scholars such as Rinduss, Piotrowski and Faust have pointed out that longitudinal studies show that "intra-family exchanges are influenced by marital status, the presence of children, having parents in the origin household, and having siblings depart from it." The obligations that many migrants have towards their families vary over a period of time and are not stable, as many people assume. This leads to a change in dynamics between the migrant and his or her family and community. Similarly, Litwaik's notion of an 'extended kin family' could be useful to understand remittances behavior, these authors suggest (Litwaik, 1960; Rinduss, Piotrowski, Entwisle, Edmeades & Faust, 2012).

Other research in this area has yielded the 'decay hypothesis,' which suggests that the amount of remittances that migrants send to the country of their origin is inversely related to the amount of time that they are in the host country, meaning that the longer they are in a new country, the lesser they are likely to remit (Bettin & Lucchetti, 2012; Brinkerhoff, 2014).

Remittances' volume around the world is estimated to be three times the volume of international aid, according to the Hudson Institute and the World Bank.

Why Focus on These Two Pairs of Countries?

Why did we pick these two pairs of countries, among all the others? The short answer is that U.S.A.-Mexico and Saudi Arabia-India represent among the most significant countries *by volume*, in terms of remittances. However, these four countries are at the heart of many debates around migration and flows of money.

As the world's preeminent destination for technological innovation and change, the U.S. is one of the leaders in regulations and norm setting. The U.S. has also played a key role in shaping the global standards in managing financial flows.

In addition, these two pairs of countries were also chosen as a convenience sample, to illustrate some of the major trends in this sector—and while not entirely representative of the population, they represent some of the major trends in remittance activity, both at the government levels as well as individual behavior.

Methodology and Data

We have used a mixed-methods approach to data collection and analysis. While some chapters contain data from the World Bank, which is largely quantitative, we have supplemented this with interviews with various stakeholders including—but not limited to—return migrants, migrants in a country, and also policy makers and advocates who work in the space of remittances. We were fortunate to have interacted with several individuals who were forthright and open, in terms of sharing their insights. This, combined with the process of snow-balling, helped us reach the required number of people, to reach 'theoretical saturation.'

We believe this process of iterative data collection and analysis, combined with a keen awareness of what is missing, in terms of data, was critical for us to complete the process of data collection and analysis. This process, which is largely inductive, is helpful in building theory and offering better explanations of what we are witnessing about the phenomenon of remittances.

Chapter-wise Breakdown—Summary of Each Chapter

This section offers a chapter wise breakdown of what we attempted and how this book is laid out.

In **Chapter 2**, we examine the motivations to send and receive money. We ask simple questions: Why do people send money to their friends, families, or other relatives, in the country of their origin? How long do they send this money for, and under what conditions do they stop doing this? This set of questions yielded some interesting and surprising answers. As scholars and observers of the phenomenon of remittances, we were pleasantly surprised by the range of answers we found—both in scholarly literature as well as the empirical data that is produced by organizations such as the World Bank, among others.

As Lucas and Stark point out in their seminal paper, the most important motive for people to send remittances is pure altruism (1985, p. 903). Lucas and Stark test three theories of possible motivations in the context of a single country and suggest that there is either pure altruism or self-interest or perhaps a need to return to the country in dignity, which is also motivated by self-interest. What this implies is that there could be more than one motivation at play as a family unit manages this process of remittances.

Chapter 3, titled "Growth of Money Transfers: Theorizing Technology, Distance, and Money," deals with the ongoing technological changes and how they impact the sending and receiving of remittances. With the rise of firms such as MoneyGram, Western Union, and others that are based in Western nations and act as conduits of the transfer of money, we seek to examine how these firms act as bridges of connection. What role do they play, besides being pure agents of money transfer? Do they lobby the government for fairer and better regulations or do they seek to just profit from this basic need of millions, around the world, to send money to their loved ones? We seek to offer a theoretical perspective of this important component of the remittance landscape, in this chapter. Based on an in-depth analysis and interviews with individuals from the remittances sector, we offer a critical perspective that delves deep into relationship between technology, policy, and governance. Our goal is not to map the historical development of technology, but to offer a nuanced and sophisticated analysis of how technology, policy, and people come together to shape this field.

We offer insights from some of the leading practitioners and thinkers in this space and suggest that based on a close examination of the sector, there is reason to be optimistic. The technology-remittances space is one characterized by high innovation with policy catching up with the demand for greater regulation from all ends: from money transfer companies to banks. Even end-users are asking for some form of regulation when it comes to crypto remittances, as it would make it easier and safer for people to transfer money.

There are cases when unregulated forms of money transfer are the lifeline of the economy. Edwina A. Thompson, a researcher who has studied issues of trust extensively in the realm of *hawala*, arguably the oldest 'technology' of transfer of money, argues that trust is the backbone of any transfer of money. Thompson, whose research covers much of the ungoverned parts of the world, points to the widespread use of hawala in Iraq and refugee or internally displaced settlements across Africa and South Asia. She writes,

> In early 2005, after the tsunami wave hit Aceh, for example, money dealers reportedly established an emergency communications system using the *flexsi* local mobile network to help migrants locate their families and arrange for the delivery of funds through bank accounts or directly to the IDP camps themselves.
>
> (2011, p. 1)

This anecdote illustrates the manner in which trust, combined with existing technologies, saved the day for millions of people who would have remained stranded, without money, if not for this structure in place.

Chapter 4, titled "Remittances by the Numbers: How Much Is Sent and Where," provides a quantitative understanding of money transfers. This chapter offers the number lens from a purely hard data driven definition. We focus on inflows of money for Mexico and India while being cognizant of outflows from the U.S.

It is common knowledge among economists and those who study remittances that money transfers are at an all-time high (2019) and they total roughly three times more than International Development Aid, while also being the largest source of funding for many nations. But what are the regional and country-specific differences of sending money? This chapter seeks to paint a quantitative, data-driven landscape of remittances. We continue our focus on Mexico and India as receivers while creating a funnel-like journey through remittance data, beginning on a global scale, moving to a regional, and then discussing the individual nations. It is our hope that by offering this layout, you will be able to see the complexities and nuanced differences in remittance. And gain an understanding of the changes, impacts, and casualties of remittance giving.

The quantity of remittances varies across time and location; there are certain trends and policy angles that have shaped and continue to emerge. This chapter contextualizes these occurrences and provides a numbers-based answer to how remittances have evolved or devolved.

Data and discussion is derived heavily from the World Bank and the latest (2019) The Global Knowledge Partnership on Migration and Development (KNOMAD) report; data points are made available in an open-access format from the World Bank. We also utilized many reports from CEMLA and sought out data discussion from academic articles to further shape this chapter and the information included.

Chapter 5, titled "Policy and Remittances: Human Needs and the Shaping of Practice With Policy," focuses on the policies around remittances and giving. This chapter pays close and specific attention to Mexico and India, offering the two different lenses as a juxtaposition to understanding the complexities of remittances giving. We venture into the realm of governmental imposed policies and how humanitarian aid is policed, discussing the frameworks that have led to the current state of remittances while also outlining the impact that regulations have on remittances and delving into how policy shapes practice. Our aim for this chapter is to explore how remittances can play a critical role in public policy, attempt to deduce trends, and further the conversation of what changes need to take place.

Policy frameworks vary from country to country and at times from state to state, but the mere fact that remittances are a huge source of funding for many LMICs (low- to middle-income countries) spurs that conversation that there needs to be a useable, viable, and sustainable framework around money transfers. The age old debate of whether practice should develop policy or whether policy has the right to shape practice is echoed in this chapter's lensing. Furthermore, we delve into the delivery and methods of sending money with the differences in associated costs and in some areas that lack of competition resulting in inflated costs of sending. Coupled with this discussion is the overarching Sustainable Development Goals 2030 that aim for a more favorable global cost of sending money (aims are slated for 3%).

While a full policy analysis with situational awareness, alternatives, proposed solutions, and a final recommendation is not designed within this chapter, the next steps and a wonderful graduate project would be to dissect the trends in policy on a country-to-country basis, tracking similarities and divergences, seeking to offer a conceptualized internationalization strategy-based framework. However, for the purposes of this chapter we provide a foundational understanding of the policies present in Mexico and India while discussing the merits and implications.

In **Chapter 6,** titled "Discourse of Remittances: How It Shapes Praxis in India, U.S.A., and Mexico," we look at purely the discourses of remittances and how it shapes practices of migration. Do migrants influence the remittances behavior of others? How does the discourse of remittance shape the lives of those who are dependent on the money sent? We examine this as well as the sustainability of continued remittances—both the giving and receiving, using a *meta-analytic review* of published government policy documents and reports. This chapter delves into the social paradigm that is created through the remittance relationship. We also pay attention to the policy discourses of remittances and how it impacts practice.

We look at how the governments of India, Mexico, U.S., and Saudi Arabia have shaped the discourses around remittances in the recent past and how this is shaping the field as a whole. We suggest that given the key role of government in regulating this largely unregulated market, it is imperative that governments keep up with the ongoing rapid pace of innovation.

Discourses shape practices. This insight from various theorists guides our analysis of what each of the governments is going, as it grapples with this phenomenon of remittances, which has existed for centuries now. Will governments frame this as an 'unregulated' and 'illegal' market that needs taming or will the policies in each nation-state adapt to the needs of each of these societies? This remains an open question.

Chapter 7, titled "Case Study: India as a Receiver," examines one of the most significant sending-receiving pairs of U.S.-India. Using India and the U.S. respectively as paradigmatic examples of the largest recipient and sender respectively, we take a close look at the dynamics of how remittances came to be. This includes historical and sociological examination of this phenomenon. We look at the forces that shaped remittance behavior and future implications of policies. Through review of documents, interviews, this chapter relies heavily on the individual experiences of those sending remittances, while offering a 'big picture' of the phenomenon of remittances. The main questions answered here in this paper are: What factors shape remittances behavior in the U.S. and what specific policies by the U.S. government hinder/facilitate remittances? What factors make the U.S. the biggest sender of recipients and India the largest recipient of remittances? Also, how is the culture around remittances being shaped by recent changes in migration policy and attitudes towards migration, both in India and in the U.S.?

Chapter 8 deals with the remittances from Gulf nations to India. This remittance corridor is one of the most significant ones. The Gulf nations are oil rich but are facing a challenge that may alter the dynamics of migration (from South Asia) as well remittances. With changes in the economy and various strategic initiatives such as Vision 2030 in Saudi Arabia, we are likely to see a significant shift in labor demands in the years to come. Given how intimately migration is tied to remittances, any change in migration patterns is likely to impact remittances flow as well.

The 1960s and '70s saw the rise of oil- and natural gas-rich Persian Gulf nations, which acted as magnets for migrant workers seeking employment. The phenomenon of the guest worker has boomed since the late 1970s. With this, we have also seen the rise of remittances to South and Southeast Asia, where a majority of migrant workers are from. However, with falling oil prices and shifts in geopolitical significance, we are witnessing a potential realignment of the remittances landscape.

We offer an up-to-date analysis of how the changing economy in states such as Qatar and the Kingdom of Saudi Arabia, with the ongoing political and economic upheavals, might impact the remittances landscape and what it might mean for the recipient states. It is also worthwhile to examine how their own economies might change. As the resource-rich Gulf nations shift their positioning in the global landscape from being a magnet for fortune seekers and seek to become hubs of innovation, we are interested in understanding how this shift may impact the millions of people working there. This specifically implies those who are the primary remittance senders. We also examine whether nation-states have a role to play in this phenomenon?

Chapter 9—"Remittances as Subaltern Giving: The Case of Mexico"—offers a theoretical perspective of remittances.

Given that much of the writing and discourse of remittances is conducted from a policy or government lens, we have argued in this paper that there is a need for looking at remittances as a 'subaltern' phenomenon. We frame remittances as 'subaltern giving' or giving by the poor and marginalized towards other marginalized populations. Even though remittances are typically given to an 'in group,' there are instances when it exhibits philanthropic characteristics such as addressing the 'common good.' We critically examine how remittances can be seen as a new form of solidarity among people who are marginalized.

This new perspective which moves beyond economic rationality and seeks to examine this behavior in terms of 'community of practice' (Page, 2012) has not been explored and examined in much depth. We frame the theory of remittances as a theory of praxis and offer a mid-range theory, using a Grounded Theory approach.

We argue that this perspective of examining remittances dispels many stereotypes and brings greater clarity to *why* people send money to their relatives or friends in the country of their origins. With this theorizing, based on 'mid-range theory' principles, using data is helpful in understanding what exactly is going on in these situations.

Chapter 10, titled "Remittances as a 'Soft Power'?: Examining the Power of Money-Flows Between Communities and Nation-States," seeks to understand the impact of remittances on nation-states. Remittances are flows of money that migrants send to their country of origin, from their country of residence. This phenomenon often is examined with the individual as the unit of analysis. In this paper, we take a different point of view—examining the countries of sending and receiving as the units of analysis. The objective of this exercise is twofold—to turn the focus on nation-states and to use concepts such as diplomacy and soft power to examine whether this lens can be used to understand remittances and its manifestations as a tool of diplomacy.

Given the rise of nationalistic rhetoric such as 'America first' and the 'Saudization' policy, whereby expatriates are being replaced by local Saudi nationals, the idea of immigration itself has come under attack. We seek to understand how remittances play in this mix, and what impact— if any—they have, on the way that national policies are impacted, as a result of remittances. We use the theoretical contributions of Joseph Nye (2010) and other international relations theorists to understand these concepts.

Chapter 11 concludes the book and offers some insights into future research and some of the limitations of the book. We offer some ideas on how these ideas can be implemented.

References

Adelman, C., Schwartz, B., & Riskin, E. (2016). *Index of Global Philanthropy and Remittances*. Washington, DC: Hudson Institute.

Almond, S. (2018). *Bad Stories: What the Hell Just Happened to Our Country*. Pasadena, CA: Red Hen Press.

Bettin, G., & Lucchetti, R. (2012). *Intertemporal Remittance Behaviour by Immigrants in Germany*. SOEPpapers 505.

Brinkerhoff, J. M. (2014). Diaspora philanthropy: Lessons from a demographic analysis of the coptic diaspora. *Nonprofit and Voluntary Sector Quarterly*, 43(6), 969–992.

CRS. (2019, Dec 2). *Remittances: Background and Issues for Congress*. Congressional Research Service. Accessible at https://crsreports.congress.govR43217

Eckert, S., Guinane, K., & Hall, A. (2017). *Financial Access for U.S. Nonprofits.* Washington, DC: Charity & Security Network.

Grabher, G., & Stark, D. (1997). *Organizing Diversity: Evolutionary Theory, Network Analysis and Post-Socialism: Legacies, Linkages and Loyalties.* Oxford: Oxford University Press. Pp. 1–23.

Litwaik, E. (1960). Litwak Eugene: Geographic mobility and extended family cohesion. *American Sociological Review*, 25(3), 385–394.

Lucas, R. E. B., & Stark, O. (1985). Motivations to remit: Evidence from Botswana. *Journal of Political Economy*, 93(5).

Nye, J. (2010). *The Powers to Lead.* Oxford University Press.

Page, B. (2012). Why do people do stuff. Reconceptualizing remittance behaviour in diaspora-development research and policy. *Progress in Development Studies*, 12(1), 1–18.

Payton, R., & Moody, M. (2008). *Understanding Philanthropy: Meaning and Mission.* Indianapolis. IN: Indiana University Press.

Rinduss, R., Piotrowski, M., Entwisle, B., Edmeades, J., & Faust, K. (2012, Mar). Migrant remittances and the web of family obligations: Ongoing support among spatially extended kin in Northeast Thailand, 1984–94. *Popul Stud (Camb)*, 66(1). Published online 2012 Jan 24. doi:10.1080/00324728.2011.644429

Thompson, E. (2011). *Trust Is the Coin of the Realm.* Oxford, UK: Oxford University Press.

Trump, D. (2017). *Pay for the Wall.* Accessible at https://assets.donaldjtrump.com/Pay_for_the_Wall.pdf. Retrieved on Dec 26, 2019.

World Bank. (2019). *Migration and Remittances Data.* Accessible at https://www.worldbank.org/en/topic/migrationremittancesdiasporaissues/brief/migration-remittances-data

2 Motivations to Send and Receive

Background[1]

Introduction

Why do people send money to their friends, families, or other relatives in the country of their origin? How long do they send this money for, and under what conditions do they stop doing this? These questions have been dealt with by many scholars. We have also written about this earlier and draw upon our earlier findings of a qualitative meta-synthesis of literature for this paper (Khan & Merritt, 2018).

While much of the study of remittances behavior occurs in the context of trying to understand it as a phenomenon of development, we suggest that there is a need to nuance this debate and look at it as a sociological phenomenon in its own right. Examining the discourses of international development, aid and related aspects is useful as we build our understanding of remittances. This tension between looking at remittances as an 'expressive' act versus that of examining this as an 'instrumental' act can be seen as a parallel to how Peter Frumkin describes the differences in philanthropic action (Frumkin, 2006). Expressive giving refers to giving to causes or issues where the donor has a personal investment and values invested in the act, whereas instrumental giving refers to a more rational and calculated giving, which may not be too personal and value driven. Several scholars have drawn parallels and contrasts with the phenomenon of remittances and philanthropy/international aid.

Czaika and Spray (2013) in their argument suggest that remittances are more stable than other forms of financial flow such as foreign direct investment, loans, etc. They also point to the work of other scholars such as Poirine (1997) who suggests that migrants send money to repay intergenerational loans. "Consequently, we would expect higher remittance volumes from short-term migrants. This has even led to calls for decreased regulation on temporary migration" (Ghosh, 2006), they suggest. We know, from various ethnographic and other studies that remittances is a complex phenomenon and the drivers of remittances are multiple: from being used for education, to paying off loans, to paying for marriages of relatives back home to even supporting aging parents.

Brown (1997) has suggested that in the case of Pacific Islands, controlling for structure of family ties, there is no 'decay hypothesis' when it comes to remittances, meaning that remittances do not come down over a period of time. Decay hypothesis refers to the notion of remittances going down over a period of time or 'decaying' as a result of loss of ties or attachment to the country of origin, as the migrant establishes himself/herself in the host country.

As Lucas and Stark point out in their seminal paper, the most important motive for people to send remittances is pure *altruism* (1985, p. 903). They test three theories of possible motivations in the context of a single country and suggest that there is either pure altruism or self-interest or perhaps a need to return to the country, in dignity, which is also motivated by self-interest. What this implies is that there could be more than one motive at play, as a family unit manages this process of remittances.

Lucas and Stark also point out that their findings mean that our understanding of a household as belonging to one specific socio-economic class is not accurate. They straddle both higher and lower economic spectrums: "they cease to be only peasants and workers and a hybrid peasant-worker group emerges" (p. 915). This understanding needs to be furthered in a world where there is increasing flow of people and money. The understanding of these complexities among policy makers and academics needs to increase as well.

In Section 1, we outline some major theories that have been proposed by others, while in Section 2, we offer an analysis of what this means for developing a better understanding, using our work in this area. In Section 3, we offer our conclusions and next steps.

Section 1: Existing Theories of Remittances and Giving

While philanthropy and giving of money is distinct from remittances, there are areas where they overlap. For instance, we suggest that similar to the phenomenon of philanthropy, that is driven by identification with the recipients, remittances are also driven by a similar logic. The identification in the case of remittances is far more immediate and bound by direct relations, familial or neighborhood. In the case of philanthropy, there is usually a degree of separation that could potentially make this identification a bit weaker.

As Lucas and Stark point out in their work, there is a strong notion of 'paying back' to one's family, either for the investment they made, in education or other such support, that the remitter would like to repay. They argue that without qualifying the altruistic aspect of remittances, there is no reason to believe that people send money only because they care. They argue that there could be 'tempered altruism' or "enlightened self-interest" at work here, meaning that the remitter is either tied in some practical ways with those who are receiving remittances and it may be that the remittances are helping keep this bond alive, whether it is just keeping up the familial ties, or even the remittance receiver and the sender having some mutually beneficial relationship.

In this section, we offer some insights into existing theories and what they point to, as forming the landscape of why remittances are sent and the motivations behind them. Note that some of the theories are drawn from 'philanthropic studies' and though scholars of philanthropy have not applied them to remittances, we suggest that there could be strong application, given the striking similarity and overlaps between the two phenomena. The boundaries between the two fields is quite clear, however; there is a need for an inter- and trans-disciplinary look at the phenomenon of remittances for us to understand how remittances function in our societies.

The Identification Model

There are many mechanisms that drive philanthropic giving (Bekkers & Wiepking, 2011). One of the major theoretical approaches to philanthropic giving is the 'identification model' as developed by Schervish and Havens (1997). Philanthropic giving, they argue, is fundamentally based on the idea that morality reaches beyond one's self. To be able to operationalize the factors that drive this morality, they propose five broad variables that drive giving. Communities of participation are the actual relationships one has; frameworks of consciousness refer to one's beliefs and values; direct requests directly evoke charitable contributions; models and experiences from one's youth shape philanthropic behavior in later life; discretionary resources are the objective and perceived resources which foster giving.

Below, we discuss the possible similarities and differences between philanthropic giving and remittances giving for each of those five factors.

Communities of Participation

The identification model states that the formal and informal relationships one has—in families, neighborhoods, schools, organizations, etc.—is the basis for philanthropic behavior. Diaspora giving is international by nature. In the host country, immigrants can be involved in ethnic organizations or informal groups around their ethnic origin which connect them to their home country. In the home country, migrants often have family and friends whom they contact and visit. Remittances are often hypothesized to decrease in time after the moment of migrating, although the evidence is mixed (Bettin & Lucchetti, 2012; Menjívar et al., 1998; Pozo & Amuedo-Dorantes, 2006; Lucas & Stark, 1985).

Motivations for Remittances

There has been a wide debate in many strands of the academic literature on the motivations to give remittances. Motives that are often distinguished are altruistic, exchange, strategic, insurance, and investment motives (Rapoport & Docquier, 2006).

Previous empirical studies are mostly case studies of a particular ethnic group in a particular country, which does not enable generalizable conclusions. Previous literature reviews have focused on the outcomes of remittances (Adams, 2010; Page & Plaza, 2006) and/or reviewed the macro- and micro-economic determinants, reviewing mostly studies that use survey data or financial statistics (Hagen-Zanker & Siegel, 2007; Rapoport & Docquier, 2006; Ruiz & Vargas-Silva, 2009; Russell, 1986). Those reviews have shed light on the quantitative evidence for different motivations of remittances that can be deducted from the available data.

However, given the large variety of research designs and research contexts in the literature on remittances, there is need for stronger theoretical ground to explain findings from quantitative and qualitative studies.

Our review takes a more in-depth approach. It reviews previous research not only to summarize previous findings, but also to compare them and to identify similarities, differences, and gaps.

Gender Dimension of Remittances: Family-Based Motivations to Send

The prevalent discourse around remittances is that male senders leave Mexico for other countries—predominantly the U.S., as the data suggests— and send money to their families. This discourse is flawed, suggests a new report by the Center for Latin American Monetary Services (CEMLA). This report, produced by CEMLA and a working group from Banorte and International Development Bank (IDB), sheds some insights on the gender aspects of remittances and also the motivations behind sending remittances (Cervantes, 2015).

The gender dimension is important as it offers new insights into who sends money to whom and why. While it was earlier conceived that the male senders of money would send it to their wives, data suggests that they send it to their parents in most cases, not their own children and spouses.

The change in the gender dynamics also complicates and nuances the discourse around remittances. The total percentage of female migrants is also increasing over the years, indicating a shift in the remittance pattern to Mexico, the world's fourth largest remittance receiving country after India, China, and Philippines (World Bank, 2015).

The percentage of women among immigrants has increased from 49.7% of the population in 2007 to 51.2% in 2013, the CEMLA report suggests. In 2013, the total percent of women in the U.S. was 51.2% of the total immigrant population, according to data from the American Community Survey (ACS), one of the most authoritative and credible sources of data on American demographics. Mexicans constitute about 28% of the total immigrant population in the U.S. and also constitute the single largest sending country from the U.S.

The biggest draw for women and men from Latin America to migrate to the U.S. is due to the wage differential. However, during the years 2007–13, there was a negative net migration into the U.S. from Mexico due to the following factors, the CEMLA report suggests:

- Low employment due to the recession
- The low demand in construction and manufacturing sectors, where a large number of Mexicans work
- Increased opportunities for work in Mexico, which may have encouraged Mexicans to stay
- A stronger border control policy which may have stopped many immigrants from coming to the U.S.

The CEMLA report also offers some insights into who the main beneficiaries are. Women are the main beneficiaries from the remittances sent. Women receive more than 71.7% of remittances sent from the U.S., with the recipients being mothers, sisters, and possibly daughters of women making these transfers (Cervantes, 2015, p. 28). This suggests a more family-based pattern of consumption, which has been theorized as one of the main motivations for sending remittances around the world.

The average amount of money sent is around $468, with the weekdays being the most significant in terms of sending remittances, the report suggests. Some other interesting findings that come out of this report are that the remittances are received more or less within a week of sending them, meaning that they were to be expected by the receiving party.

Status Hypothesis of Remittances

Mariano Sana, a professor of sociology, argues that remittances can be a way of gaining status and earning what they have lost, for the Mexican immigrant (Sana, 2005). While the move to the U.S. represents for many Mexicans a loss of social standing, status, comfort, and, in many cases, even loss of citizenship, the phenomenon of remittances can be a way of gaining some of this lost status. Sana has called this phenomenon 'status hypothesis' and seems to hold true in the case of Mexican immigrants.

Sana points to data from Bank of Mexico that between 1990 and 2004, the average rate of worker remittances tripled that of Mexican oil exports during the same period. This reached a total amount of $16.6

billion, equivalent to 78% of the total value of Mexican oil exports or 2.5% of its GDP.

Sana has argued that the increase in remittances can be seen as the combination of three factors: change in migration, in remitting propensity, as well as in the average amount of money sent. As he rightly points out, there was massive migration in the 1990s and this was mainly responsible for the growth of remittances. However, this has been changing, with the amount of remittances being sent also increasing, along with the remittances propensity. The macro effects of remittances are due also to economic conditions, how the government of Mexico makes policies regarding remittances and also outreach by Mexican groups and communities.

The phenomenon is also true in the case of Indian migrants who make the journey to Saudi Arabia and other oil-rich economies in search of better job prospects.

Assimilationist Theories of Migration and Remittances

There is a substantial body of literature that examines the change in remittances across generations or the impact of time and associated 'assimilation' in a host country (Stark, 1991; Khan, Merritt, & DeWit, forthcoming). This theorizing posits that there is a decrease in sending remittances over a period of time, or if there is no one that the migrant knows in the sending country. In other words, loss of social capital and connections in the host country reduces the amount of remittances.

This is contrasted with the assimilationist perspective. As Portes and DeWind point out, the formation of transnational communities that rely on the diaspora communities for development leads to them becoming powerbrokers of sorts (Portes & DeWind, 2004).

Many immigrants transfer money to relatives and friends in their country of origin, and they do so with considerable generosity. The World Bank estimates worldwide remittances between countries to be worth $441 billion USD (KNOMAD, 2016).

There are an increasing number of initiatives in the U.S. and Western world that are trying to involve diaspora communities to 'give back' to the countries of their origin. The U.S. State Department led diaspora initiatives (for example the International Diaspora Engagement Alliance) and those at the World Bank (for example the Global Remittances Working Group) are noteworthy, both in their scope and ambition. Given the conflicts in the Middle East and Africa, in particular the ongoing war in Syria and Iraq, there has been a lot of attention to this issue.

Research on remittances often focuses on the impact of private transfers to developing countries or on the role of those transfers in broader labor migration processes. There is growing interest in how 'mobile money' remittances and the intersection of technology and philanthropy can increase opportunities for the rural poor around the world (Munyegera & Tomoya, 2016). The role of household level giving and its impact on development has received a lot of attention among scholars (Erdal, 2012; Adams, 2010; Page & Plaza, 2006). Another stream of literature explores remitting as a sociological phenomenon with economic, social, and psychological determinants (Najam, 2006; Rapoport & Docquier, 2006; Lucas & Stark, 1985).

As Lacroix points out, the debate about belonging citizenship and the 'rights to have rights' has been a paradox of sorts in the European context. This is because states that do not follow or put emphasis on human rights norms are excluded from EU membership, but also, individuals who are denied full membership of European nation-states are denied these full constitutional protections (Lacroix, 2015). There is, it seems, an underlying tension in terms of how immigrants and migrants are conceptualized and their sociological behavior in the context of how they are to behave, as citizens and subjects of European nations. Notions of belonging, rights and duties are part of this discourse, though not explicitly spelled out in most studies.

Graphical exploration shows that transfers to family members decrease over time, whereas transfers to non-family members remains stable or increases after the moment of migrating. When controlled for age, income, and other background characteristics, results from regression models show that remittance giving initially decreases, but increases among migrants who live in the Netherlands for three decades or more, which contradicts earlier studies supporting the decay hypothesis (Bettin & Lucchetti, 2012; Pozo & Amuedo-Dorantes, 2006; Brown, 1997; Lucas & Stark, 1985).

People send money to their home country when they know someone out there and when they plan to return. This may reflect remittances giving as a way to participate in communities that include family and friends overseas. Our paper builds on the work of Page and Mercer (2012), who have argued that remittances are part of 'communities of practice' and not merely individual acts. While this is true, there are individual motives as well; that should be taken together with the social dimensions of sending and receiving money.

While remittances may be perceived as a form of philanthropy, donations to international aid organizations are to some extent different from remittances. If one's social network is concentrated in the country of residence, one is more likely to give to international aid organizations. International aid donations initially increase after migrating, but then decrease. This is a rather surprising finding which could be perceived as evidence that social integration fosters international transfers through more 'traditional' charitable organizations. Remittances often follow a combination of different 'scripts' (Carling, 2014), and it is difficult to distinguish specific remittance practices from broad survey measures.

Yet, our results suggest that there is a substantial prosocial component in international money transfers.

We must point out that the model of 'assimilation' versus 'integration' could be different in the American and European contexts, respectively. While the U.S. is seen as a 'salad bowl,' European integration is historically described as a 'melting pot' of cultures, especially where ideas of multiculturalism are dominant (Glazer & Moynihan, 1971). With the rise of nativist movements both in the U.S. and parts of Europe, it remains to be seen how these ideas of integration and assimilation will change over time.

Without essentializing this phenomenon or generalizing this trend, we can confidently assert that this sort of social capital can have a limited, if not major influence on the philanthropic efforts of these Afghan, Turkic, and other diaspora communities in The Netherlands. As Snel et al. (2006) points out, the challenge with the study of remittances to theorize about the whole field is very difficult, given that it may be impossible to carry out studies that cover the entire world. While empirically that may be a challenge, theoretically combining various assumptions and analyses to form a meta-theory of remittances remains a possibility. Reading of this philanthropic behavior through various forms of 'remittances scripts' is one way to theorize about the field, in addition to paying attention to the south-south dynamics of giving and alternative forms of economic rationality, as some researchers have pointed out (Pollard & Samers, 2011).

Further follow-up and continuation studies should be explored to determine if there are other underlying or group-related causes or correlations associated with the findings included in this study. It is the hope and plans of the authors to continue this line of inquiry delving further into motivation evidence related to remittance giving and specifically remittances as a form of philanthropic behavior internationally.

Weak Altruism?

Another 'mid-range' theory that is used to explain remittance motivations is that of 'weak altruism.' Brown (1997) suggest this theory, in which the children are seen as remitting to their parents as a form of repaying their debts to them (Adams, 2010). Their study shows that the level of remittances is positively correlated with the level of migrant income and the intention to return. Similarly, de la Briere et al. (2002) point to insurance as one of the main motives to remit among Dominican migrants. This is also the phenomenon observed among migrants from rural Mali, who remit more in the case of a death in the family or other natural calamities such as crop failure, etc. Adams (2010) raises the question that all of these studies have methodological weaknesses given that they either have the problem of omitted variable bias or sample selection biases.

Yang and Choi (2007) seem to have addressed this issue, by incorporating new innovations in their research design, Adams points out. Yang and Choi (2007) use rainfall as a natural experiment that causes a change in household income. Secondly, they use panel data from the Philippines to reduce the impact of time-observed data from households. These innovations are novel and can account for some of the changes noted. Their research reveals the insurance of one's income as primary motive to remit. Their research points to the fact that over 60% of declines in income are replaced by remittances (Adams, p. 814).

Section 2: What All of This Means

Identification Still Important, But in a More Complex Way

Identity, in the form of a hyphenated identity—whether it is Ghanaian-American, Indian-American, Chinese-American—is important for any form of diaspora remittances or philanthropy. When thinking about the difference between remittances and philanthropy, identification is seen in both respects (Figure 2.1), but there is ultimately a difference that emerged from the analysis. Without a conscious effort on part of the diaspora communities to engage in this form of identity creation, or the existence of pre-existing family ties, such giving does not occur; as the books demonstrate. Does the longing for one's identity increase the longer one

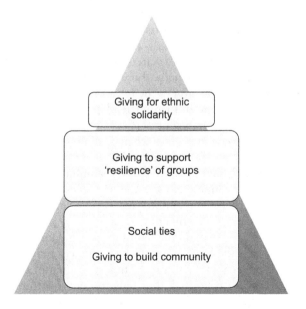

Figure 2.1 Hierarchy of motivations—remittances and philanthropy
Source: Implications for theory

lives in a different country? This question can be answered through using remittances and philanthropy as a metric. As our literature review has shown, there is mixed proof that giving decreases over a period of time. On the other hand, the process of 'identification' or the process of creating a new identity—in the adopted 'home'—and its impact on remittances and philanthropy has not been theorized much. We suggest, based on our analysis and our own research, that perhaps 'identification' is a continuum that *expands and contracts* over a period of time—and is extremely contextual. For instance, during times of crisis (such as a humanitarian disaster), the identification with one's own kin and people of one's country of origin goes up. There is reason to believe this is the case, as people give to causes that they identify with—from this framework—rather than to other causes. In the research of one of the researchers, he has seen this phenomenon playing out in more than one case.

Economic Impact of Remittances

In his exhaustive literature review of the economic impacts of remittances on developing countries economies, Adams (2010) points out the disparate methods and techniques that have been used to examine this phenomenon.

Adams cautions us that there is a distinction between studying remittances and migration and this distinction must not be conflated in any studies of remittances. We are cautious about conflating these phenomenon as well and have—in our empirical work—sought to make the distinction between the two phenomenon clear, while looking for how migration impacts remittances. These are interrelated and co-dependent phenomenon, which could, in some circumstances be conflated. Adams's review points to the fact that only about half the migrant households send remittances. A good portion of the remittances received are not necessarily from direct relatives, but from friends, extended family, etc. And this can be towards loan repayments, etc.

Adams points to some of the issues when dealing with remittances from a methodological perspective: simultaneity, reverse causality, selection bias, and omitted variable bias (p. 810). By simultaneity, here we mean phenomena that occur simultaneously. Adams suggests that the migration of the oldest male to a foreign country may occur simultaneously at the same time that the youngest member of the family may go to school. These variables both cause and explain the remittances behavior. By reverse causality, one means that the large amount of remittances may be because of the high level of poverty in a country. "Thus, any attempt to analyse the impact of remittances on poverty that fails to consider the reverse causality between these two variables might lead to erroneous conclusions" (p. 811). This also implies that one has to take into account the context in which this phenomenon is occurring, before we draw any conclusions.

Speaking of the 'omitted variable bias,' one can think of factors such as risk averseness or related factors. In addition, we hypothesize that factors such as awareness of the country of destination, cultural or diplomatic relations between the people of the countries and historical ties also play a significant role in how potential migrants and remitters see their role. In the context of the U.S.A., the election of Donald Trump is said to have increased remittances among certain migrants, as the migrants are feeling a sense of insecurity in their situation, given the migration policies in the U.S. These can also be considered variables that are not often considered in empirical analysis, but can end up having an enormous impact on remittances.

Section 3: Conclusion

To sum up, the idea of identification is key to understanding each of the ideas under discussion here—philanthropy and remittances (Figure 2.1). While the process of identity formation has been extensively studied by anthropologists and sociologists, we have seen that the process of identification, as it plays out in the field of philanthropic contributions and how it impacts or is impacted by philanthropy, has not been studied as much.

It is the conclusion of this research that there is a hierarchy of motivations when thought through the concepts of remittances and philanthropy (Figure 2.1). These tiers or levels of motivation include "Giving to build community" as a foundational step that crosses all cultural populations reviewed. This is followed by "Giving to support 'resilience' of groups" and finally "Giving for ethnic solidarity." These reasons for giving or motivations were clearly discovered through the primary sources and understood across all immigrant/refugee groups.

Our paper has tried to nuance the arguments made by several scholars and to synthesize some of their key ideas, to form a more holistic framework to understand each of the processes on their own terms (Figure 2.1). While Schervish and Havens (1997) have argued for operationalizing the factors that drive this morality, by proposing five broad variables that drive giving, one cannot ignore the role that changing identities or multiple identities or identities in flux can impact the way that people find their own 'community.' This is particularly important, given the role that changing citizenship has on identity or community. While theorists have proposed ideas such as a human community with no claim to identity, such as in the work of Giorgio Agamben in his classic 'The Coming community' (1999), the work of Schervish and Havens (1997) and other sociologists is on the opposite spectrum, where they argue that people primarily claim their 'belongingness' through their identity. A belongingness that is agnostic of identity may be a theoretical possibility but not a practical reality, they contend.

Stuart Hall's conception of identity as something of a 'process' and not fixed in time may be a better analytical framework to understand the phenomenon at hand (Hall, 2000). His argument that one needs to go beyond one's ethnocentrism to define 'identity,' whether it is European-ness or Americanness, is more urgent than ever. Given the massive flow of people, ideas, and money; given the refugee crisis that we are witnessing; given other catalysts for remittances and philanthropic giving, there is an urgent need to nuance this debate around identity and identification. Going beyond binaries, acknowledging the full validity of hyphenated identities such as Somali-American, Chinese-American, etc. is not only a crucial part of this process, but an important element in how we frame and understand 'philanthropy' and 'remittances.' Moving beyond fixed categorization of ideas and persons may be a first step in this process.

The insights and arguments presented above challenge us to reconsider the notion that remittances to family cannot be considered as 'philan-thropy.' There is empirical proof that families that benefit from remittances have a better standard of living and are able to send their kids to school, more often than those that don't receive these remittances. How is this not 'philanthropy' if in the long run these remittances translate into a 'public good' of having a more educated town/village? The positive externalities of these private acts, which are often driven by kinship behavior, we believe force us to reconsider these binaries. While we are not making the claim that remittances and philanthropy are the same and that these two catego-ries should be collapsed, we are arguing for a closer reexamination of these two phenomena—as we have attempted—in an effort to look for common ground, rather than points of differences (refer again to Figure 2.1).

When comparing explanations for remittances giving with the identi-fication model for charitable giving (Sana, 2008; Sana & Massey, 2005; Schervish & Havens, 1997), all five explaining factors (communities of participation, frameworks of consciousness, direct requests, models and experiences from one's youth, and discretionary resources) can be recog-nized in the literature on remittances giving. However, there are at least two features of diaspora giving that makes it different from philanthropic giving as it is traditionally understood. First, instead of the traditional dependency relationship between donor and recipient, remittances are often poor-to-poor giving. Second, most migrants do not have a single identity, but rather a 'hyphenated identity' that cannot be understood in a single variable. Our analyses show that remittances are a multi-faceted phenomenon driven by a combination of economic, cultural, social, reli-gious, and political motivations and surrounded by pressures from gov-ernments, religious organizations, and financial institutions.

Another example of such remittances that we haven't included in our study but that bears mention is Jane Pollard's framing of the Somali's philan-thropy in London as 'resilience.' Her framing is another theoretical attempt at making sense of the charity and remittances that occur among the most vulnerable and poor, who are on welfare themselves (Sana & Hu, 2006).

Finally, as we wrap up our arguments, it is important to remember that the field of philanthropy and international aid remittances needs a broader range of methods. While positivist methods and reliance on numbers can tell us part of the story, we suggest that we need a more pragmatic, intimate, and closer look at the stories of giving aid and remittances, which incorporate a more qualitative methodology. Perhaps Merton and Flyvbjerg's reminders to focus on the pragmatic, mid-range aspects of data are key to our better understanding of each of these phenomena (Flyvbjerg, 2001; Merton, 1949). While we believe that positivist methods are a key and integral part of research efforts, more synthesis or mixed methods of research can yield richer results, as well.

Should we use frameworks of 'resilience' or 'solidarity' more than purely use categories of 'remittances' and 'philanthropy' in describing these sorts of giving behavior? Our synthesis of arguments seems to suggest that perhaps being sensitive to these categories when we discuss remittances and philanthropy will certainly be helpful and nuance the arguments as we formulate them.

Note

1. Sections of this paper are from our earlier papers titled "Remittances and philanthropy: Findings from a qualitative meta synthesis" (Khan & Merritt, 2018) in *The Journal of Social Science* and "Does social integration hinder immigrant giving to the country of origin?" (Khan, Merritt, and DeWit).

References

Adams, R. (2010, June). Economic impacts of remittances on developing countries using household surveys: A literature review. *Journal of Development Studies,* 47(6), 809–828.

Agamben, G. (1999). *The Coming Community*. Minneapolis: Minnesota University Press.

Bekkers, R., & Wiepking, P. (2011). A literature review of empirical studies of philanthropy. Eight mechanisms that drive charitable giving. *NVSQ*, 40, 924–973.

Bettin, G., & Lucchetti, R. (2012). *Intertemporal Remittance Behavior by Immigrants in Germany*. SOEP papers 505.

Brown, R. P. (1997). Estimating remittance functions for Pacific Island migrants. *World Development*, 25(4), 613–626.

Carling, J. (2014). Scripting Remittances: Making sense of money in transnational relationships. *International Migration Review*, 48, 218–262.

Cervantes, J. (2015). *Female Integration and Remittance Flow to Mexico*. Mexico City: CEMLA and BANORTE.

Czaika, M., & Spray, J. (2013). Drivers and dynamics of internal and international remittances. *Journal of Development Studies*, 49(10), 1299–1315.

De la Briere, E., Sadoulet, A., de Janvry, A., & Lambert, A. (2002). The role of destination, gender and household composition in explaining remittances: An analysis for the Dominican Sierra. *Journal of Development Economics*, 58, 309–328.

Erdal (2012). Who is the money for? Remittances within and beyond the household in Pakistan. *Asian and Pacific Migration Journal*, 21(4).

Flyvbjerg, B. (2001). *Making Social Science Matter*. UNESCO Report.

Frumkin, P. (2006). *Strategic Giving*. Chicago: University of Chicago Press.

Ghosh, B. (2006). *Migrants' Remittance and Development: Myths, Rhetoric and Realities*. Geneva and The Hague: IOM.

Glazer, N., & Moynihan, D. P. (1971). *Beyond the Melting Pot: The Negroes, Puerto Ricans, Jews, Italians, and Irish of New York City*. Cambridge, MA: MIT Press.

Hagen-Zanker, J., & Siegel, M. (2007). "The Determinants of Remittances: A Review of Literature." Working PapeMGSoG/2007/WP003. Maastricht Graduate School of Governance, Maastricht University, The Netherland.

Hall, S. (2000). Who needs identity? In P. du Gay, J. Evan, & P. Redman (Eds.), *Identity: A Reader*. London: Sage. DOI: 10.4135/9781446221907.n1

Khan, S., & Merritt, D. (2018). Motivations for remittances: Findings from qualitative meta-synthesis. *Journal of Social Sciences*, 14(2), 81–90.

Khan, Merritt & DeWit (n.d). Does social integration hinder immigrant giving to the country of origin. *Journal of Integration and Migration*. Under review.

Knomad (2016). Migration and remittances factbook 2016: Third edition. Retrieved on Feb, 2018. Washington D.C.

Lacroix, J. (2015). The rights to have rights in French political philosophy: conceptualizing a cosmopolitan citizenship with Arendt. *Constellations*, 22, 79–90.

Lucas, R. E. B., & Stark, O. (1985). Motivations to remit: Evidence from Botswana. *Journal of Political Economy*, 93(5).

Menjívar, C., DaVanzo, J., Greenwell, L., & Valdez, R. B. (1998). Remittance behavior among Slavadorian and Filipino immigrants in Los Angeles. *International Migration Review*, 32, 97–126.

Merton, R. (1949). *On Sociological Theories of the Midrange*. New York: Blackwell Publishing.

Munyegera, G. K. & Tomoya, M. (2016). Mobile money, remittances and household welfare: panel evidence from rural Uganda. *World Development*, 79, 127–137.

Najam (2006). Portrait of a giving community: Philanthropy by the Pakistani-American diaspora. Cambridge, MA: Global Equity Initiative, Asia Center, Harvard University.

Page, B., & Mercer, C. (2012). Why do people do stuff? Reconceptualizing Remittance behavior in diaspora-development research and policy. *Progress in Development Studies*, 12, 1–18.

Page, J., & Plaza, S. (2006). Migration remittances and development: A review of global evidence. *Journal of African Economies*, 15, 245–336.

Poirine, B. (1997). A theory of remittances as an implicit family loan arrangement. *World Development*, 25, 589–611.

Pollard, J., & Samers, M. (2011). Governing Islamic Finance: Territory, Agency, and the Making of Cosmopolitan Financial Geographies, Annals of the Association of American Geographers. doi:10.1080/00045608.2011.628256

Portes, A., & DeWind, J. (2004). A cross-Atlantic dialogue: The progress of research and theory in the study of international migration. *International Migration Review*, 38(3), 828–851.

Pozo, S., & Amuedo-Dorantes, C. (2006). The time pattern of remittances: Evidence from Mexican migrants. *Well-Being and Social Policy*, 2, 49–66.

Rapoport, H., & Docquier, F. (2006). The economics of migrants' remittances. In S. C. Kolm & J. M. Ythier (Eds.), *Handbook of the Economics of Giving, Altruism and Reciprocity*. Amsterdam: Elsevier, 1135–1198.

Ruiz, I., & Vargas-Silva, C. (2009). To send, or not to send: That is the question-a review of the literature on workers' remittances. *Journal of Business Strategy*, Forthcoming. https://www.emeraldgrouppublishing.com/products/journals/journals.htm?id=jbs

Russell, S. S. (1986). Remittances from international migration: A review in perspective. *World Development*, 14, 677–696.

Sana, M. (2005). Buying membership in the transnational community: Migrant remittances, social status and assimilation. *Population Research and Policy Review*, 24(3), 231–261.

Sana, M. (2008). Growth of migrant remittances from the United States to Mexico, 1990–2004. *Social Forces*, 86(3), 995–1025.

Sana, M., & Massey, D. S. (2005). Household composition, family migration and community context: Migrant remittances in four countries. *Social Science Quarterly*, 86(2), 509–528.

Sana, M., & Hu, C.-Y. (2006). Is international migration a substitute for social security? *Well-Being and Social Policy*, 2(2), 27–48.

Schervish, P. G., & Havens, J. J. (1997). Social participation and charitable giving: A multivariate analysis. *VOLUNTAS: International Journal of Voluntary and Nonprofit Organizations*, 8, 235–260.

Snel, E., Engbersen, G., & Leerkes, A. (2006). Transnational involvement and social integration. *Global Networks*, 6(3), 285–308.

Stark, O. (1991). *The Migration of Labor*. Oxford and Cambridge, Mass.: Basil Blackwell.

World Bank. (2015). *Remittances and Migration Data*. Washington, DC: World Bank.

Yang, D., & Choi, H. (2007). "Are Remittances Insurance? Evidence from Rainfall Shocks in the Philippines." *World Bank Economic Review*, 21(2), 219–248.

3   Growth of Money Transfers
Theorizing Technology, Distance, and Money

Understanding that there are multiple determinants of why people remit, who sends money and the overall spectrum of definitions pertaining to the interactions between remittances and philanthropy, it is only natural to want to uncover or at least theorize some causal impacts on money transfers. Within this chapter, we draw on academic articles, media sources, and first-person accounts to attempt to make possible an understanding of what today's environment has on remittances. While we as a society are continually evolving and changing through the development of our daily lives, one of the biggest influencers of our actions is technology. Technology is an actor used to accomplish our everyday functions.

Just this morning, when I woke up, I checked my email, my banking account balance, and the local news alerts, all from the convenience of my smartphone while sitting on the couch with my kiddo and a cup of tea. Then we read the national news and checked the weather to plan out our daily activities, again all from the convenience of a conduit of technology. This is all to say that we as a global society are influenced by technology and are avid consumers of it as well. While I may live in the Western world and teach at a technology-heavy institution, I am no different than many of you reading this book, nor is my account of my morning activities different from my friends, East, South, North, or West of me. Civil society and the expansion of our definition of the local community is expanding and with it the spread of accessibility and user-ability of technological resources. Therefore, we seek to understand what impacts this is having on the evolution of the household sector, the donor-recipient use, and simply the ways in which support is offered, transmitted, and received within diaspora communities.

Technology and Know-How

How to define technology can be as simple as 'know-how' or advancements. However, when attempting to place this concept in a tangible realm and seeking to understand if, how, and why there may be technological influences on remittance giving within migrant communities, the definition of 'know-how' lacks a solid line of inquiry. Technology is not limited to a computer or smartphone interface; it includes medical advancements, agricultural innovations, industry evolutions, and information and communication technology as well. While changes, evolutions, and know-how increase globally, they beg the questions: Does this have an impact on the economics of a nation? Does technology offer opportunities or increase boundaries between individuals? And where does money transfer suffer or benefit?

Definitional Antecedents

Before we can find answers, we must understand the epistemological changes that have been theorized regarding remittances. When we look at different philanthropic projects from multiple countries, the sociological concept of transnationalism surfaces. Transnationalism in the sense of "multi-stranded activities created by immigrants across national borders" (Basch, Glick-Schiller, & Blanc-Szanton, 1999; Glick Schiller, 1999; Portes, Escobar, & Radford, 2007). The rise of the concepts of transnationalism overtook the previous line of thought surrounding assimilation theory (Basch et al., 1994), whereby migrants went through a gradual process of acculturation and amalgamation to their new country; transnationalism offered a new conceptualization by which migrants continually lived between their country of origin and their new host society. Sociologists coined this new society as a 'deterritorialized community' (Bach et al., 1994). However, the sociological and anthropological binders of the definition of transnationalism have quarreled for many decades, primarily as a result of the variables used to study the concept. With the introduction and the availability of mass communication, ease of travel, and accessibility of news across borders, the influences of technology on a small scale have aided in the concepts of transnationalism to further understand the participation of migrant communities across civil society. Without the advances in technology, the limits of study and limits of understanding migrants' integration within their countries of origin and host societies would continue to be limited. Though it should also be noted that the availability and use of technology as a means to secure funds and propagate need is not limited to the individual, the above discussion was merely an attempt to situate the introduction of know-how advancements within a theoretical lens focused on the household sector. In Chapter 5, we will further delve into the political, socio-political, and economic influences of remittances, whereby technology has presented many immediate opportunities.

The 21st century has shown a fortitude and aptitude for innovation and adaptability. The use of technology within the economic realm has continued to be discovered as a means to further connect a seemingly already connected world. When we look at the use of social media and the impacts it has on civil society, there hardly seems to be a nation untouched by the changes, challenges, and the introduction of social media within their society (see Nigeria—Armstrong & Butcher, 2018; Carribean—Harrison & Hinds, 2014; Sweden—Scaramuzzino & Scaramuzzino, 2017; Japan—Kaigo & Tkach-Kawasaki, 2017; plus many more country-specific articles). As we have discussed in the opening chapters, our aim is to contextualize and understand the impact of remittances looking at specific countries. Within the data collected, both primary and secondary, there have been mentions of technology as a factor to consider. Especially when looking towards the future. Interview data from researchers in Mexico have suggested that political interactions play a particularly heavy role in how remittances are defined and utilized. Specifically, legislation that is proposed and 'rhetoric' used in the U.S. has a large impact on the remittances seen in Mexico. Additionally, organizations such as Banxico, the World Bank, and the Bureau of Labor Standards have been collecting data on money transfers and availability so that data is also dependent on the current political climate in the U.S. Specific interview data points that we conducted provide a feeling and overall sentiment that while quantitative data points lead us to know that remittances are on the rise, there is an uncertainty of sustainability given the U.S. president's current stance on U.S.-Mexico relations.

'The War on Cash' and Impact on Remittances

The rapid changes in the remittances sector has coincided with a big trend that has gone unnoticed by the money transfer companies—this is one colloquially called the 'war on cash,' meaning that governments around the world, and in particular Asia and the West, have gone on a frontal assault on the use of cash. While cash is easily accessible, fluid, and is guaranteed by the Central Bank of the particular nation, it has a few drawbacks: it can be counterfeited, physically stashed away—thereby impacting its supply—and also is liable to misuse by bad actors such as criminals and terrorists. This 'war on cash' is not an altogether new phenomenon, but something that has gone on for the past few decades.

There is an implicit understanding among practitioners in the space of money transfer that there is an ongoing 'war on cash' around the world (Mohr, 2019). As the *war on terror* became more aggressive, in a post-9/11 attack world, cash transactions were the first to come under close scrutiny. In 'quasi-states' or states that are failing, cash is often the only way to function and if one looks at the cases of Afghanistan, Somalia, and other such nation-states, this is clearly visible. Cash, one can argue, provides liquidity and legitimacy for those that seek to govern a place (Thompson, 2011, p. 240). However, it is seen with increasing suspicion due to its fluid nature. Cash cannot be tracked easily, is versatile, and can be counterfeited, making it harder to regulate.

Photo 3.1 A sight of the ubiquitous money transfer agencies in Kochi, Kerala, India

As Lawrence White explains, the war on cash is, of course, an exaggeration, in the sense that there is no actual war on the use of paper currency; rather, governments around the world have instituted policies that discourage the use of cash and would rather have citizens use electronic payment systems (White, 2018). White points to Kenneth Rogoff's assertion that there need not be a war on cash, but only on bills of high denomination—which is exactly what the Indian government did, in its 'demonetization' efforts in 2016. This move coincided with a move to digitize all payments, from small vendors on the street to farmers, selling their produce in the agri-markets.

This effort, which shocked the Indian economy and is reported to have cost over 1.5 million jobs, did not accomplish the stated objectives—i.e., uncovering illegal cash, stacked away by greedy businessmen (Safi, 2018; Rogoff, 2016). The manner in which this effort played out is interesting in itself. Mr. Narendra Modi, the Prime Minister of India announced in November 2016 that the government would take out the older Rs.500 and Rs.1000 out of circulation, so as to starve illegal trades and terrorists of a lifeline. As Safi points out, the impact was quite unintended and severe:

> As India's massive informal economy reeled, Modi implored the country to give the policy time to work, arguing it would flush out untaxed wealth being hoarded by wealthy Indians, help to digitize the economy—one of the most cash-based in the world—and starve terrorists and criminal gangs of cash.
>
> (Safi, 2018)

This, observers point out, did not happen. This move by the Indian government amounted to withdrawing over 86 % of the cash in circulation, in an economy that was 90% reliant on cash. The said objective of Mr. Narendra Modi's move was to get rid of corruption in the system by removing the illegal money that was in circulation. However, as Harvard Business Review points out,

> As of December 3, about 82% of the demonetized bills, amounting to about $185 billion, had been deposited in bank accounts and validated to be legitimately earned money (or legitimized after any additional taxes owed are accounted for). In other words, very little of the estimated $2 trillion black money estimated to be stashed overseas has been captured.
>
> (Chakravorty, 2016)

There were several unintended consequences to this move. What did happen was the loss of lives—several people are reported to have died—and an estimated 1.5 million people across the country lost their jobs.

India's former Finance Minister P. Chidambaram added that India's GDP lost about 1.5% due to this move and there was general anxiety and lack of liquidity in the markets. As the Guardian reports,

> Digital transactions have grown, but the RBI found the value of banknotes in circulation had also increased in the past year by

37.7%. Counterfeiters had also shifted to recreating smaller notes and were now able to replicate en masse the new 500 and 2,000-rupee notes, it said.

(Safi, 2018)

This seems like a contradictory result to what the government expected. Further, the most impacted were the poor and unbanked, who had to forego salaries and payments for many months. This move can be said to have had an impact on the long-term growth of India's economy as well. There are also similar efforts in other parts of the world that are attempting to reduce the use of cash in favor of digital payments.

So, who benefits from a reduction in the use of cash? As Lawrence White points out, there are organizations such as Better than Cash Alliance (BTCA) that advocate for the removal of as much cash as possible, and they suggest that it would benefit the poor and is part of the 'financial inclusion' strategies. He points out that the Bill and Melinda Gates Foundation and Omidyar Network may have the interests of the poor at heart, but suggests that Visa, MasterCard, and other players may be eyeing the transaction fees as part of the incentives to be in this space in their advocating for a cashless society (White, 2018).

Many of the regulations and laws that exist can criminalize a normal transaction. White points to the "Bank Secrecy Act," which says "a U.S. financial institution must file a 'Currency Transaction Report' (CTR) with FinCEN for any deposit, withdrawal, currency swap, or transfer involving $10,000 or more in currency, whether or not the institution employees handling it consider the transaction suspicious" (White, 2018). This can lead to unnecessary paperwork and also regulating personal transactions which are often above the board, he suggests. For example, breaking up the deposits of $10,000 into smaller amounts and depositing can be considered 'structuring,' a crime as well, he argues. White's example of dairy farmers who got caught in this mix is illustrative of what can go wrong when such laws are implemented. He points out that

> In the notorious case of dairy farmers Randy and Karen Sowers, who frequently deposited cash income from sales at farmers' markets, Treasury officials seized $29,500 in February 2012, charging the couple with structuring, without suspecting them of any other crime.
> (White, 2018)

The family was finally able to get their money back, but only after much hassle and action from their end.

The government amended the rules about structuring in 2014 to exclude individuals if they were not evading tax, etc. when carrying out transactions of $10,000 or more. These cases illustrate the challenges of regulating cash and the inevitable clashes that emerge in this space. The need for liquidity in contexts where there is insufficient technology infrastructure, to maintain and run financial institutions is in conflict with the need for a 'cashless' society.

The Technology Landscape and Use

The landscape available and the terrain accessible to remittances have broadened the reach of diaspora aid. No longer are money transfers limited to hard cash flows via a direct mail system, nor wired money via a third-party intermediary. Recently aid has been transferred in the form of crypto technology vehicles. In recent news, blockchain technology is emerging as what could possibly be a disruptive technology and possible advancement to philanthropy and specifically remittances. First of all, and simply stated, blockchain is digital information stored in a public database. Through the use of e-commerce and the development of Bitcoin banking, remittances are now being secured and transferred worldwide via this new modality. Blockchain technology provides reduced transaction costs, increases transaction security by mitigating fraud and increasing transparency, offers faster transactions, and reduces the need for multiple transactions (BankingTech, 2018). In 2015, India was regarded as the largest receiver of remittances worldwide, with an estimated $72 billion USD; note that this figure accounts for 12% of the world's remittances (World Bank). Private banks have emerged to offer lower exchange rates, cutting the industry average by 80% and partnering with country-specific banking firms to offer transfers of Bitcoin as well as local currency (IMTPC, 2016). To further the understanding and availability of money transfers, in 2016, the International Money Transfer and Payments Conference took place in New Delhi, India, with the aim of bringing the cross-border money transfer industry together to network, share information, and collaborate. This organization continues to hold annual conferences, that in recent years have been more specific in how technology plays a prominent role in remittances. This is all to say that in the daily life of remittances, there is no longer a single avenue for success, but through emergent tech, the global money transfer industry (including individuals, firms, banks, and non-governmental organizations), is large and expanding. The industry as a whole is scattered but interconnected through networks and growing with the help of technological advancements and innovations.

To supply a general glance at the scale and breadth of remittances, in 2017 global transfers were estimated at $633 billion USD and recent numbers from 2018 report a record high of $689 billion, USD (World Bank). Technology and the ease of transfer is the main variable in understanding this growth. In this book, we look specifically at four nations: Mexico, India, Saudi Arabia, and the United States. Chapter 4 will delve into the quantitative data.

Remittances are not a new concept and as discussed in Chapter 1, private money transfers have existed in every culture since bartering. However, the phenomena that we are working to understand is the realm in which remittances are prevalent in civil society and, furthermore, the interactions that the act of remitting creates. While the emergence of technology has offered a way to shape remittances and giving, it is the impact that technology has on giving and sending and what implications it has on the relationship of donor and recipient that are intriguing.

When looking at roles, there are many participants within the industry. The individual and the recipient are the two that immediately come to mind, but there are also the firms that make possible the long-distance money moving. Firms such as MoneyGram, Western Union, Coinsecure, OK Coin/OKLink, etc. are all actors in the exchange of monies. What role do intermediaries play? What are the pros and cons of using different modes of transfer? Above we discussed the use of blockchain technology as a means of lowering the costs, but overall what are the costs associated with remittances? Is that a factor to take into account, and how about the intangible cost, regulations, and limitations due to legislation or lack thereof?

Organizations have started to network, collaborate, share information, and partner in the endeavor of acting as agents of money transfer (International Money Transfer & Cross-border Payments Conferences, or IMTC). While informal networks have most likely existed between firms since their conception, it is the now formalized connections that are making news headlines, allowing for easier access to information and data, and allowing the farther country-to-country partnerships. Policy pressure has been seen in many low- and middle-income countries to formalize the remittance process, which created the externality of stimulation and innovation in the market (Siegel & Fransen, 2013). In the African market, there has been a surge of mobile remittance services whereby you can make financial transactions via mobile phones. The usage of mobile phones has risen in African nations and is seen as a benefit within the development process (Scott, Batchelor, Ridley, & Jorgensen, 2004). In the seven-year period between 1999–2006, the usage of mobile phones increased by over 50%; to further put this into context, in sub-Saharan Africa more people have mobile phones than bank accounts (World Bank, 2016). The avenue of use for mobile devices as a mean of money transfers offers multiple opportunities. However, while the opportunities exist, it is not always the goal or intended strategy for the banking institutions to create an avenue for remittance giving. Many times, the facilitation of remittances is considered an externality or a side-effect of banking. As found by Siegel and Fransen, many banking institutions in Africa are concerned with getting the non-bank account holders to become active banking members, versus money transfers (2013). Furthermore, expansion efforts are placed on small businesses, not the individual. And limitations to the individual wishing to send funds further hinders the ease of remitting. Limitations have been studied in the form of who a customer can send money to, how remittances can be initiated, where monies can be routed. Specifically, financial regulations of many developing nations restrict international money transfers, further limiting remittance support. It was theorized that given the expansion of the mobile phone industry in Africa, that mobile remittances would increase and favorable regulatory framework would surface (Harrison & Hinds, 2014). This hope or expectation leads one to further surmise that the companies that are agents of money transfer play a role more intricate and highly vital to the success of global remittances and thereby act not solely as pure agents of money transfers, but rather as advocates for policy and network or link between the remitter and recipient. If you consider these roles, the process may not be linear or as simple as a one-way street.

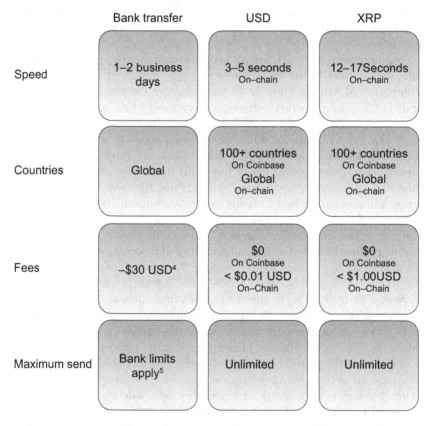

Figure 3.1 Comparison of speed of transfer of money via various sources

Source: Harrap (2019)

Technology and the Future

Given the above analysis of technology and the multifaceted interactions between remittances and technology, it should come as no surprise that there are concerns when we look towards the future health of global remittances. While first-person data from industry agents of money transfers are scarce, interviews revealed that internally, organizations are not seeking to participate in the making of policies on a national or international level regarding remittances. Interviewees made specifically clear that banking institutions (Mexico) were independent of government while interviews also specifically noted that it is a normal industry (banking) practice to have a "close relationship with federal public administration" (Khan & Merritt, 2018). This contradictory or rather convoluted information is most likely typical among many nations. Therefore, while a generalization about the relationship and the ability to enact change within the remittance regulatory frameworks may not happen directly, there seems to be some ability to influence and interact with policy formulation, while not actually shaping it directly. We will delve specifically into the U.S. conceived policies and their intricacies as well as implication woven throughout the legislation in Chapter 5.

Hugo Cuevas-Mohr, the founder of International Money Transfer & Cross-border Payments Conferences (IMTC), a firm that organizes money transfer conferences that bring all the key players in this space together. He points out how the technologies—starting with faxing—have evolved and how people are trying to keep a track of these changes. "While the individuals, the end-users are trying to keep up and use these technologies, sometimes, the pace has been too fast for people to keep up," he says as he summarizes the trends in technology and transfer of money mechanisms. He points out that due to this lag, sometimes there can be gaps in understanding. He suggests that some of the money transfer agents discourage or even exaggerate the usage of their channels—the traditional money transfer firms, rather than using the newly developed phone apps or other online methods.

> I've heard several agents warn their customers not to use the online platforms, as they can lead to bad exchange rates or even in some cases, the recipients not receiving the money. Many of these are just stories—made up to scare people to stick to them,

Mohr points out. This gap in knowledge, understanding is not conducive but again, there are no shortcuts to fixing them. A better-informed consumer is the solution, but when ignorance is bliss (and lucrative), money transfer agents are happy to keep the status quo.

"Trust Is the Coin of the Realm"—Edwina A. Thompson

"It all boils down to trust, whether it is a hawala agent or an agent using TransferWise to transfer money, the bottom line is—how much do I trust the technology and the people managing it," Hugo Cuevas-Mohr says, pointing to the history of how technologies have evolved, over the decades and how they have shaped the money transfer industry, around the world.

Edwina A. Thompson, a researcher who has studied issues of trust extensively in the realm of hawala, arguably the oldest 'technology' of transfer of money, argues that trust is the backbone of any transfer of money. Thompson, whose research covers much of the ungoverned parts of the world, points to the widespread use of hawala in Iraq and refugee or internally displaced settlements across Africa and South Asia.

> In early 2005, after the tsunami wave hit Aceh, for example, money dealers reportedly established an emergency communications system using the *flexsi* local mobile network to help migrants locate their families and arrange for the delivery of funds through bank accounts or directly to the IDP camps themselves.
>
> (2011, p. 1)

This anecdote illustrates the manner in which trust, combined with existing technologies, saved the day for millions of people who would have remained stranded, without money, if not for this structure in place.

Thompson's account of the use of hawala as an ancient system that has survived centuries of usage is quite emblematic of technologies that grow and evolve.

> Some companies in the wire-transfer business operate like the hawala. There is obviously no physical movement of money, but there is the transfer of credits, balances etc. and viola—the person at the other end—often, thousands of miles away receives the money they need.

pointed out a participant at the IMTC Conference, in Miami, in November 2019. What makes the transfer of money so seamless can also be the factor that makes it so insidious and subject to suspicion and scrutiny.

In the U.S. and the Western world in a post-9/11 context, *implicitly* there was recognition of the use of hawala for state-building and emergency relief, as illustrated in the example above but an *explicit* disavowal of hawala as a potentially dangerous network tied to terrorists (Thompson, p. 3). A similar pattern is emerging with the newer forms of technology such as crypto-currencies, which are having to struggle for legitimacy while trying to remain viable models for money transfer and remittances.

"The financial system has left billions of people unserved and it is our role to bring this access to millions around the world," Brian Armstrong, the co-founder of Coinbase points out (Armstrong, 2018). Armstrong points out that Bitcoin solved the problem of verification—to avoid double-spending—and allows one to prove that a transaction is real. "It created a global version of cash, seamlessly" (Armstrong, 2018). The fact that crypto is new brings new challenges to the table. Coinbase has over $20 billion in crypto being traded and is one of the most significant sources of crypto trading on the internet.

The potential for cryptocurrencies to be used for remittances is being discussed. Several countries such as Venezuela are already deploying Bitcoin for remittances transfers. As Aguilar writes, "With an estimated $3.7 billion in remittances sent in 2019, money from abroad is an increasingly large source of income for Venezuelan families. As such, bitcoin and crypto currencies have assumed a larger role in facilitating cross-border transactions" (Aguilar, 2019). The restrictions placed on trade and U.S. sanctions have made much of the trade and other activity go underground. This process of using cryptocurrencies is part of the trend. The use of cryptocurrencies is prevalent for Venezuelan migrants living and working in other parts of Latin America. In addition, this is also a reliable mode of sending money where a recent migrant doesn't have a bank or other institution through which to transfer money, Aguilar suggests. See Figure 3.2 for a basic overview of the cryptocurrency remittance process.

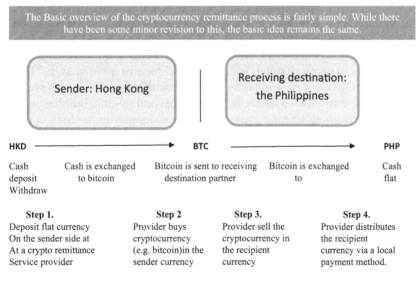

Figure 3.2 The basic overview of the cryptocurrency remittance process is fairly simple

Source: Harrap (2019)

While there are some who are using cryptocurrencies for remittances, others are cautious, as the government tracks these payments and in some cases has tried to extort people, Aguilar points out when discussing the dangers associated with this platform.

Cryptocurrency and the Future of Remittances

Hugo Cuevas-Mohr's point that the money transfer industry is the backbone of several countries is key to remember. While countries such as Somalia and Uzbekistan, receive more than 23% of their GDP from remittances, the methods of transfer of money in these countries range from the very traditional hawala to the modern cryptocurrency mechanism (World Bank, 2016). The inter-governmental agencies have historically played a role in providing access to those who have not been part of the banking system. However, with emerging phone-based technologies, there are newer players, who are gaining more influence and reach when it comes to remitting money.

With innovation outpacing policy-making in most countries, there is a risk that most countries will not know how to deal with the challenges before them, as far as the flow of money. Dan Torrey from Genesis owned by Digital Currency Group (DCG), one of the firms in the space since 2013, does institutional trading. "We are in the business of digital lending and we are just shy of $600 mn and it is fun to watch an asset class, and cool to build the first world's first institutional lender," Torrey points out. "Every conference in the early 2000s in Latin America was hype, but we are getting more realistic," Cuevas-Mohr says. "Bitcoin started as a global phenomenon and not one country had an advantage. This is similar to what's going on around the world. Trading is our focus and this industry has so many channels for growth and for entrepreneurship," Tim Byun from OK Coin mentions. Byun says that this stage of crypto is the building stage and use-cases are being built beyond mining, building, and trading. "It is going to take some time, but all levels—individual, enterprise and countrywide acceptance will take place," he adds. To Byun, compliance with local regulations is key. "Billions are moving through us, and aside from the Bear market, you can start to forecast your business on, this is exciting," Fernando Martinez from OSL says (LABITCONF, 2019).

Mohr points to how important the work of bridging the traditional world of moving money to the new one, which is all in bytes. "We see the light shining and there are ups and downs, the realistic problems that exist in this space" (LABITCONF, 2019). Fernando Martinez points out that the market for cryptocurrencies is growing and in the emerging markets, this is visible in the remittances space as well. Mohr adds that it is hard to settle money using wire transfers, and increasingly firms are using crypto for settling accounts. "This year, more and more firms are getting on-board. Banks are also coming onboard" (LABITCONF, 2019). The question of taxing and regulating these transactions is also taking place and there is a need for that, as well. The convergence of traditional banking infrastructure with the newer infrastructure is key, point out Mohr and Torrey.

Experts mention that social media is a good precursor to where crypto technologies can go. "WeChat allows you to pay at various merchants, and my prior employer Visa's business model may be disrupted," Byun argues (LABITCONF, 2019). What Thompson says about policy challenges in the traditional world with hawala may also be true in the case of cryptocurrencies, as they are used in remittances. She points out that often policy responses are quick, knee-jerk, and meant to ameliorate an immediate threat and are often not thoroughly thought-out options (Thompson, 2011, p. 3). As the groundwork is being laid for the use of cryptocurrencies and other advanced technologies around the world, there is the danger of this becoming hegemonic. Access to technology, power, and resources are crucial even in the case of cryptocurrencies, even though they are seemingly more democratic.

As George Harrap, the CEO of Bitspark, a cash-to-Bitcoin company, says, over 90 percent of the money in remittances flows originate as cash payments (Harrap, 2019). Harrap further reminds us that just under 30 percent of the people in the world have a bank account, which means the potential for those who are unbanked to be brought into the financial system is huge and largely untapped. Four companies are working in the space of cash-Bitcoin transactions: Bitspark, Bitpesa, Rebit, and CoinsPH, with the Philippines leading the global market in this space. Some of the problems in this space are related to buying and selling crypto instantly, lack of application program interfaces (APIs), difficulty in converting Bitcoin into local currencies, scalability of the service, etc. (Harrap, 2019). Bitspark closed its doors in March 2020 as a result of the Coronavirus, protests in Hong Kong and internal company restructuring (Partz, 2020).

A viable model that would help work around these problems should find solutions for all these problems. Regulations are needed for greater acceptance of these models and for wider adoption of these mechanisms.

As others have also pointed out, not many countries have meaningful regulation in cryptocurrency remittances, with the Philippines being the only exception (Mohr, 2019; Harrap, 2019). This took place because of the rapid use of cryptocurrencies in remittances, which forced the government to adopt these regulations. As Harrap points out, ultimately, governments will come around and realize that given the volume of money in the space, they will have to come around and adopt norms and regulations, sooner than later. Harrap adds that "the emergence of uncensorable peer to peer applications is higher in transaction volume than regulated platforms anyway, as in the case of India, Pakistan, Venezuela and Iran" (Harrap, 2019).

With the 'war on cash' that many advanced economies have indulged in, there is reason to believe that more people will move to digital platforms for payments (Mohr, 2019). Some of the upcoming developments in this space include bill payments, developing cash agent networks, etc. (Harrap, 2019). The challenge for most players in this space has been to onboard traditional players and bring them into the crypto fold. "The more bitcoin adoption continues to expand, the greater the pressure on traditional players to investigate newer forms of settlement," Harrap adds.

The future is as unpredictable as the present is dynamic. This is the situation in the world of crypto remittances and no one seems to be complaining as this sector evolves and grows organically. What is striking is that individual initiative seems to be the driving force. Just as the centuries-old technology of hawala originated the business of remittances, and was the product of a businessman's ingenuity, so are the technologies of the future—ingenious inventions meant to solve an immediate problem.

Regulating Crypto Remittances: Mission Impossible?

A recent report from the Library of Congress in Washington, D.C. laid out the landscape of regulation with respect to cryptocurrencies around the world (LOC, 2018). The report covers over 130 countries and is one of the first attempts of its kind to map the emerging regulatory framework in this sector. As the report points out, there is a vast diversity in how each country or region describes the cryptocurrency space.

> Some of the terms used by countries to reference cryptocurrency include: digital currency (Argentina, Thailand, and Australia), virtual commodity (Canada, China, Taiwan), crypto-token (Germany), payment token (Switzerland), cyber currency (Italy and Lebanon), electronic currency (Colombia and Lebanon), and virtual asset (Honduras and Mexico).
>
> (LOC, 2018, p. 1)

This being the case, there are attempts by the central banks at educating the citizens of the said country, this report says. However, much of the framing of cryptocurrencies is in the context of money laundering and financing terrorism and the central banks expect the agencies transacting with these currencies or tokens to carry out the due diligence necessary for these purposes. This is a herculean task by any measure, especially given the amount of information that exists on the internet and other social media outlets.

The Library of Congress report points out that "For instance, Australia, Canada, and the Isle of Man recently enacted laws to bring cryptocurrency transactions and institutions that facilitate them under the ambit of money laundering and counter-terrorist financing laws" (p. 1). Algeria, Bolivia, Morocco, Nepal, Pakistan, and Vietnam have banned cryptocurrencies while Qatar and Bahrain have barred their citizens from transacting in these currencies within their borders. The report also adds that several countries such as Spain, Belarus, the Cayman Islands, and Luxemburg, although not friendly towards cryptocurrencies, are developing mechanisms and regulatory frameworks to attract investors in this space in the near future. Belgium and South Africa have shown indifference towards the entire sector, considering it to be too insignificant to make a dent in the real economy. However, there are other nation-states that have gone on to develop their own cryptocurrencies. These include the Marshall Islands, Venezuela, the Eastern Caribbean Central Bank (ECCB) member states, and Lithuania. At least in the case of Venezuela, it is driven by volatility and a desperate need to access liquidity, given the economic situation in the country and the continued American economic sanctions.

The main question that arises in this context on earnings from mining coins is one of taxation. However, these earnings are not covered under value-added taxes, the report points out. The most progressive governments seem to be in the Swiss Cantons of Zug and a municipality in Ticino, where government agencies accept cryptocurrencies. "The Isle of Man and Mexico also permit the use of crypto currencies as a means of payment along with their national currency," the authors of the report from Library of Congress add (LOC, 2018, p. 3).

The situation in India, one of the countries we examine, is also one of caution. The Reserve Bank of India (RBI) has issued several notices warning people who would like to purchase these assets to exercise caution and also that these are not legal tenders in India. The government has taken a proactive step in pursuing the use of blockchain technology while being cautious about promoting the use of cryptocurrencies. This cautious optimism seems to be the trend around the world, with very few countries putting a total ban on this new and emerging technology.

The question of regulation in the context of cryptocurrencies is not a straight-forward one, as the most important factor in favor of these currencies is that they are not centralized (Jayachandran, 2019). Jayachandran elaborates on this argument and suggests that

> While many crypto proponents argue that crypto currencies should not be regulated, as the technology is decentralized (some are designed

to be censorship-resistant), many aspects such as exchanges, governance around issuance of new tokens, and marketing are highly centralized in nature, requiring standardized oversight to prevent and punish impropriety.

This begs the question: who is in charge? The question of legitimacy is one of the most significant ones, in this space and one that needs to be worked out in the near future, if cryptocurrencies are to be widely accepted.

This problem may be closer to being solved, with the People's Bank of China and the Bank of England moving in the direction of releasing their own digital currencies in the near future. The RBI is rumored to be experimenting with its own digital currency but has banned any crypto transactions in the country. The middle ground seems to be one of having technologists and government regulators agree on a shared taxonomy or nomenclature, such as the Token Taxonomy Initiative.

With an economy that is well integrated into information technology infrastructure, countries such as India and Mexico may well open up to embrace cryptocurrencies in the near future. As we have seen, even with technological changes, much remains the same. The very traditional and old challenges of settling payments remains, even with newer forms of digital payments. Old problems invite new approaches to the table, but the fundamental challenges remain. It seems that only with coordination and collaboration among the various parties—the government, money transfer agencies, and regulators—can we find real solutions to the most vexing issues in remittances. And if not anything else, technology can certainly speed up the process!

References

Aguilar, D. (2019). *Venezuelan Migrants Are Deploying Bitcoin for Remittances, But There's a Catch*. Accessible at www.coindesk.com/venezuelan-migrants-are-using-bitcoin-for-remittances-but-theres-a-catch. Retrieved on Dec 17, 2019.

Armstrong, B. (2018). Coinbase CEO on the future of crypto. *YouTube*. Accessible at www.youtube.com/watch?v=xABO3BKUxG8. Retrieved on Dec 17, 2019.

Armstrong, C., & Butcher, C. (2018). Digital civil society: How Nigerian NGOs utilize social media platforms. *International Journal of Politics, Culture, and Society*, 31(3), 251–273. doi:10.1007/s10767-017-9268-4

BankingTech. (2018, June 18). *How Blockchain Could Change the Global Remittance Industry*. Accessible at www.bankingtech.com/2018/06/how-blockchain-could-change-the-global-remittance-industry/

Basch, L. G., Glick-Schiller, N., & Blanc-Szanton, C. (1994). *Nations Unbound: Transnational Projects, Postcolonial Predicaments, and Deterritorialized Nation-States*. Langhorne, PA: Gordon and Breach.

Chakravorty, B. (2016). India's botched war on cash. *Harvard Business Review*. Accessible at https://hbr.org/2016/12/indias-botched-war-on-cash. Retrieved on Dec 26, 2019.

Glick Schiller, N. (1999). Transmigrants and nation states: Something old and something new in the U.S. immigrant experience. In C. Hirschman, P. Kasinitz, & J. DeWind (Eds.), *Handbook of International Migration: The American Experience*. New York: Russell Sage Foundation. Pp. 94–119.

Harrap, G. (2019, Nov). Interview at IMTC. Miami.

Harrison, K., & Hinds, H. (2014). Virtual shop fronts: The internet, social media, and Caribbean civil society organisations. *Globalizations*, 11(6), 751–766. doi:10.1080/14747731.2014.90416

International Money Transfer and Payment Conferences. (2016). Accessible at https://imtconferences.com/

Jayachandran, P. (2019). Crypto currency regulation: An Indian perspective. *Coin Telegraph*. Accessible at https://cointelegraph.com/news/cryptocurrency-regulation-an-indian-perspective. Retrieved on Dec 26, 2019.

Kaigo, M., & Tkach-Kawasaki, L. (2015). Social media for enhancing civil society and disaster relief: Usage by local municipalities in Japan. *JeDEM: eJournal of eDemocracy and Open Government*, 7(1), 1–22. doi:10.29379/jedem.v7i1.371

Khan, S., & Merritt, D. (2018). Motivations for Remittances and Philanthropy – Lessons from a Qualitative Meta-Synthesis of Literature. *Journal of Social Sciences*.

LABITCONF. (2019). How does crypto money flow around the world. *YouTube*. Accessible at www.youtube.com/watch?v=7Fnaw0oCO-Y&feature=youtu.be. Retrieved on Dec 17, 2019.

LOC. (2018). *Regulation of Cryptocurrency around the World*. Washington, DC: The Law Library of the Library of Congress.

Mohr, H.-C. (2019, Nov). Interview at IMTC. Miami.

Partz, E. (2020). *Bitspark Shuts Down Amidst Coronavirus and Protests*. Accessible at https://cointelegraph.com/news/bitspark-shuts-down-amid-restructuring-coronavirus-and-protests

Portes, A., Escobar, C., & Radford, A. W. (2007, Spring). Immigrant transnational organizations and development: A comparative study. *The International Migration Review*, 41(1), 242–281. Published by: Sage Publications, Inc. on behalf of the Center for Migration Studies of New York, Inc.

Rogoff, K. S. (2016). *The Curse of Cash*. Princeton, NJ: Princeton University Press.

Safi, M. (2018). Demonetization fails to uncover "black money." *The Guardian*. Accessible at www.theguardian.com/world/2018/aug/30/india-demonetisation-drive-fails-uncover-black-money. Retrieved on Dec 18, 2019.

Scaramuzzino, G., & Scaramuzzino, R. (2017). The weapon of a new generation?- Swedish civil society organizations' use of social media to influence politics. *Journal of Information Technology & Politics*, 14(1), 46–61. doi:10.1080/19331681.2016.1276501

Scott, N., Batchelor, S., Ridley, J., & Jorgensen, B. (2004). *The Impact of Mobile Phones in Africa*. Paper prepared for the Commission for Africa. Accessible at http://gamos.org/couksite/Projects/Docs/Mobile%20phones%20in%20Africa/Full%20Report.pdf

Siegel, M., & Fransen, S. (2013). New technologies in remittance sending: Opportunities for mobile remittances in Africa. *African Journal of Science, Technology, Innovation and Development, 5*(5), 423–438. doi:10.1080/20421338.2013.837287

Thompson, E. (2011). *Trust Is the Coin of the Realm.* Oxford, UK: Oxford University Press.

White, L. (2018). The curse of the war on cash. *CATO Journal.* Accessible at www.cato.org/cato-journal/springsummer-2018/curse-war-cash. Retrieved on Dec 18, 2019.

World Bank. (2016). *World Bank Makes Progress to Sending Remittances to Somalia.* Accessible at www.worldbank.org/en/news/press-release/2016/06/10/world-bank-makes-progress-to-support-remittance-flows-to-somalia. Retrieved on Dec 17, 2019.

4 Remittances by the Numbers
How Much Is Sent and Where

Introduction

Monetary transfers are not new to the financing of a country, the well-being of a region, or the daily budget of a family. The flow of monies is as old as any tradition, but tracking those monies is a newer practice that has yet to be completed in all areas and encompassing all modes of transfer. This chapter looks at the data points available and discusses the quantitative numbers from a U.S. perspective. There are multiple different stakeholders who collect data on remittances, from the World Bank, whose data we heavily rely on for this book, to regional centers such as the Center for Latin American Monetary Studies who have specific country data. While access to these rich data pools is available to the public, other monetary hubs such as faith-based organizations or private transfer offices, including post offices, telecommunication companies, and bank data are harder to come by. We will do our best in this chapter to paint the picture of the movement of money on a global scale using quantitative data points. To start the discussion and given the country of origin of this book, Graph 4.1 depicts outflows monies from the United States, 2007–2017.

Worldwide Monies

The ever-moving inflow and outflow of monies to and from countries have been on an upward climb over the last two decades, but increases have been significant over the last two years. In 2017, low- to middle-income countries (LMICs) have gone from 8.8% to 9.6% and reached over $500 billion USD. This increase can be linked to positive increased growth of the United States while also a rebound in infrastructure from Russia and some Gulf Nations (World Bank, 2019). To further emphasize the increased flow of remittances, in LMICs money transfers have become the largest source of foreign monetary exchanges, surpassing foreign direct investment (with the exception of China).

Discussion of money transfers within this chapter is primarily focused and reported for LMICs and estimated in consideration of a country's

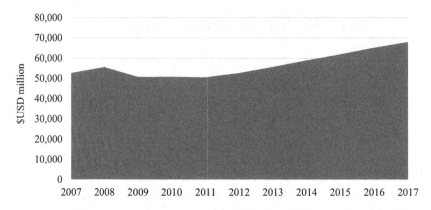

Graph 4.1 United States remittance outflows 2007–2017

gross domestic product (GDP), with data used from the World Bank and through the KNOMAD report on migration (The Global Knowledge Partnership on Migration and Development, 2019) report. We do not, nor have we been focusing on high-income nations. This is not to exclude those interactions, but monetary flows into high-income nations are large but the impact is minimal compared to their GDP. If interested further in high-income nations who are recipients of remittances, there are open-access data from the World Bank and individual country data from those respective nations.

From World Bank estimates, IMF statistics, and World Development indicators, Graph 4.2 has been derived to give a visual understanding of the top remittance recipient countries in 2018. The World Bank divided the entire globe into nation regions: East Asia and Pacific, Europe and Central Asia, Latin America and Caribbean, Middle East and North Africa, South Asia, and sub-Saharan Africa. In the derived graph you can see the different regional money flows. Within these figures, India and Mexico are part of the top ten countries receiving remittances. Though before we move into specific country data, as this book is primarily offering a United States lens on Mexico, India, and to a lesser extent Saudi Arabia, it would be beneficial to set a worldwide view of remittance inflows. And the definitional parameters around money transfers and impacts.

Within the context of this book and what is typical within academic research studies of remittances, we focus on the inflows of remittances. Our targeted discussion and analysis are offered using USD currency. And we discuss money transfers as whole dollars as well as the percentage of

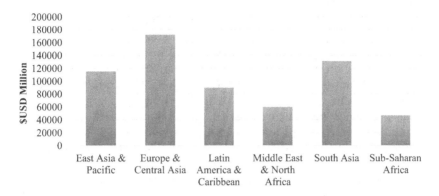

Graph 4.2 Regional money flows 2018

GDP. Given the domestic U.S.A. lensing of this entire book, in this chapter, we also offer data on United States remittance outflows. And from available 2017 data, the United States remains the largest contributor to remittances recording $68 billion USD in remittance outflows. To further emphasize the number of monies recorded that flow from the U.S.A., the next highest contributors are the United Arab Emirates and Saudi Arabia, at $44 billion USD and $36 billion USD, respectably. To further delve into remittance outflow, there seems to be a tie between economic growth, migration, multinational enterprises and ventures, and remittance outflows. For example, with the rebounding of the Russian Federation, Russia offered $21 billion USD in remittance outflows in 2017. This is notable as the Russian Federation is a middle-income country that has a large migrant population (European and Asian descent). And China recorded $16 billion USD in outflows for 2017, which may be a result of the international opportunities for multinational enterprises and ventures.

Regional Lens of Money Transfers

Refocusing the conversation back to inflows of remittances, quantifying in terms of the region offers a visual that is easier to grasp. So while we are still focusing on the three primary areas of Mexico, India, and Saudi Arabia within our pointed focus, we also wanted to offer a regional approach to further frame the discussion and understanding. If we take a look at the last decade, again focused on low- to middle-income regions, we can divide the world into East Asia and Pacific, Europe and Central Asia, Latin America and the Caribbean, Middle East and North Africa, South Asia and Sub-Saharan Africa. These regional categorizations come from the World Bank. Looking strictly at dollars, on a worldwide scale growth has been realized from a 2010 flow of $470 Billion USD to $633 Billion USD in 2017, to a forecasted $714 Billion USD in 2019 and $746 Billion USD in 2020. Further work has been tabulated and completed utilizing projections for remittances through the World Bank and open access if any reader wishes to dive into their raw data sets. When focusing on the regional constructs, from 2010 to 2017 there has been overall positive growth and forecasts for 2019 and 2020. While conservative, this also notes the growth in each region. Data offers us a rather positive slope. Starting in 2010, $342 billion USD flows to low- to middle-income regions was documented, moving to $51 in 2015, to a slightly lower $444 in 2016, a rise to $483 in 2017, continuing to increase to $529 in 2018, and forecasted to reach $574 in 2020.

Pinpointing Latin America and the Caribbean, we can see that in 2010 there were $55 billion USD remittance flows, then an increase to $67 (2015), $73 (2017), and forecasted to reach $95 billion USD in 2020. Though from a regional perspective, the largest increase in monies over the last ten years was in South Asia, reporting $82 billion USD in 2010 and forecasted to reach $142 billion in 2020. While the reasoning for this large growth rate is not directly correlated and only a relationship can be surmised, one would argue that internationalization and increased globalization strategies of multinational enterprises have an impact on money transfers. South Asia is not alone in its increase of remittance flows, as all regions have seen rather steady growth over the last decade with only a lessening or dip in growth rate in 2016. Again reasoning cannot be directly linked but political climates in the U.S.A. changed in 2016 and there could have been a relationship between leadership turnover and monetary flows, though this angle has not been further validated, simply a musing of the authors. For furthering the discussion we now turn to look at the general cost of sending funds.

As we noted in the opening of this chapter, it is one thing to want to send money earned in one country to one's origin nation, but there are several cost factors involved: economic, social, physical, and emotional, as well as political. In Chapter 5 we seek to further understand the policy angle and political interactions, while this entire book weaves in the social, physical, and emotional aspects. We will continue to hardline the quantitative and more concrete realities in this chapter.

There are different avenues for sending and receiving monies between nations. Most individuals initially seek out banks in order to send monies as it 'makes the most sense' to send money where you house your funds; however banking institutions tend to be among the most expensive or costliest modes of transferring remittances. In 2019 sending money via a banking institution had an average cost of 10%, whereas postal offices offered 7.6%. There is a political interaction here whereby some national postal offices have premiums added to the transfer of funds that can be linked to policy initiatives geared towards the sending of funds overseas

(World Bank). These premiums can be as high as 4.4%, which happens to be the case for India. These premiums for sending remittances at national post offices are linked with partnership agreements that offer exclusivity to a dominant money transfer operator. This could be an area for advocacy on behalf of other companies wishing to offer money transfers through money transfer operators and thereby limiting the exclusivity and potentially alleviating the premium surcharge. However, as a baseline, the average cost of sending monies is 7%, which has remained steady over the last year and seen a decrease over the last five years. When we break down the costs to send remittances based on the regional areas, we find that Sub-Saharan Africa (average of 9.3%, 2019) has the highest cost point while South Asia has the lowest (average of 5%, 2019). For Latin America and the Caribbean, costs level out at around 6%, dipping to 5.9% in 2018, and rising to 6.2% in 2019. Bringing some political headway into this discussion, there are global efforts to reduce these costs. The Sustainable Development Goals which are planned for 2030 aim for a 3% cost of sending funds. It needs to be noted here that we are discussing averages. Meaning that there is an extremely higher and lower cost point for sending remittances. For example, the World Bank notes that to send money to certain areas of Sub-Saharan Africa can cost over 20%. These elevated numbers play a major role in the global efforts of the Sustainable Development Goals, 2030 to find ways to reduce this burdensome cost.

Data available and open to use by researchers is varied and aggregate to a certain level. Individual countries keep their own measures, evaluations, and accounts of monetary transfers, while data for this book is mainly derived from the World Bank. To this end, we will continue our quantitative discussion on the analysis of the regions, specifically the regions that include Mexico and India: Latin America and the Caribbean and South Asia, respectively.

Latin America and the Caribbean

Remittances to Latin America and the Caribbean are on the rise and continue to grow (see Graph 4.3). This growth can be connected (again) to the strength of the United States' current economy and specifically the labor market in the U.S. In 2018 remittance flow in Latin America and the Caribbean saw a near 10% growth, though market conditions and forecasts expect the growth to level out to 4% in 2019. This parallels the projections for the U.S. economy as well. Within this region and of most interest to the authors is that Mexico received the largest dollar amount of remittances. It is estimated that in 2018 Mexico received $35.7 billion USD which is an 11% growth. Furthermore, Mexico is the third-largest recipient of remittances worldwide. Given historical migration patterns of migrants who settled the region of Latin America and the Caribbean as

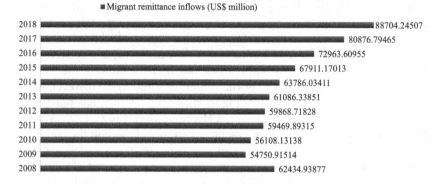

■ Migrant remittance inflows (US$ million)

2018	88704.24507
2017	80876.79465
2016	72963.60955
2015	67911.17013
2014	63786.03411
2013	61086.33851
2012	59868.71828
2011	59469.89315
2010	56108.13138
2009	54750.91514
2008	62434.93877

Graph 4.3 Latin America and the Caribbean remittance inflows 2008–2018

Note: Data from the World Bank, depicting the inflow of remittances over a ten-year span (2008–2018) to the region of Latin America and the Caribbean.

well as the strong U.S. connections for this region, money transfers from both Spain and the U.S. favor Latin America and the Caribbean. Costs associated with transfers (as noted earlier) have hovered around 6% with a slight increase in 2018. And to continue to tie in the political angle connected to remittances, in a 2019 study by Warren, the undocumented Mexican population in the U.S. fell in 2017. That may be linked to a change in leadership and focus on migrant policy within the U.S. federal government. Additionally, trends in South America continued, with the political unrest of Venezuela resulting in a migration of millions.

South Asia

Similar to all regions discussed, South Asia has seen an increase of remittance inflows, reporting 12.3% in 2018 which outpaced the 5.7% growth in 2017 (see Graph 4.4). India is the largest recipient of remittances worldwide and accounts for a large part of this growth. Remittances have grown in India by 14% in 2018, resulting in $78.6 billion USD in transfers. Some of these fund transfers can be linked to the crisis and national disaster, while other components can be tied to philanthropic endeavors that encourage religious and familial support of a person's country of origin. The growth in trade and entrepreneurial activities in India is also an avenue for the encouragement of international investment and promotion of needs, which has an externality of furthering private money transfers.

The inflow of remittances to LMIC reached a record high in 2018 with expectations that this trend will continue in 2019 and become the largest source of external funding for those countries. While the cost of sending monies remains high and off-target for the World Bank's Sustainable

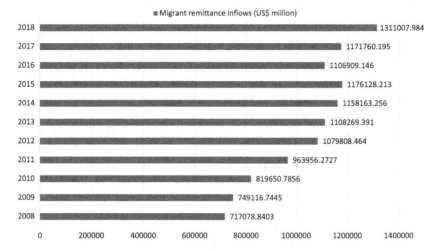

■ Migrant remittance inflows (US$ million)

Year	Value
2018	1311007.984
2017	1171760.195
2016	1106909.146
2015	1176128.213
2014	1158163.256
2013	1108269.391
2012	1079808.464
2011	963956.2727
2010	819650.7856
2009	749116.7445
2008	717078.8403

Graph 4.4 South Asia remittance inflows ($USD million) 2008–2018

Note: Data from the World Bank, depicting the inflow of remittances over a ten-year span (2009–2019) to the region of South Asia.

Development Goals 2030, there remains a high variance of costs to send monies depending on the country receiving.

Dilip Ratha, head of KNOMAD summed up the latest World Bank reports,

> Remittances are on track to become the largest source of external financing in developing countries. The high costs of money transfers reduce the benefits of migration. Renegotiating exclusive partnerships and letting new players operate through national post offices, banks, and telecommunication companies will increase competition and lower remittance prices.

(2019)

Individual Country Focus

Moving this chapter's discussion back to the individual country, we have been funneling the information on costs of remittances and dollar amounts of money transfers from a worldwide view to regional and now we return to the specific focal areas: Mexico and India.

Mexico

The Center for Latin America Monetary Studies (CEMLA) has compiled country-level data on remittances for Mexico that is steeped in rich quantitative data points. Inclusion in their data is gender differences, regional (within Mexico) changes, and the ability to view differences over time trends. Dr. Jesus A. Cervantes Gonzalez is the lead author and expert on *remesas* in Mexico. The authors of this book have had the distinct pleasure of interfacing with him on multiple occasions to further their knowledge and the contents of this book. Mexico has seen a rise in remittances over the last two years, which was predicted, though at the time a worrisome point.

While we know that in 2018 Mexico received $37.7 billion USD and is the third largest recipient of remittance globally (World Bank; see Graph 4.5), it wasn't less than a decade ago that there was a decline in remittances to Latin America and particularly Mexico. This decline was attributed to the recent recession (U.S. Great Recession, 2007), but statistics forecasted that by 2013 remittances to Latin America would again rise, which they did, except to Mexico. In 2013, remittances to Mexico were $22 billion USD, still below their 2006 peak by 29%; whereas the rest of Latin American countries were slightly surpassing expectations (Pew Research Center, 2013). Potential links to why there was a lack of remittances reaching Mexico from the U.S. was hypothesized to be the crash of the housing market, where many U.S.-living Mexicans were employed in construction jobs. And with the lessening of housing needs, the construction market declined as well, leading to less money available for remitters to send abroad. However, a 2013 study from the World Bank concluded that the housing market's connection to remittances has

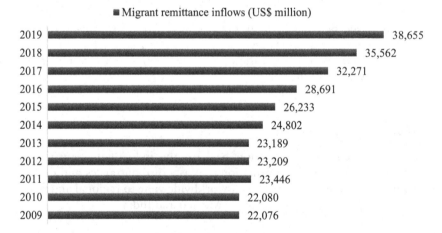

Graph 4.5 Mexico remittance inflows ($USD million) 2009–2019

Note: Data from the World Bank, depicting the inflow of remittances over a ten-year span (2009–2019) to Mexico.

weakened. It was also hypothesized that the Mexican population in the U.S. has declined and therefore fewer persons send money back to Mexico. To further support this factor, in a 2012 study by Passel, Cohn, and Gonzalez-Barrera, they noted that 1:10 Mexican-born people live in the United States. And that same study found that there was a decreased number of arrivals to the U.S. and interestingly enough an increased number of departures, while the latter did include deportations. And since the U.S. is the source of nearly (98%, in 2012) all the remittances to Mexico, each of the above-cited factors could have been contributing factors to the unsteady and declined remittance amounts to Mexico from 2007–2013.

Mexico did rally and increased its efforts of tracking remittances and researching multiple levels, through various lenses, of the remittance market. One of the factors looked at is a gender differential and gender motive in remittance giving in Latin America (Cervantes, 2014). Globally, women total approximately 50% of migrants and this is not different in Latin America and the Caribbean. In 2013, CEMLA researchers utilized the Grupo Financiero Banorte, SAB database to analyze remittances—BANORTE is one of Mexico's primary remittance payer banks. Results indicated that in Mexico, women are the primary beneficiaries of remittances, receiving about three-quarters of the remittances from the U.S. (Cervantes, 2015). And 30% of the remittances analyzed (2.9 million) were sent by women, and 72% of private money transfers sent to women by women, were the main group benefiting. Results further delineated that remittances sent by women were typically less in amount than men remitters (for Mexico). And that the average remittance sent was $468 dollars USD, though interestingly enough the study also shed light on the amount of income earnings from Mexican immigrant workers in the U.S. and there was not a difference found between men and women (Cervantes, 2015).

Overall, remittances to Mexico from the U.S. play a vital and important role in the daily lives of both immigrants in the U.S. as remitters and Mexican citizens as receivers. These numbers are not expected to dwindle but are rather forecasted to continually grow. Multiple programs have been crafted between the U.S. and Mexico to assist in the transfer of funds (Directo a México) while also seeking to find a common ground between the movement of people from Mexico to the U.S. and sustainability of economic opportunities in Mexico as an option as well (Partnerships for Prosperity). We will discuss these in further detail in Chapter 5 and seek to offer an understanding of how such programs further expand on the quantitative data interpretation.

An interesting fact about remittances in Mexico is the use of bank accounts as well. According to the World Bank, only 9% of persons in Latin America and the Caribbean use a bank account to receive remittances, while CEMLA research sheds light that in Mexico 18% utilize a bank account to receive monies. And to further this finding, if a bank account was used to receive funds and the remitter was a man, a higher amount was sent than a women remitter.

The dynamics in Mexico are an interesting case that continues to be shaped by political, economic, and social changes both within the country and by the neighboring United States. This is not a discussion that will cease to exist anytime soon, but one that takes into account hard numbers and connects them to already established theories of remittances. There is a connection between identification and motivation that is also affected by economic forces outside of one's country of origin (as well as inside, see the case of India below for further examples), as seen through the U.S. Great Recession beginning in 2007 and the dramatically lowering of remittances to all of Latin America and Mexico. But through this and perhaps despite this, there are still strong links and connections between the U.S. and Mexico that shape the remittance landscape.

India

As India's economy evolves into a market that is stimulated by opportunities to grow, policies that may or may not encourage spending (see Chapter 5) and with a population that is eager to seek out the next new idea, it is no wonder that remittances are highest in India. Entrepreneurial ventures such as Flipkart are entering the market and utilizing a localization strategy that allows for insider knowledge of Indian traditions, customs, and desires to sell goods online with near-immediate local delivery. Their business model is similar to that of Amazon, and while we in the U.S. are familiar with the powerhouse of online sales (Amazon), Flipkart is now a local household name in India, reaching a larger market share than Amazon and garnering the attention of Walmart (Joshi, 2020). This is just one such example of how India's economy is evolving and opening up to international companies that work on a virtual platform, thereby making it easier to pave the way for technology introductions into the country as a whole. And as detailed in Chapter 3, technology and remittances go hand in hand. With the expanding innovative offerings to remit through tech ventures, India is continuing to see a rise in money transfers.

While we have discussed the quantitative numbers as linked to India and remittances, we also want to link the conversation with the premise of this book, remittances through multiple lenses and see-through models of identification and motivation. In the case of India, while we know that India is the top recipient of remittances globally, we saw a statistically large spike in 2018 (see Graph 4.6). In South Asia, while there was a 12.3% increase of remittances which outpaces the 2017 growth. And India recorded a 14% growth in 2018. Part of this is due to the connections that remitters have with their country of origin. As previously mentioned, there were floods in the southern Indian state of Kerala. When we interviewed individuals from that region and organizations connected to

■ Migrant remittance inflows (US$ million)

Year	Value
2019	82,203
2018	78,609
2017	68,967
2016	62,744
2015	68,910
2014	70,389
2013	69,970
2012	68,821
2011	62,499
2010	53,480
2009	49,204

Graph 4.6 India remittance Inflows ($USD million) 2009–2019

Note: Data from the World Bank, depicting the inflow of remittances over a ten-year span (2009–2019) to India.

the region, we found that when we look at the data of remittance growth in 2018, there may be a link to humanitarian aid and a purposeful outpouring of support as well as solicited requests for support directly following the disaster. While the interviews offered a different non-objective lens to think about the growth of remittances in 2018 to India, they also brought to light that it may be the remitters' country of origins struggles that fuel (at least in part) remittance giving. And this directly ties into both identification and motivation theories of remittance giving.

Furthermore, in the case of India, the remittance market is flooded by multiple parties that not only include banks (they have the largest share of the market), but also are non-bank money transfer organizations, foreign exchange bureaus, cooperative banks, and the post offices in India. Each of these entities has a stake in the remittance market in India and plays a part in the growth of remittances received. However, there is a severe lack of transparency and financial inclusion in India. In 2015, there were 950.8 million people in India, age 15 or higher with a 1,670 GNI per capita (Global Findex, 2017). And while 79% of adults report having a bank account, India is still labeled as 'underbanked.' The Global Findex also noted that in 2015, 28.7% have made or received a digital payment which rose nearly 10% from the previous year (19.3% in 2014). And this number is higher when compared to all of South Asia, 27.8% in 2015 and 16.7% in 2014. However, it was also noted that 38.5% of adults have an inactive account in the past year (2017). India through the Reserve Bank of India (RBI) has set numerous regulations that aim to assist in remittances both internationally and domestically (Trading Economics, 2018). To accomplish this they (RBI) have started to allow third-party, non-bank actors to offer services that include door-to-door financial transactions. Innovative financial strategies such as this may also be a contributor to the increase of remittances in India, as the number of banks, ATMs, and digitized machines have increased since the on-start of the program. Primarily help is through offering access to financial systems, which still continue to be an issue in rural India. The downside of these outreach programs and connections with third-party financial services is that there is little to no incentive for the continued use of savings or bank accounts. So while an individual may utilize these agents for money transfers, there are not sustainable or continual reasons to keep banking with these services, thereby not actually addressing the 'underbanked' concept. And this might simply come down to a concept of access and addressing the need of the consumer versus standardizing the practice globally.

Conclusion

Understanding the quantitative numbers associated with remittances is an important part of the conversation of impacts, externalities, and influences. This is true on the global scale; as we have detailed in the first part of this chapter, remittances have effects on an international scale. Remittances total over $500 billion USD (Pew Research Center, 2019), a number that has never been documented so high. This includes numerous methods of transaction, each with their own positives and negatives, particularly in the policy realm. We discuss these interactions and powers of remittances on and surrounding policy in Chapter 5. We do not, however, come to concrete or one-size-fits-all recommendations for further policy advancements; rather we detail the recent history of policies, practices, and procedures in both the Mexican and Indian contexts. With the global effects of remittances, it is no wonder that in some countries, the contribution of remittances is upwards of 7, 8, 9 and more percent of their GDP. In the cases of Mexico and India, 3.1 and 2.8% respectively (World Bank), though if we were to look at the Philippines where remittances are 9% of their GDP or Guatemala whose 2019 remittances accounted for 13% of their GDP, we would further see not only the impact but economic reliance on these money transfers. This also brings to the conversation the reliance on such money and the sustainability of such practices. While we know that philanthropic giving practices have roots that date as far back as recorded history, we do not have a measure of how much and for how long these giving practices will last. When we look at the tradition of hawala, it is largely undocumented and specifically anonymous in its foundation. But this also means that there is little to no concrete data available that gives researchers, or economists for that matter, a handle on the country's reliance on these funds. Furthermore, from our own ground interviews with persons who remit, researchers who delve into the nitty-gritty of a specific country data points, and organizations that service money transfers, we can conclude that the practice of sending and receiving remittances is not likely to dwindle anytime soon. We also know there is a connection between humanitarian aid and remittances; when a country experiences a natural disaster, it is nearly expected that people from all over the globe who have origin ties to the affected communities will show their support through monetary contributions. As previously mentioned this was the case in Kerala after the 2018 floods. While this is excellent in infrastructure re-establishment, it is not sustainable for day-to-day operations of a nation.

References

CEMLA. (2018). *Total Amount of Remittances Received in 2017: By Country in Millions of USD*. Mexico City. Accessible at www.cemla.org/PDF/remesaseinclusion/2018-06-Remittances-LAC-2017.pdf

Cervantes, J. (Junio, 2014). *La mirgacion latinoamericana de genero femenino a Estados Unidos y las remesas*. Mexico City: Centro de Estudios Monetarios Latinoamericanos.

Cervantes, J. (2015). *Female Integration and Remittance Flow to Mexico*. Mexico City: CEMLA and BANORTE.

Cohn, D., Gonzalez-Barrera, A., & Cuddington, D. (2013). Remittances to Latin America recover- but not to Mexico. *Hispanic Trends*. Pew Research Center. Accessible at www.pewresearch.org/hispanic/2013/11/15/remittances-to-latin-america-recover-but-not-to-mexico/

Global Findex. (2017). *The World Bank*. Accessible at https://globalfindex.world bank.org/node

Joshi, D. (2020). Walmart's acquisition of Flipkart: A paradigm shift in retail management strategy—Current and future implications for various stakeholders. In *Paradigm Shift in Management Philosophy*. Cham: Palgrave Macmillan. Pp. 65–86.

Pew Research Center. (2019). Remittance flow worldwide in 2017. *Global Attitudes & Trends*. Pew Research Center. Accessible at www.pewresearch.org/global/interactives/remittance-flows-by-country/

The Global Knowledge Partnership on Migration and Development (KNOMAD). (2019). *The World Bank, Remittances Data* [digital, open access]. Accessible at https://www.knomad.org/data/remittances

Trading Economics. (2018). *India Remittances: Reserve Bank of India*. Accessible at https://tradingeconomics.com/india/remittances

White, L. (2018). The curse of the war on cash. *CATO Journal*. Accessible at https://www.cato.org/cato-journal/springsummer-2018/curse-war-cash Retrieved on Dec 18, 2019.

World Bank Group. (2019, Apr). *Migration and Remittances: Recent Developments and Outlooks*. KNOMAD, Migration and Remittances Team, Social Protection and Jobs. World Bank. Accessible at https://www.knomad.org/sites/default/files/2019-04/Migrationanddevelopmentbrief31.pdf

5 Policy and Remittances

Human Needs and the Shaping of Practice With Policy

Even with the increase of technological investments and know-how, concerns of security risks and costs have risen to become prevalent concerns for many migrants sending money transfers as discussed in Chapter 4. These issues and concerns also bring into question public policy and the construction of policy around remittances. In this chapter, we take a domestic, United States, view of policy initiatives, public good, and delve into implications for foreign receivers where information is available.

Remittances and the need to send money have increased over the last two decades but significantly over the last two years. With the rise of low-to middle-income countries (LMICs), flow in remittances has reached $500 billion USD (World Bank, 2019). However, in order to send money, there is a cost associated with the transfer of funds that vary widely depending on the location monies are sent, the method used to send funds, and the mode used for delivery. These costs to send are not strictly monetary, but consist of social, physical, political, and economic impacts. And it is within the policy arena where the monitoring of remittances is created. But even with constructed guidelines, policies, and procedures, the actual practices, again, vary widely between nations.

In this chapter we will first define and outline several major concepts, then present the cases of Mexico and India as related to policy initiatives. While we are not crafting a policy brief or offering action plan recommendations, we are laying out a timeline approach of the different frameworks created by policy endeavors that shape remittance practice.

In order to fully develop this discussion on policy, policy implications, and the ways policies are shaping practice, it is imperative we refer back to the original conversation (placed in Chapter 2 of this book) regarding philanthropy and remittances, understanding that at times there is an overlap of motivation and who gives, resulting in similar reasons of giving and factors that have been used to operationalize giving (Lucas & Starke, 1985; Schervish & Haven, 1997; Bekkers & Wiepking, 2011). We also look towards the concept of humanitarian aid and its role in philanthropic studies. The aid of this type can be seen within the identification model of philanthropy and we suggest these concepts of identity shift and fluctuate depending on the time, place, and circumstances. An example of how humanitarian aid fits into this discussion is when natural or humanitarian disasters strike one's country of origin and the identification with one's own kin and people of one's own country goes up. While this is a single type, an example is when we saw monetary transfers rise in India after the flooding disaster in Kerala, southern India (2018), which was most likely a contributing factor in the rise of over 14% of remittances to India in 2018.

The policy that surrounds the private transfers of money is not standardized nor is it limited to a single type of transaction or location. Policy enactments have trends and tend to be politically bound in their foundation, use, and conception. In the next sections of this chapter, we strive to present the cases of Mexico and India, delving into a timeline approach of the different initiatives, endeavors, policy struggles, and action plans that have been proposed and implemented. The planning, execution, and eventual results of the multitude of policy frameworks have produced varied outcomes and at times the policies were discontinued without any impact studies or follow-through. As mentioned in the opening of this chapter, this discussion arises from a U.S. outflow of remittances to a Mexico and India inflow. Whereby policies are implemented on both the sender and receiver countries and then melted together, creating at times more ebbs than flows, and trials and tribulations, nonetheless they offer a perspective to view another force that is shaping remittances globally. Further, this extends the notion that there are multiple invisible forces for and against each other in remittances.

Mexico: The Situation for Remittances

Our neighbor to the south has had trials, tribulations, and triumphs in its relationship with remittances and particularly with the interaction of public policy in regards to governance and regulation of remittances. There has been and continues to be a strong link between monetary policies and the current political regime in office, both in Mexico and in the U.S. But throughout these political changes there is a continued migratory flow of emigrants from Mexico, predominantly to the U.S., and this meshing and melding of cultures plays an integral role in the formation of policy, which in turn impacts the private money transfer practices.

In this section, we aim to provide a timeline view of the major policy impacts regarding remittances within the Mexican context. We have been fortunate to interact with key researchers, academics, policy entities, private money transfer organizations, and to interview numerous migrants to obtain a mixed-methods approach in understanding the actual practice of remittances.

Migratory flows into and out of Mexico are steeped in history and can be traced back to the indigenous population. This flow has been tracked for the last hundred years and in total Mexico is second in terms of the number of emigrants, with India third. There are an estimated 37.5 million people of Mexico origin in the U.S. when second- and third-generation Mexicans are considered in this figure. The migratory patterns of Mexicans have fluctuated over the recent past with the return migration—at times voluntary and others forced—many times including parents with children born abroad. This return migratory pattern has a cultural and economic impact as well with the unplanned or unexpected arrival of citizens. While Mexico's history is steeped with migratory movement out of a region, there is a little history and even fewer policies related to the return or reception of migrants, i.e. returning Mexicans (Arenillas, Ling, & Serrano, 2018).

Reviewing the current history and outlining policy influences and impacts on remittances is the goal of the below section. We aim to contextualize the push and pull between U.S. and Mexican policies and the practices that are occurring as a result of those. When attempting to understand policies and flows of remittances in Mexico, we must consider the institutions that deal with money transfers, governance, regulations, and policies. Consideration needs to be placed on partnerships, nonprofit or third-sector advocacy efforts, formalized initiatives, and political relationships. Some noteworthy endeavors include U.S.- Mexico Partnership for Prosperity, Directo a México, Institute of Mexicans Abroad, Mexican hometown associations, Mexican National Policy on Financial Inclusion, National Remittance Plan (G20–2015 and 2017), Tres por Uno program, and the current U.S. administration migration policies. We will delve deeper into these below.

U.S. and Mexico's Relationship in the Political Context

It is hard to offer an unbiased, politically correct, and public acceptable answer to this above section title. While we can view many media sources from a plethora of different outlets, there are overwhelming conflicts in information available and too many opinions to solicit enough for any type of generalized assumptions. However, what we can do is look at it from a 36,000-foot viewpoint and discuss the policy proposals and interactions.

There are uncertainties surrounding the new economic policies that are being proposed in the U.S. and their impacts on Latin America; however, there are three parts of these new economic policies that may directly influence Latin America: alteration in policies on trade, immigration, and remittances. Note that a standardized policy is not blanketed to a specific region; rather, given Mexico's close proximity to the U.S. and their close relationship, Mexico tends to be the most affected nation when it comes to changes in U.S. global policies.

On Wednesday, January 25, 2017, President Donald J. Trump signed two executive orders regarding immigration:

- "Border Security and Immigration Enforcement Improvements," detailing the construction of a border wall and enhancements to border security
- "Enhancing Public Safety in the Interior of the United States," enabling and enacting measures to detect and deport illegal aliens from inside the U.S.

While we are not aiming to pursue a political argument or intense discussion within the context of this chapter, it is needed to set the stage for where the relationship is between the U.S. and Mexico to then better understand where we came from and the shaping of remittances. The above executive orders do not directly mention remittances but they focus on migrants who are both the senders and receivers of over $27 billion USD in 2016 and $35.7 billion USD in 2018, and forecasted remittances for inflows to Mexico are expected to continue to rise (World Bank Group, 2019).

According to some research outlets (BBVA) as of September of 2018, there have not been any negative effects in Mexican remittances given the change in U.S. administration or the increased focus on migrants in the U.S. And it is further estimated by BBVA that because of the low unemployment rate in the U.S. plus the favorably high peso (Mexican currency) to dollar (U.S. currency) exchange rate, an 11% growth will continue in remittances to Mexico.

We have discussed the impact of Mr. Trump's rhetoric around using taxes on remittances to build the border wall with Mexico. While this initiative didn't gain traction and he had to dip into funds from other U.S. government sources, the fact that this initiative was on the table means that remittances are viewed by both sides—the U.S. and Mexico— as being important. With remittance amounts totaling the revenues from oil exports, the phenomenon of remittance from the U.S. to Mexico is not easy to ignore (BBVA).

With that being stated and the potentially favorable economic conditions assisting towards a positive growth of remittance outflows from the U.S. and inflows to Mexico, and despite the hostile (there is not a better or more descriptive term to use in this context) attitude towards migrants in the U.S., it seems that this is not slowing down support, motivation, or identification with one's own country of origin and the dedication to connecting with that spirit of giving.

However, there are still a multitude of factors that are present in Mexico that shape remittance practices.

Banking Governance, Regulation, and Policies

The federal government in Mexico oversees all banking and financial institutions in Mexico. Banxico regulates money transfer services, though only those that follow a formal channel (Federal Banking Law in Mexico). The banking system as a whole in Mexico is regulated by four different governmental agencies: Bank of Mexico (Banxico), the central Mexican bank; Ministry of Finance and Public Credit (SHCH), the ministry within the executive branch of the federal government with the duties of regulating all financial institutions; National Banking and Securities Commission (CNBV), an agency that works with the SHCP; and the Financial Consumer Protection Commission (CONDUSEF).

In order to be authorized as a banking service or any financial service, a company must file with CNBV. All retail banking institutions in Mexico are required to be incorporated as a corporation under Mexican law and this must be approved by the CNBV; additionally, once approved for incorporation, it is required to be published for public knowledge through the Federal Official Gazette.

Security Concerns and Consumer Protection

In June 2000 Mexico joined FATF, the Financial Action Task Force. This inter-governmental body was established in 1989 and objectives include setting standards for more effective application of legal, regulatory, and operational measures to mitigating money laundering, terrorist financing, and other threats to a country's financial system. Essentially the FATF offers policy frameworks and guidelines for member countries (FATF, 2019). According to Mexican law history, money laundering was criminalized in 1996 and in 1997 the Financial Intelligence Unity (FIU) was organized to investigate money laundering. All banks and financial institutions are subject to anti-money laundering regulations, which require them to not only maintain records of all transactions but also identify customers. Through these regulations, banks must report unusual activity and any transaction over $10,000 USD. Mexico is actively implementing standards as recommended by the FATF; for example, the Federal Penal Code (Articles 139 and 140) was updated in 2018 to link terrorist financing with money laundering.

Existing regulations that were published in 2004 in the Federal Official Gazette were created to strengthen the financial system and promote transparency and imposed on credit institutions, exchange bureaus, money transfer operators, and all money service businesses. The regulations include:

- Reporting of unusual or suspicious operations and transfers
- Establishing internal policies for identifying customers
- Utilizing a computerized system to save and track information
- Keeping records of every transaction, archived for at least ten years
- Developing and offering training and informational sessions
- Maintaining confidentiality regarding transactions

Again in 2014, Mexican President Enrique Peña Nieto set forth financial reforms that redefined the mission of development banks to promote private financing using lower financing rates. Results from these reforms have reduced borrowing costs and increased access to credit. Outlined in the 2014 reforms were four goals:

1. Promote lending
2. Expand credit
3. Increase competition
4. Ensure security

As with all new or recently implemented reforms, there are concerns about timeliness of results, capacity issues, and sustainability. The 2014 financial reforms in Mexico continue to have the same trepidations. But slow results have been already actualized.

Policy Initiatives Between the U.S. and Mexico

U.S.–Mexico Partnership for Prosperity

In 2001 President George W. Bush and President Vicente Fox met for the first time and through that meeting and subsequent discussions, the U.S.-Mexico Partnership for Prosperity was created. It was seen as a benefit for both the U.S. and Mexico to craft a concrete action plan to promote economic development, specifically in areas of Mexico where growth lagged. This turned into a private-public alliance that aimed to yoke the power of the private sector to foster an environment in which a Mexican citizen would not feel the need to leave his or her home because of a lack of jobs or opportunities. It took six months of work and the Partnership yielded an action plan for leveraging resources.

The action plan seeks to facilitate investment into multiple projects within small business ventures, housing, agriculture, roads, ports, airports, and information technology. The Partnership was designed to hold itself accountable, measure results, and produce outcomes.

Directo a México

Directo a México is a service for sending money from a U.S. bank account to any bank account in Mexico. In the early 2000s, the Bank of Mexico and the U.S. Federal Reserve undertook a study to seek a recommendation of whether to link both countries' payment systems as a direct response to the Partnership for Prosperity's action plan. Effectively this connection between banking systems would allow for efficient interbank exchanges and create a mechanism to process payments between counties. In 2003, the link was established. The Bank of Mexico and the U.S.

Federal Reserve established a payment system. In 2004, payments were able to be sent from any enrolled U.S. financial institution to any individual bank account in Mexico. In 2005, this payment service was registered and authorized through CBNV and named Directo a México.

Directo a México's (DM) purpose was to help U.S. financial institutions reach and assist customers with a low-cost and convenient way to remit funds to Mexico. Further, it provides U.S. financial institutions with customizable, dual-language marketing material and offers consumers an affordable alternative to costly money transfer organizations. And DM assists U.S. financial institutions in capitalizing on the growing U.S.-to-Mexico remittance market.

Interestingly enough there have not been many studies conducted on the usage, operationalization, outcomes, or efficiency of Directo a México as a mechanism for remittances.

National Policy on Financial Inclusion

In June of 2016, the National Policy on Financial Inclusion was published. Its goals were for the adult population of the country to have access to financial services. Specifically, at minimum half of the adult population was to become part of the formal financial system. Mexico was included by the World Bank as a top 25 country priority to achieve Universal Financial Access by 2020. While there have been some efforts to achieve financial inclusion, the telecommunications sector has a long way to go in developing and offering virtual access to financial products and services.

The Financial Inclusion Program for Migrants, part of the initiative, offers an innovative way for Mexican citizens repatriating from the U.S. to gain financial services, in the form of bank accounts and other direct support. The National Savings and Financial Services Bank (Bansefi), a development bank, opened 11 strategically located service branches along the U.S.- Mexico border and one in Mexico City to provide financial services and education as part of the repatriation. Since the initiation of this program, Bansefi's services have been well received, resulting in quicker repatriates, meaning a quicker return to being productive Mexican citizens and restarting labor activities to generate income and further provide for one's family's well-being.

Institute of Mexicans Abroad

El Instituto de Los Mexicanos en el Exterior—Institute of Mexicans Abroad, or IME—was formed in 1990 by the Ministry of Foreign Affairs to encourage involvement in Mexican communities abroad. Information was encouraged to be provided for services in health, education, culture, and community organizations. Their mission is to promote activities that raise the standard of living for Mexican living abroad in the form of their communities. Programs that stem from the institute tend to be civil society organizations and collaborations between the institute and U.S. entities such as school districts, hospitals, universities, and foundations. Multiple projects have resulted from these partnerships, all with the common outcome of collaboration and information sharing among common groups.

Mexican Hometown Associations

"In the Americas, U.S.-based Mexican migrant organizations are one of the most visible forms of grassroots philanthropy aimed at supporting migrants' communities of origin" (Duquette-Rury & Bada, 2013). These voluntary civic associations are an avenue for migrants to come together and connect with others from their communities of origin. In the late 1980s, several Mexican states started to participate in a federal matching funds program that turned into the formalized Tres por Uno or 3x1 Program for Migrants, formalized in 2002 by President Vincent Fox's administration. The 3x1 Program offered a peso-for-peso contribution match for Mexican migrant clubs, up to 1 million pesos. The public-private partnerships developed sustainable working programs that spread across all Mexican states. The 3x1 Program is a national social spending program where not only are contributions matched, these contributions are mainly remittances. Funds are sourced with the aim to improve public services through cross-border partnerships.

National Remittance Plan (G20–2015 and 2017)

Highlights from the 2015 plan include an aim to increase remittance market competition, improve financial systems infrastructure, and improve transparency and consumer protection of transfers. In 2017, the Mexican government focused on promoting innovative business models utilizing business technology to increase capacity and become more cost-effective for remittance transfers. The plan directly promotes the continued use of Directo a México program from the Central Bank, where the commission is extremely low (0.21%). Currently, there is a FinTech Law in the Mexican Government waiting for approval; once passed it will offer protection to customers, provide legal platforms and fiscal certainty to ensure compliance with policy standards in financial services.

Mexico and Future Policy

As seen in the above discussion on policies related to financial services and specifically remittances, there is a large overlap between plans, programs, and initiatives in Mexico. Several of the government-led policy proposals create further projects that turn into programs that are later supported or focused on in other policy endeavors. Whether this is by design or happenstance, there are numerous frameworks that are geared toward the collection, sustainability, and effective use of remittances within Mexico. This is further supported by the close relationship (though unstable at times) with the U.S. government and partnerships with private sector organizations.

India: Remittances and a Changing Economy

India is the top recipient of remittances worldwide, reaching over $78 billion USD in 2018 according to the World Bank. These monies come from a variety of diaspora Indian migrants, concentrated in the Gulf region, the U.S.A., U.K., and Canada. Interestingly, India received more than 50% of its total remittance from the Gulf Region. Remittances play an integral role in the economy of India, financing the trade deficit for example. Despite this, India's dependency (measured through GDP) on remittances remains stable at 3%, which is interesting because of the high amount of remittances and the fast-changing macro-economic structure and pace of the Indian economy. By contrast and to shed a different light, in many low-income countries, remittances play a role in the development of and also shaping of external policies, though in these cases remittances account for over 10% of their (respective) country's GDP.

Given the large amounts of monies flowing into India, one would think there are solid structures and frameworks in place to govern and dictate private transfers. However, according to many studies, there is an absence of coherent policy frameworks on dealing with these remittances, which results in a decrease in realizing a high level of utilization, creating negative impacts for India. If utilized productively, through institutional and public support, remittance has the potential to become an instrument for creating alternative livelihoods and a mechanism for sustainable development in many states within India (Pande & Yan, 2018). As mentioned the economic structure of India is changing and the latest numbers,2016, show that the amount of Indians with a banking account is on the rise (CGAP, 2019).

The timeline of policy related to remittances in India is varied, but in 2006, some state-level governments were experimenting with electronic cash transfers from bank accounts, which required delivery from a bank agent. In 2013, the federal government attempted to target some of the largest cash transfers and move them to an electronic cash transfer. This shift has resulted in ease and better accountability for the sender and receiver. It has gained popularity and through the newly elected national government has gained momentum through renewed policy efforts. In terms of numbers, while we mentioned that remittances accounted for 3% of India's GDP, the World Bank has kept data points on the percentage of GDP regarding remittances since 1975. The lowest percentage was 0.44 in 1975 and the highest 4.21 in 2008 (World Bank Group, 2019).

In India, remittances and remittance-related activities are broken down and apart, resulting in various authorities for each activity. These include the Reserve Bank of India (RBI), the Ministry of Finance (MoF), the Ministry of Overseas Indian Affairs (MOIA), the CCI, and the Ministry of Consumer Affairs, the latter coming into public discourse and general conversation when the national online seller Flipkart partnered with the global powerhouse Walmart in a billion-dollar transaction in 2018. However, the MoF, the MOIA, and the RBI are the central players within the remittance discussion and the driving forces behind moving the needle to improve remittance serviced and improve market conditions for remittances. Here it should be noted that the MOIA was created in 2004 for the direct purpose to "promote, nurture and sustain a mutually beneficial and symbiotic relationship between India and overseas Indians" (MOIA, 2010). This ministry has been in charge of initiatives such as the Pravasi Bharatiya Divas, among others, which seek to engage the Indian diaspora to invest in India and also to stay connected.

Remittance Market in India

The remittance market in India is serviced by multiple parties: commercial banks, non-bank money transfer operators (MTOs), foreign exchange bureaus, cooperative banks, post offices, and a variety of other commercial entities acting as agents (in some cases sub-agents). In India, the term collectively used for these actors is Remittance Service Providers or RSPs.

The Actors

Banks

Banks are typically the first place visited to send and receive remittances. Banks have as much as 80% of the market share for remittances within India. Banks also yield the highest costs associated with remittances according to the World Bank (2019).

Money Transfer Operators (MTOs)

These include multinational enterprises such as Western Union (WU), MoneyGram, and others. MTOs are the second most widely utilized RSPs in India. If we break down this particular market share, WU is the leader. This is not surprising given their globalization efforts, their longevity in the global arena, and their ability to utilize a localization or glocalization strategy of expansion within multi-country areas (Robertson, 1995). This strategy allows for the understanding of a worldwide view of expansion while taking the local view of said expansions into equal account. This view of globalization further considers that while there is a trend towards global markets and political interactions between nations and nation-states, there is an associated need to recognize increased diversity, the importance of community. Back to the market share of WU, there are more than 50,000 locations in India, operating out of 7,000 cities. WU has a partnership with upwards of 30 banks in India as well.

India Post

India's post has established its own set of offerings when it comes to remittances, primarily in the form of money order (MO) and postal order (PO) services. Both MOs and POs are ways to send money from across the 160,000 post offices around India.

Internet

Private banks in India have become players in this remittance area. Banks such as HDFC and ICICI have begun offering e-commerce type remittance services. This trend has spread to state-owned banks as well, such as SBI and Bank of India, with branded offerings to include e-remit and star-e-remit.

Other Actors

While this list is not exhaustive in the area of remittance service providers, we wanted to add in other actors, to include courier transfers, in-kind remittances, and hawala/hundi. You will note that a deeper discussion of hawala and in-kind remittances occurred in Chapter 2. But it should be noted here that these are other types of avenues for giving and receiving remittances in the case of India. These methods often include low transaction costs, speed in receiving funds, a way to perform giving anonymously, and specifically in the case of hawala a strong tradition is steeped within this method of monetary transactions.

To contrast the speed and efficiency of the hawala system of transfers, courier transfers are much less efficient and come with more risk. As there are no tangible guarantees that your monies will make it to the destination on the sending end of the transaction; nor a guarantee that monies will arrive at their destination on the receiving end of the transaction. This risk is due to the physical need to handle the cash and cross border. On the flip side, the hawala system does not have a tracking mechanism which is unfortunate in events such as this book where data is key to understanding the expanse and impact of differing systems, though some academic studies have estimated that the hawala market in India may be as much as 30 to 40% of the recorded remittances.

Regulatory Systems in India

The regulatory system in India in regards to remittances is overseen by the Foreign Exchange (FX) Department. The FX Department established two approval systems that administer the process of remittance services: the Rupee Drawing Arrangement (RDA) and Money Transfer Services Scheme (MTSS). Below is a synopsis of the different structures of the approval systems (Afram, 2012).

RDA

The RDA has a business arrangement that offers a bank in India to link with a financial services company in a different country. The foreign financial services company is not necessarily a bank, but sources the funds from the remitter. The Indian bank then disburses the funds in India using their already established bank branches. In order for a bank in India to operate with foreign financial companies, the Indian bank has to apply to the FX Department. Under the RDA, the source of countries includes the Gulf Cooperation Council (GCC) countries, Singapore and Hong Kong SAR, China. Under the RDA system, it is determined that the foreign financial services companies are regulated effectively by the individual local monetary authority. Otherwise, there are no particular partnership restrictions nor are there specific appointments of agents within the partnership agreement. While there is a necessary collateral guarantee requirement under the RDA scheme, in order for a foreign financial service company to qualify for partnership through the RDA approval system, it must be a financial institution that is monitored and regulated by their own nation's monetary authority. Remittance transfers approved through RDA may be for any reason which includes business transactions. Payout modes include interbank payment instruments, but no direct cash is permitted under RDA. Under the RDA there are quarterly statements compiled and collected on all remittances received.

MTSS

The MTSS approval system works with foreign banking and non-banking services. These foreign financial companies partner with both banks and non-banking companies in India. Through these partnerships a principal-agent is appointed; this agent then appoints sub-agents. The foreign financial company sources the funds from the remitter and the recipient is able to collect funds in cask form from the agent/sub-agent. The recipient also has the option to receive funds using other interbank payment methods. In order for a principal-agent to receive funds, an application must be completed for approval through the FX Department. In this case, the foreign financial company is termed "Overseas Principal" and must submit an application for a license to the Payment and Settlements Department under the FX Department. It should be noted that there is only one "Overseas Principal" per foreign company, and each agent/sub-agent need not apply and be approved individually. Furthermore, there are no country-based restrictions through the MTSS system though there are amount limits on remittances for the recipient. A maximum of $2500 USD per remittances with a limit of 12 remittances per recipient per annum is allowed. And a distinctive point regarding the MTSS approval system is that the remittance service may only be used for remittances for family or personal expenses within India. This means that remittances for business transactions under the MTSS are strictly prohibited. There must be a capital guarantee or collateral of $50,000 USD or three days average worth of remittances (whichever is higher), but there are no restrictions on the type of partnerships. And under MTSS there are required quarterly reporting of the transaction volume as well as listings of all agents and sub-agents currently operating.

Authorization Institutions

To further delve into who has what type of authority over money transfers within India, each of the aforementioned actors and approval schemes has overlaps. But all foreign money transfers must conform to the Foreign Management Act (FEMA), 1999. FEMA was specifically crafted and implemented for the purpose of promoting the development and maintenance of a foreign exchange market in India. Through the act, it empowers the RBI to regulate and monitor foreign currency payments in and out of India, which includes remittances. It is under this act that foreign financial service companies are required to obtain a license. There are five main types of licenses: Authorized Dealer (AD) I, divided into non-bank and bank institutions: AD I non-bank and AD I bank; AD II and III, and Full-Fledged Money Changer (FFMC). AD IIs are money transfer agents and AD IIIs are specialized financial institutions. FFMCs purchase foreign exchange currency and resell it to Indians traveling abroad.

Regulation, Policies, and Enactments

There have been several frameworks that have been crafted in India to assist, mature, and sustain the entrance and exit of monies within India.

The Foreign Contribution (Regulation) Act (FCRA) of 1976 was enacted shortly after Indira Gandhi imposed the Emergency, which suspended civil and political liberties (see further research on India's history and links to civil discourse studies). While the Emergency was abrogated, the FCRA continued though it was frequently amended. The FCRA has regulated the Indian nonprofit sector without a political party or coalition affiliation since its conception. The FCRA regulates the acceptance and use of foreign contributions by Indian third-sector institutions, political parties, journalists, and other individuals. The interpretation and enforcement of the FCRA are overseen through the Ministry of Home Affairs. As mentioned there have been multiple amendments, which were often levied to enforce stronger regulation. Indian nonprofits are required to apply to the government through the Ministry of Home Affairs in order to accept foreign money transfers or contributions. If a nonprofit is not registered it cannot accept remittances on a continual basis. Nonprofits can apply for a one-time prior permission option, but the Ministry of Home Affairs is strict as to what organization qualifies to accept such contributions. The wording of the policy leads to further scrutiny and generally undefined wording. Through a 1984 amendment, contributions subject to the FCRA include donations to an Indian organization as well as direct foreign donations. This also meant that Indian organizations who received funds from another Indian organization, yielding indirect donations, must comply with the Act's registration or prior permission regulations as well. This addition to the Act impacted thousands of local non-governmental organizations. The further amendment enacted in 1996 required approval of officeholders within an organization by the Ministry of Home Affairs.

The FCRA is not only overseen by the Ministry of Home Affairs companies. The role of the courts in state-nonprofit relations is further supported through policy such as the FCRA. However, the courts at times can end up on both sides of a conflict, defending the nonprofit when it seeks to block state action or offensively when a nonprofit seeks to assert rights against a state entity (Ministry of Home Affairs, 2019).

The Foreign Contribution Amendment Rules

The Ministry of Home Affairs issued the new rules that allow for the entire registration of Indian organizations to be completed online (2015). This new rule is another addition to the FCRA. It now stipulates that the Indian nonprofits must report all foreign contributions they receive through their websites and provide the Ministry quarterly updates. Banks must also inform the Ministry within two days of receiving a transaction from a foreign remitter. Furthermore, the Ministry of Home Affairs has created a 'watch list' of donors who cannot offer any financial assistance to Indian organizations without clearance from the ministry. In 2016 there were a total of 18 major foreign donors on this 'watch list.'

The crackdown on International NGOs working in India over the past few years has been particularly glaring, also a cause for concern for scholars and activists around the world. As Sujeet Kumar, a Research Fellow at Jawaharlal Nehru University (JNU), one of the most prestigious universities in India points out, the FCRA was enacted in the 1970s to prevent foreign interference in Indian politics, but since 2010 it has become weaponized against any civil society organization that is working to empower people to question the actions of the government (Kumar, 2019). Kumar points out that in 2014, an intelligence bureau report accused foreign NGOs such as Greenpeace, Oxfam, etc., of being 'anti-development' and of negatively impacting India's GDP.

Kumar adds that

> In late 2018, it was revealed the Modi government had canceled the licenses of nearly 20,000 NGOs receiving foreign funds under the FCRA. According to a report on India's philanthropic landscape by the consultancy Bain and Company, there was around a 40% decline in foreign funding between 2015 and 2018.

This negative trend in philanthropic support (and some coming from remittances) has impacted the NGO landscape in India. More pervasive has been the fear of being on the wrong side of the law, whether by supporting these NGOs or financing them in any way.

Other Regulations Impacting Philanthropic Giving

Societies Registration Act, 1860, detailed the requirement for an organization to be fully registered and governed by the state.

Indian Trusts Act, 1882, is a federal law regulating trusts. It applies in Indian states that do not have their own designated Trust Acts. An example of a state-specific law is the *Bombay Public Trusts Act*, 1950 which applies to the states of Maharashtra and Gujarat.

Income Tax Act, 1961, is a federal law offering tax exemptions for nonprofits and deductions for donations.

Prevention of Terrorism Act, 2002, is a federal law that offers definitional parameters to 'terrorism' or 'terrorist acts' and provides additional authorization to counter-terrorism officials.

Characteristics of Remittances in India as Understood Through the Committee on Payments and Settlements System

Transparency and Consumer Protection

There is a push and general principle that remittances in India appear transparent and that consumers are informed about the different aspects of transactions.

Payment System Infrastructure

Continual improvements to the Payment System Infrastructure are being made to increase the efficiency of remittances. The Reserve Bank of India

(RBI) plays an integral role in this standard and in the overall opera-tion of India's payment systems. To this end, the RBI in conjunction with banks in India has established the NPCIL or National Payment Corpo-ration of India, a nonprofit that will establish a domestic payment card network for ATM usage.

Legal and Regulatory Environment

Through the Reserve Bank of India Act, 934, the RBI is empowered to make statutory regulations to electronic fund transfers between banks and other financial institutions.

Market Structure and Competition

The remittances market in India is dominated by banks with about 80% of the market share of inflow remittances being consumed by banks. Remittance services by MTOs are focused on cash payouts. Interestingly the demographics of remitters who use banks are predominantly white-collar workers whereas mainly blue-collar workers use MTOs. While the remittance market is dominated by banks, there is still a high level of competition in the bank-operated schemes. Leaders in the banking com-petition are ICICI Bank, SBI, Federal Bank, HDFC Bank, and the Bank of India. While the banking level of competition is high, in the MTO segment dominance is by WU with MoneyGram and UAE Exchange also competing.

Governance and Risk Management

The FX Department is responsible for the oversight of all remittances; therefore governance is provided through their oversight. Specific guide-lines related to fraud and operational risk management for remittance services do not exist in India.

Future Promises and Developments

As in the discussion that began "India: Remittances and a Changing Economy," there are several new developments and outlooks for the future of money transfers for India. Many banks have started rural bank-ing projects to provide services to the rural poor. Through the expanded use of mobile phones, even people of low income in remote areas are encouraged to utilize banking services. With the introduction of mobile networks in rural poor areas, partnership opportunities exist for mobile service providers to launch products that further utilize mobile phones. This can be seen as links or partnerships with banking institutions. Banks have already started to evaluate e-commerce style money transfers for payment schemes. Furthermore, India's Union Cabinet approved a proposal to extend proxy voting to non-resident Indians (NRIs) by amending electoral laws. Note that NRIs and overseas Indians are already allowed to vote in constituencies where they are registered, but now they will be able to use a proxy. Via a web-based service, NRIs may register themselves as voters. This service is offered in multiple languages, further-reaching untapped voting potential. This new policy is further connecting different nationals, overseas individuals and may offer new avenues for private money transfers as migrants are being offered another connection to their country of origin.

Further Discussion and Next Steps

Policies have a way of shaping practices, and this at times is the case with both the nations of Mexico and India, though there are many times where policy is shaped by practice as well. This was the case when the U.S. Federal Reserve and the Central Bank of Mexico noted the need for a low-cost alternative to money transfer companies to remit and receive payments across the border, and the creation of Directo a México was established. Whether policy comes first or second, there are multiple mechanisms in place to measure, oversee, and guide (though not always efficiently, as seen in the FCRA of 1976 in India). It is imperative that these policies be amended, updated, and monitored. Just as they set out to regulate and oversee the financial transactions, so too do they need to be understood and kept in check as well.

References

Afram, G. (2012). The remittance market in India: Opportunities, challenges, and policy options (English). In *Directions in Development: Finance*. Washington, DC: World Bank.

Arenillas, D. C., Ling, J. J., & Serrano, C. (2018). *Mexico: Yearbook of Migration and Remittances, 2018*. BBVA Research, Banco Bilbao Vizcaya Argentaria, S. A. Accessible at https://www.bbvaresearch.com/en/publicaciones/mexico-yearbook-of-migration-and-remittances-2018/

Bekkers, R., & Wiepking, P. (2011). A literature review of empirical studies of philanthropy. Eight mechanisms that drive charitable giving. *NVSQ*, 40, 924–973.

CGAP. (2019). *Research & Analysis*. The Consultative Group to Assist the Poor. Accessible at https://www.cgap.org/research

Duquette-Rury, L., & Bada, X. (2013). Continuity and change in Mexican migrant hometown associations: Evidence from new survey research. *Migraciones Internacionales*, 7(1), 65–99.

FATF. (2019). The Financial Action Task Force. *Who We Are*. Accessible at https://www.fatf-gafi.org/about/whoweare/#d.en.11232

Kumar, S. (2019). India: Decades of hostility against NGOs have worsened under Narendra Modi. *The Conversation*. Accessible at http://theconversation.

com/india-decades-of-hostility-against-ngos-have-worsened-under-narendra-modi-113300. Retrieved on Dec 27, 2019.

Lucas, R. E. B., & Stark, O. (1985). Motivations to remit: Evidence from Botswana. *Journal of Political Economy*, 93(5).

Ministry of Home Affairs. (2019). Government of India. Accessible at mha.gov.in

MOIA. (2010). Annual Report, 2009–2010. Government of India: Ministry of Overseas Indian Affairs.

Pande, A., & Yan, Y. (2016). Migration of students from India and China: A comparative view. *South Asian Survey*, 23(1), 69–92. https://doi.org/10.1177/0971523118764971

Robertson, R. (1995). Glocalization: Time-space and homogeneity-heterogeneity. In M. Featherstone, S. Lash, & R. Robertson (Eds.), *Global Modernities*. Thousand Oaks, CA: Sage. Pp. 25–44.

Schervish, P. G., & Havens, J. J. (1997). Social participation and charitable giving: A multivariate analysis. *VOLUNTAS: International Journal of Voluntary and Nonprofit Organizations*, 8, 235–260.

World Bank. (2015). Remittances and Migration Data. Washington, DC: World Bank.

World Bank Group. (2019, Apr). *Migration and Remittances: Recent Developments and Outlooks*. KNOMAD, Migration and Remittances Team, Social Protection and Jobs. World Bank. Accessible at https://www.knomad.org/sites/default/files/2019-04/Migrationanddevelopmentbrief31.pdf

6   Discourse of Remittances

How It Shapes Praxis in India, U.S.A., and Mexico

Introduction: Remittances Are Beautiful?

Remittances have been part of human existence for a long time. As a phenomenon that accompanies migration, there have been forms of payment or money sent by people to their relatives and friends from time immemorial. However, the form in which it occurs and the speed of transaction has definitely transformed over the years. The technology boom as well as easier access to sources for sending and receiving remittances has made a huge difference. With the emergence of newer forms of technology there is also talk of the use of blockchain technology for remittances transfer, which may revolutionize this space. Crypto remittances are a reality and firms such as Coinbase are at the forefront of this digital transformation, as we discuss in other chapters in this book.

This paper is meant to offer a synthesis of the various discourses that exist in the realm of remittances and offer the reader an overarching view of what sorts of discourses exist and help the reader understand how these discourses were shaped.

In this paper, we focus on the discourse of remittances: how the senders, receivers, the policy makers, and all other key stakeholders frame it. Are remittances a means to support a family, or are they a 'beautiful' tool for development (Kunz, 2008) or a way for people to show solidarity towards their own kind? What exactly is this phenomenon? Is it a dangerous trend that empties out countries of their capital or does it fuel terrorism and financing of gangs? There are multiple and competing discourses of remittances and in this paper, we tease this out using both empirical data as well as existing theories and discourses around remittances.

We use the methods of analysis that include framing and discourse analysis to point out and examine critically how these remittance practices are being developed and the implications for practice.

What Do We Mean by Policy Discourse?

Before we define what we mean by policy discourses, we need to clarify how we are using the term 'discourse.' As Sarah Mills points out in her book *Discourse* (Mills, 2004), the meaning of the term depends on the context in which it is used. For instance, the term may mean 'holding forth' on giving a speech, etc. in a general sense, but may mean all language units in linguistics, as defined by David Cristal (Mills, 2004, p. 3). What this implies is also that discourse is defined by what "it is not, what it is set in opposition to; thus, it is often characterized by its difference from a series of terms, such as text, sentence and ideology" (p. 3).

We have used Michel Foucault's definition, referring to "the general domain of all statements," meaning all utterances or texts have a meaning in a specific context. His other definition of discourse is the one that seems most useful, reminds Mills. This one is that of a discourse being "a regulated practice which accounts for a number of statements" (p. 6). This implies viewing language as a system that has its own rules and constraints that determine how individuals express themselves. "The use of the term discourses perhaps more than any other signals a break with past view of language," Mills tells us (p. 9).

The work of Michel Pecheux is also important in this context, as he points to how discourses are often created in conflict and contradiction to one another. Mills points to the usage of environmental activism discourse that is often created in direct response to that of governmental policy.

We use the notion of discourse to point to ways in which government regulation shapes behavior. This follows from a Foucauldian reading of discourse as one that regulates practice. With increased demand for regulation of remittances—and a crack down on 'illegal' practices such as hawala and other informal forms of sending money to foreign countries, the entire field of remittances has come under very strong regulation—both internationally as well as nationally. Sovereign states have often responded to requests from the U.S. (Department of Treasury) or to international initiatives or norms such as the 'Global War on Terror' (GWOT) or other measures that have had a disproportionate impact on the flow of money worldwide.

We argue in this paper that the American and European Union's move to regulate the flow of money through nonprofits, hawala, and other civil society groups, etc. has had a very large and disproportionate impact on the phenomenon of remittances. The trickle down of these norms of governance as well as 'best practices' that have been put in place at the level of banking, transfer of money protocols, etc. is something that is part of this regime.

However, the focus here is not in covering all the measures that have been taken to prevent the illegal flow of money, but rather in identifying how those measures have impacted the norms as well as values around remittances. How do people understand the flow of money and their contribution towards this process? We have taken a critical perspective in analyzing the existing policy discourses and subjecting them to close scrutiny, towards understanding how and under what circumstances they facilitate the actual process of remittances and when they hinder or obstruct this phenomenon.

The Discourse of Remittances in the Countries We Study

- **India:** Given the huge amount of remittances that Indian expatriates send back to India, the discourse of remittances has largely been a positive one. Indian government officials see this both as a tool for development as well as one that contributes to the Indian economy, more generally. The Non-Resident Indians (NRIs) are wooed by the Indian investment sector as well as government, as cash-rich investors. This phenomenon has become salient over the past few decades. We will examine some of the changes in this discursive shift over the past decades in this paper.
- **U.S.A.:** As the world's largest economy and one of the most favored destinations for migrants, the U.S. still retains obvious advantages that other countries do not when it comes to earning money and repatriating those funds to other countries. Given the freedoms that exist both in wealth creation and in sending money outside of the

Photo 6.1 Migrant workers in California

country, the U.S. capitalist framework has created a generally conducive and positive discourse regarding remittances.

- **Saudi Arabia:** With a presence of a large number of migrant workers from South Asia, Saudi Arabia has been a magnet for remittances. While in the past decade or so, there has been talk of 'Saudization' policy, of replacing the foreign labor with Saudi workers, the overall trend has still been positive. The leaders and media in the Kingdom realize that they need the migrant labor to keep the economy going and there needs to be a conducive work environment for these workers to thrive and do well. We will see how this trend has changed over the years and what it means for migrant workers from South Asia living and working in the Kingdom today.

- **Mexico:** Mexican remittances are shaped by two forces: internal discourses in the country and policy frameworks—including banking regulations in Mexico and secondly, the regulations in terms of sending money and state of the economy in the US. This complex dynamic has been in flux for several decades and has also impacted migration to the U.S.

How Current Policy Discourses May Shape Remittance Behavior: Saudi, India, and Mexico

Some developed countries—remittance-sending countries—are considering taxing remittances. According to a new report by The World Bank's KOMAD, this is being considered by countries such as Bahrain, Kuwait, Oman, Saudi Arabia, the United States of America, and the United Arab Emirates (UAE). Malit and Nofal in their explanatory note on the issue point this out and explain that the dropping oil prices and warnings from several quarters including the IMF indicate the region has to buckle up and ensure there is financial liquidity in the years to come. This has led the governments to think of various means of taxing the resident—often non-citizen—populations (Malit & Nofal, 2016).

This includes the proposals for introduction of new income tax as well as other forms of value-added taxes that might boost revenues for the government. There is a general consensus among the ruling elite that remittance flows out of the Gulf countries are bad for the local economies, Malit and Nofal point out. However, there is proof to the contrary, they assert. They add that:

In the GCC countries, remittance outflows are seen as leakages of money that could be otherwise circulated and invested in the domestic economy. Therefore, large remittance outflows prompted the GCC governments to seriously consider introducing taxes on money transfers. In fact, only one existing empirical evidence suggests that remittance outflows can actually be beneficial to local economies due to their ability to "exert deflationary pressures on inflation in GCC countries."

(p. 4)

The GCC region is one of the most significant when it comes to remittances origin. As Malit and Nofal explain, about 23% of the world's $400 billion USD remittances came from this region and this figure of $90 billion is quite significant. The Kingdom of Saudi Arabia, with $34 billion, came first followed by the UAE. The countries in the Gulf are beginning to see this outflow as a potential source of revenue, given that that average remittance per month from the remitter is about $320.

The proposed policy change in taxation is being suggested to address the budget deficit of these countries. But this could have a negative impact on the labor flow, especially among the lower income segment, the authors of the World Bank report point out. World Bank estimates also show that there has been a dip in flow of remittances in the years since 2017, given the impact of migration policies in the US. Though the region is different, the impact on migration policy, labor flow can have an adverse impact on remittances as well (World Bank, 2017).

This phenomenon of imposing taxes on remittances, coupled with the increased drive to hire locals—the policy of Saudization for instance—can

Photo 6.2 A welcome sign in Oaxaca, Mexico

have adverse impact on the country. Given that Saudis tend to avoid low paying jobs, there is a danger that the expatriate population that works in these Gulf countries may not find the incentives to work in the country if there is the extra burden of taxation, critics have argued.

It is interesting to note that there is no consensus among the ruling elite about the need for greater taxes, even though there is a need for increasing the tax base. There is fear that this new tax may deter potential employees from picking these countries as destinations. The diplomatic costs involved—with the existing agreements being impacted by new taxes—are a very real fear that most GCC countries have.

In the U.S., there are a few states that tax remittances. Currently, Oklahoma taxes remittances and Georgia and Iowa are considering taxes that are wider in scope (Cuevas-Mohr, 2019).

Discourse Analysis of Policy Documents, Media Documents

We have carried out a discourse analysis of policy documents and media reports of remittances in the target countries, with a view to arrive at the following initial conclusions that further our understanding of how remittances are framed—both in popular understanding, as well as through governmental and official records and policy documents.

The discourse of remittances as related to development is somewhat new (Kunz, 2008). The earlier part of this century did not witness the same kinds of discourses about migration or remittances. Flow of people and money was a bit more fluid, with the Southern border of the U.S. being more open and porous than it was. This means that the way we understand migration, remittances, and flow of resources is also different. With the bracero program and the flow of thousands of able-bodied Mexican men and (some women) to the U.S., the flow of people and money was also quite prevalent in the middle part of the 20th century. Added to this is the fact that crossing the border without a visa was not a criminal act until recently.

The same could be said about the Kingdom of Saudi Arabia (KSA) that used several currencies in the first part of the 20th century, before formation of the Kingdom as we know it. The Austrian Taller, the Indian Rupee, the Turkish Riyal, and the French Riyal were all in circulation (Sama, 2018).

These historical facts have also shaped the flow of people and money between the countries examined. For instance, the trade relations between the Indian sub-continent and the Saudi Arabian region go back centuries and so do the flow of people and remittances.

We suggest that an awareness of these historical facts is important, given the impact of discourses in shaping behavior. While the discourses of remittances among the sending individuals and communities may be different, there is an effort, on part of the official or administrative apparatus, to shape them in a way that serves the nation-state, as we are increasingly seeing happening in the case of 'remittances for development' discourse in all the receiving countries that we have examined. The objective of this exercise is also to tease out the various discourses that exist and examine closely how they impact our thinking of remittances, especially when it comes to shaping policy processes.

Based on an analysis of the media reportage, policy documents and other sources between 2008–2017, we offer the following as the four main categories of discourses that are prevalent in the countries we studied. These discourses are amongst the most common and prevalent ones and this list is by no means exhaustive, but is rather meant to be indicative of the entire range of discourses that are in circulation:

1.   Remittances are beautiful: the development discourse
2.   Remittances can cause us harm: conservative discourse in sending countries
3.   Remittances are linked to illegal flows of money
4.   Remittances as a social obligation and responsibility among sending countries
5.   Remittances as 'resilience' builders

Let us in turn examine each one closely to see what are the implications of each one on policy-making and praxis.

1. Remittances Are Beautiful: The Development Discourse

This is the mainstream development discourse of remittances, in which they are framed as 'beautiful' or necessary for economic development of depressed regions (Kunz, 2008). While the reality of remittances cannot be denied, its 'framing' by governments, nonprofits, and other agencies involved in this process is something that needs examining, according to Kunz. We agree with her call for a more gendered understanding of remittances. A recent study by Mexico City-based CEMLA also points to this fact, where they suggest that the number of women migrating to the U.S. has been consistently increasing over the years and this needs more analysis and understanding (CEMLA, 2017).

A recently launched 'Index of Global Philanthropy and Remittances' by the Washington D.C.-based Hudson Institute is another example of a new mechanism to contribute to the remittance's regime. This index measures, quantifies, as well as offers insights into regulatory environment for philanthropy and remittances in over 64 countries around the world. The Index in 2016, for instance, captured financial flows from the emerging economies to the developing world. The hope, they point out, is that together with the financial data collected by the Center for Global Prosperity from the 28 members of the Organization for Economic Cooperation and Development (OECD) Development Assistance Committee (DAC), the Index reveals a more complete picture of countries' total economic engagement with the developing world. CGP hopes that the Index will improve civil society around the world by strengthening philanthropic infrastructure, including private charities, foundations, religious organizations, volunteer associations, social entrepreneurship and corporate giving.

(Hudson Institute, 2017, p. 2)

Kunz points to the new framing of remittances and migration as one of understanding of these phenomena as aiding development. In the 1990s, this led to a new 'migration-development nexus,' where migration was starting to be seen not as a problem but rather as an opportunity for development. How this framing will shift in the new context with increased nationalism, the rise of ultra-nationalist parties in the U.S. and Europe, where a majority of remittance-sending populations exist is also something to keep an eye out for.

Arusha Cooray (2014) has examined the impact of skill levels on the Gross Domestic Product (GDP) of a country and said that

The results suggest that migration and remittances have an important significant effect on the GDP of the countries under study. Of the skill categories, the unskilled category has the largest robust indirect effect on GDP. The effects of migration on GDP by country of destination suggest that migration to the Middle East has a robust and significant impact on GDP. There is some evidence of a combination between the altruistic and self-interested motives of migrants to remit.

(p. 1190)

Cooray's work also points to the social networks that are embedded in the transnational flows of money and that make the entire process possible. Cooray points to research by Phongpaichit (1993) that has shown that women remit more than men, in terms of percentage of their income, and women from lower-income brackets are known to have greater altruism than males from high-income households.

As we have pointed out in earlier chapters, remittances are seen as forming some sort of an insurance system—albeit an informal one—in societies where forms of social security or retirement plans do not exist or are too weak for the general population to trust them as a safety mechanism for when they retire.

As Rahel Kunz writes in an article about remittances' mainstreaming, the focus on gender has been largely absent and this can lead to adverse impacts such as gender exclusion (Kunz, 2008). Kunz identifies a 'Global Remittances Trend' that

> refers to the process whereby government institutions, international (financial) organizations, non-governmental organizations and private sector actors have become interested in migration and remittances and in their potential for poverty reduction and development, have started to devise institutions and policies to harness this potential.
>
> (p. 1389)

Kunz goes on to point out how this trend in decreased multilateral development aid has spawned a further interest in the processes of increasing remittances for 'development.'

2. Remittances Can Cause Us Harm: Protectionist Discourse in Sending Countries

There has also emerged, in some countries, the discourse that remittances ought to be curbed. The outflow of money from the sending countries is seen as a net loss for these countries and the argument goes, these monies should be minimized as much as possible, and in some cases even taxed (Hernandez, 2017).

Several countries in the Gulf Cooperation Council (GCC) have sought to curb the flow of remittances or have sought to impose taxes on these flows. While there is no consensus within the GCC on this issue, there are certainly bills and proposals that have been forwarded to pursue this issue.

This trend could be seen as a part of the effort by the GCC countries to curb the flow of money out of their countries, given the decline of world's oil and gas prices. The taxation on remittances is seen as a way to address the budget deficits that these governments are facing (GLEM, 2016). As the GLEM report "Taxing Remittances: Consequences for Migrant populations in the GCC" points out, "Approximately 23 percent of the world's $400 billion official remittances in 2013 came from the GCC region, totaling nearly $90 billion and making it the top remitter in the world" (p. 5). This is a very significant source of money for the receiving economies, hence the focus on making sure that this flow of money remains steady.

Gulf countries also host about 18 million migrants—who are documented—from Sri Lanka, India, Bangladeshi, Pakistan, Jordan, Egypt, and Yemen. Short-term development projects such as the Doha World Cup 2022, Dubai Expo 2020, and other projects attract temporary workers who are brought in for their completion. This creates another layer of migrants who may not be in the region for a long time, but for short periods.

Estimates by GLEM point to the average amount of remittances from each worker to be in the range of about $300 per month. The taxation money from remittances is being seen as an "investment reserve that could contribute to the domestic and economic growth and development" (p. 5).

This fear of remittances leaving the sending countries can be seen in the context of the budget deficits that some of the countries are experiencing: Saudi Arabia is facing a $38.6 billion budget deficit, and has recently tapped into sovereign wealth funds. Oman is more vulnerable to shocks to other countries, given the small size of its reserves. Across the Gulf countries, there is growing realization that there needs to be economic diversification and a pursuit of alternative resource revenues.

While none of the proposed taxes have taken effect, as of this writing, Oman was considering a 2% tax on remittances. But it was rejected in 2014. Saudi Arabia has already imposed a $52 per month per non-Saudi employee who is based in the country, as a way to address the Saudi unemployment problem. UAE proposed a similar tax in 2015, through the Federal National Council, but that proposal has not been implemented yet. Kuwait also has in the pipeline a 5% tax on remittances.

The pushback to all these efforts seems to be the labor shortages in these countries. While there is a budget deficit and dire need for increasing revenues from non-oil based sources, there is also a growing realization that imposing more taxes can cause upheaval in the labor market, with the migrant labor leaving. This could cause tremendous chaos for the local economies if the disruption is too fast or too dramatic.

3. Remittances Are Linked to Illegal Flows of Money

While the GLEM report discourages the use of taxation in the Gulf countries, it also points to the phenomenon of illegal flows of money that could increase should taxes be imposed (GLEM, 2016). The authors of the report warn policy makers that

> Remitters would also make use of the existing and active hawala system in the region for cost-efficiency purposes. Such undocumented money transfers will not only raise serious security and policy concerns for the GCC countries but also derail efforts by international organizations and local governments to constructively document and examine remittance effects in the long run.
>
> (p. 9)

Hawala is a mechanism of sending money through informal networks and has existed for centuries. As a recent report from the Department of Treasury (Jost & Sandhu, n.d.) points out, there are several advantages to using a hawala type of system: cost efficiency, lack of bureaucracy, speed of transactions, and reliability. As compared to a regular bank transaction, hawala transactions are very quick and more efficient, and the sender can give a receiver a greater amount of money than through a regular bank transaction.

But given that hawala transactions are not usually conducted through legal channels or occur through manipulation of existing business practices, these are considered 'illegal' and are often considered part of money laundering.

However, there are other perspectives from scholars who have studied hawala that point to the crucial role that hawala plays in the flow of money in conflict and post-conflict zones. As Edwina Thomas points out,

> Indeed, over the past six years in Afghanistan alone, *hawaladars* have facilitated the movement of hundreds of millions of dollars of "humanitarian money" to ensure the smooth running of the national democratic elections in more than three decades, the construction of hundreds of kilometres of road that had fallen into disrepair, the implementation of agricultural assistance programmes, and the building of educational facilities in a country suffering from some of the lowest literacy rates in the world, and where less than half the children aged 7–12 years are enrolled in school. Financial analysts speculate that between 500 and 2000 unregistered *hawaladars* exist within Afghanistan today.
>
> (p. 83)

Her argument points to the necessity of these hawaldars in the country, where formal infrastructure such as banking, etc. does not exist.

Thomas points to the existence of such networks in Iraq and other parts of the world, where these informal networks have played a crucial role in delivering life-saving resources to people, on time.

In Indonesia, for example, hawala transactions helped in connecting people to resources as well as helping people reconnect with their family networks. She writes,

> In early 2005 after the tsunami wave hit Aceh, for example, money dealers reportedly established an emergency communications system using the *flexsi* local mobile phone network to help migrants locate their families and arrange for the delivery of funds either to functioning bank accounts or directly to the IDP camps themselves.
>
> (p. 85)

Thompson goes on to say that the invisible nature of these transactions is what makes them suspicious and in a post-9/11 world, these transactions have been increasingly seen as being linked to terrorist financing. She does acknowledge that this is a problem that faces hawala transactions, as if implying that all transactions are illegal or illicit.

The debate is, as it were, between the Western notions of an 'established order' or formal institutions that conduct transactions, or those that are 'indigenous' and homegrown, that cater to the local needs and are by nature informal and unregulated.

As other scholars such as Medani (2002) have pointed out, the word hawala entered the Western lexicon and imagination with the war on

Photo 6.3 A return migrant from the U.S. (who owns a weaving business)

terror and the blame game that started, in terms of who should be held responsible for the attacks. Thompson writes that the financing of the attacks was also of particular interest to those investigating these attacks (Thompson, 2008). De Goede (2003) points out how the 'hawala discourse' became criminalized in the aftermath of the terrorist attacks of September 11.

4. Remittances as a Social Obligation and Responsibility—Among Sending Countries

While the relations between the migrant sending and receiving countries are cordial, at least in the Gulf, there is a growing realization that the politicians and policy makers in these countries want to maintain cordiality. There is a shared sense of destiny and culture among the countries involved and this also creates a sense of obligation, to make sure that this long history of cordiality and diplomacy is not disturbed.

> Your blood and sweat has built this country. I am so happy to see that you have played your part with dignity, togetherness and tolerance. Before coming to this meeting, I met his Highness the leader of Dubai. Somebody who has spent more than 50 years, given his whole life and vision for Dubai,

Rahul Gandhi, the President of Indian National Congress (INC), said to a group of NRIs in Dubai in January 2019 (Rahul Gandhi, 2019). Gandhi pointed out that 2019 is the 'Year of tolerance' in UAE. He used the moment to remind Indians present of the growing intolerance in India with the current right-wing government and its policies to alienate minority communities.

Gandhi pointed out that the work of Indian migrants is part of a long chain of migration. The migration across both countries—both ways—has been possible due to tolerance.

> I want you to know that you are India's biggest strength, not only here in Dubai; but I am speaking to every single Indian, whether in Canada, US, Europe, Africa, Middle East, I am speaking to all of you and I want to tell you that you have a played a big role in making India what it is today. I want to say clearly, that without your help, without the help of NRIs, it would be impossible for India to be where it is today.

Invoking Mahatma Gandhi, Rahul Gandhi pointed out that the fight for independence was carried out by an NRI. Gandhi talked about the importance of including the voice of the NRIs in defining the manifesto of the INC.

Photo 6.4 A return migrant from the U.S. in Oaxaca

GLEM also points to the diplomatic tensions inherent in any attempts to impose taxes on remittances. The authors write that these taxes have the potential to create diplomatic divisions in the sending countries. They say, "In Oman, for example, the government rejected the proposed tax because imposing fees will pose a problem for its existing international agreements with labor exporting countries" (p. 7). They go on to say that this form of taxation could also change the dynamics of labor and how migrant laborers may decide to move, depending on the tax environment in a particular country. This could impact the competitiveness of the labor market for the GCC and in the long term have other negative externalities, for which these countries are not prepared.

5. Remittances as 'Resilience' Builders

Some scholars have argued that remittances can, in many cases, reduce corruption. Tyburski (2012) argues that remittances mitigate corruption by increasing government accountability and providing other incentives to reform. Using data from Mexico in 2001–2007, this study shows that corruption trended downward in states receiving larger remittance sums, after controlling for political competition, divided government, and market openness. The results are robust to instrumental variable analysis testing for potential endogeneity between corruption and migration. These findings bring attention to remittances as an exogenous resource for reform-minded groups and suggest that they may operate as the converse of the resource curse.

Conclusion

The recent spurt in remittances from Mexico to the U.S. can be hypothesized as a reaction to the negative discourses about migration from the Trump administration. Jesus Cervantes of CEMLA pointed this out as a possible explanation, suggesting that perhaps other explanations are also possible (Cervantes, 2018). The fact that the American economy is doing better than it was in previous years is an indication that the Mexican migrants have more disposable incomes. The other fact is that that fear of being deported can lead many of the migrants to send more money back, resulting in an increase in remittances.

Several factors are shaping how we understand remittances. The discourses about remittances are also impacted by policy discourses, discourses of migration, and other tangible and intangible forces. How emerging trends in technology such as blockchain are going to influence this realm is another consideration that we should keep in mind.

References

CEMLA. (2017). Remesas y communidades locales. Mexico City. https://www.cemla.org/english.htm

Cervantes, J. (2018, June). Interview in Mexico City.

Cooray, A. (2014). Who Remits? An Examination of Emigration by Education Level and Gender. *The World Economy*. doi: 10.1111/twec.12154

Cuevas-Mohr. (2019). Interview at IMTC Conference. The Platinum Network.

de Goede, M. (2003). Hawala discourse and the war on terrorist finance. *Environment and Planning D: Society and Space*, 21(5), 513.

GLEM, Gulf Research Center. (2016). *Taxing Remittances: Consequences for Migrant Labour Populations in the GCC Countries*. Accessible at http://gulf migration.org/media/pubs/exno/GLMM_EN_2016_01.pdf

Hernandez, K. L. (2017). How crossing the US-Mexico border became a crime. *The Conversation*. Accessible at http://theconversation.com/how-crossing-the-us-mexico-border-became-a-crime-74604

Hudson Institute. (2017). Index of Global Philanthropy and Remittances. Washington D.C.

Jost, P., & Sandhu, M. (n.d.). *Hawala: How the Alternate Remittance System and How It Works*. Washington D.C.: Department of Treasury.

Khan, S., & Merritt, D. (2018). Motivations for Remittances and Philanthropy – Lessons from a Qualitative Meta-Synthesis of Literature. *Journal of Social Sciences*.

Kunz, R. (2008). "Remittances are beautiful" gender implications of the new global remittances trend. *Third World Quarterly*, 29(7), 1389–1409.

Malit, F., & Nofal. (2016). *Taxing Remittances: Consequences for Migrant Labour Populations in the GCC Countries*. Explanatory Note. Gulf Research Center.

Medani. (2002). Financing terrorism or survival? Informal finance and state collapse in Somalia and the US war on terrorism. *Middle East Report*, 223, 2 et seq.

Mills, S. (2004). *Discourse: The New Critical Idiom*. New York: Routledge.

Phongpaichit, P. (1993). 'The Labour-Market Aspects of Female Migration to Bangkok', in the United Nations. Department for Economic and Social Information and Policy Analysis (ed.), Internal Migration of Women in Developing Countries: Proceedings of the United Nations Expert Meeting on the Feminization of Internal Migration (Aguascalientes, Mexico) (New York: United Nations).

Rahul Gandhi. (2019). *Speech in Dubai*. Accessible at www.youtube.com/watch?v=zIe5WmmXJpU

Sama. (2018). *Saudi Currency: Historical Background*. Accessible at www.sama.gov.sa/en-US/Currency/Pages/HistoricalInfo.aspx

Thompson, E. A. (2008). An introduction to the concept and origins of Hawala. *Journal of the History of International Law*, 10(1), 83–118. doi:10.1163/157180508X308509.

Tyburski, M. D. (2012). The resource curse reversed? Remittances and corruption in Mexico. *International Studies Quarterly* 56(2), 339–350.

World Bank. (2017). Remittances & Migration Report. Washington, D.C: The World Bank.

7   Case Study
India as a Receiver

Everything about India is massive, its population at 1.33 billion people, its land mass which makes it the seventh largest country in the world. In terms of remittances, India received about $80 billion USD (World Bank, 2018). A study of India is a study of the ongoing complexities and dynamic changes in one of the most diverse nations in the world and its diaspora spread in all four corners of the globe.

Using India and the U.S. respectively as paradigmatic examples of the largest recipient and sender respectively, we take a close look at the dynamics of how remittances came to be. This includes historical and sociological examination of this phenomenon. We look at the forces that shaped remittance behavior and future implications of policies. Through review of documents and interviews, this chapter relies heavily on the individual experiences of those sending remittances, while offering a 'big picture' of the phenomenon of remittances. The main questions answered here in this paper are: What factors shape remittances behavior in the U.S. and what specific policies by the U.S. government hinder/facilitate remittances? What factors make the U.S. the biggest sender of recipients and India the largest recipient of remittances? Also, how is the culture around remittances being shaped by recent changes in migration policy and attitudes towards migration, both in India and in the U.S.?

> I live in Washington D.C., but I grew up in a village in India. My father was a governmental worker and my mother could not read and write, but she'd say that a king is worshipped only in his kingdom, but a poet is respected everywhere. I didn't go to college until my aunt offered financial help.

So, begins the story of Dilip Ratha, the head of KNOMAD at the World Bank. He goes on to explain,

> I landed in the U.S. with borrowed money and a $20 bill in my pocket. I took graduate level classes while working at a research

Photo 7.1 A sign from Jew Town in Kochi, Kerala, pointing to the shared history and migratory patterns in Southern India

center and then, with the little money I had left, I'd send money to my brother and father.

Ratha describes his own journey as someone who sent money from the U.S. to his relatives in India, his country of origin. For someone who is one of the foremost experts on remittances, his research on this phenomenon is also a personal journey (Ratha, 2014).

Ratha says,

> My story is not unique. There are millions who migrate and with the help of family, they cross rivers, mountains and risk their lives to realize a dream—and that dream could be as simple as having a decent job, which can help their family, that has helped them before.

However, his story indeed is unique among the millions who come to North America in search of fortune and a good life. It is unique in that it is one among the million voices that are heard and articulated.

While the discourse of remittances is shaped around numbers and statistics and macro-economic analysis of how remittances impact development, variously defined, what is missing in the academic and scholarly literature is a broader analysis of how remittances shape culture, attitudes towards migration and policy. These influences, we argue, are not unidirectional, but take place in a complex environment, with policy-shaping remittances and vice versa.

We focus on the 'social remittances' phenomenon and also the policy environment surrounding remittances in our discussion and analyze how policies have shaped (and continue to do so) the phenomenon of remittances. This phenomenon can be understood in the context of discourses shaping practices of behavior (Foucault, 1973). From a theoretical standpoint, Foucault's concept of 'governmentality' can be useful in understanding how practices of remittance are being regulated (Välikangas & Seeck, 2011). Following this line of argument, it is key to focus on power and power relations between people and the regimes that govern them, to understand how they are shaped and behave. The current policy debates and discourses around remittances, migration are all part of this discursive regime mix that governs the behavior of subjects.

* * * * * * *

In this short paper, we will try to offer insights into two issues: how has the policy landscape on remittances changed in India, and secondly, how (if at all) are the remittances between the two countries impacting relations between the two nations, both between the communities—diaspora and Indians as well as the governments involved? This focus on 'social remittances' is crucial, as it is a neglected area of scholarship and study, while most studies and reports focus on the volume of remittances (Levitt, 2015). We build on the argument that Levitt makes that too much has been written on the financial aspects, and not much on the "ideas, practices and social identities that circulate between them" (p. 233). Remittances flow between nations have created a vast cultural and financial network that goes beyond the purely econometric measures that are offered by most scholars.

We hypothesize that remittances have a net positive impact on the way that these countries relate to each other, by building 'soft power' between the sending and receiving countries. In cases where there is tension or a policy that negatively impacts remittance, the interest groups in the said country lobby to ensure that there is action on the issue and that they are able to move the policy in a more favorable direction.

A recent report from the Global Partnership for Financial Inclusion (GPFI) points out that

> As per the India-G20 National Remittances Plan, according to the latest World Bank estimates on remittances (April 2017), India remains a top recipient of remittances with around US$ 62.7 billion from a diverse diaspora of Indian migrants which are mainly concentrated in Gulf region followed by the USA, UK and Canada.
>
> (GPFI, 2017)

India is definitely one of the largest players when it comes to remittances and the Indian diaspora continues to send money to India for various purposes—whether it is personal charity, helping local community development, or for religious purposes. There has been some scholarly work since 2000 on the impact of diaspora philanthropy in the political sphere and also how right-wing nationalism has grown as a consequence of diaspora giving and remittances (Anand, 2003). This is definitely the 'dark side' of diaspora giving.

This report from the GPFI goes on to point out that India receives more than 50% of its remittances from the Persian Gulf countries and that remittances are a key part of financing India's trade deficit. Despite this, with the changing macro-economic conditions, there is a reliance on remittances—contributing to over 3% of India's Gross Domestic Product (GDP). As the report further argues, in "contrast, in case of various low-income countries, remittances not only play a developmental role but also predominantly shape up their external sector policies and account for more than one-tenth of their GDP" (GPFI, 2017).

Despite the India-G20 National Remittances Plan, some studies show that the absence of a coherent policy framework on dealing with these remittances has not only impeded their optimum utilization but also led to certain negative impacts in India. If harnessed productively, through institutional backing, remittances can actually become viable instruments for creating alternative livelihoods and sustainable development in the rural areas of the country (Pande, 2018).

******

Writing in their literature review article about transnational diaspora, Tan, Liu, Rosser, Yeoh, and Guo (2018) point out that there are five different types of transnational linkages—familial, political, economic, socio-cultural, and subjective. This framework is an interesting one to remember, as we try to understand the working of remittance as a transnational phenomenon. We argue, building on their theorizing, that the phenomenon of remittances cuts across all these five dimensions and can play a crucial role in building and sustaining transnational networks. Tan et al.'s analysis is based on a close examination of over 600 publications involving transnationalism, diaspora, development. In their review, scholars point out that there is insufficient evidence on the impact of development through transnational migration. They argue for a closer examination of how "diaspora from single homelands is internally differentiated and distributed across multiple transnational spaces and the need to identify data sources for more robust quantitative analyses" (p. 1). Their call for examining how countries such as India that have a significant diaspora and are influential in the diaspora space are important to consider.

The term 'transnationalism' was coined by Schiller et al. in the 1990s and this term has come to signify ways in which migrants establish social fields that cross geographic, cultural, and political borders. This framing, which has come to be seen as interdisciplinary, has extended the research focus into areas of sociology, geography, etc., thereby expanding how one uses this term and what it signifies, in terms of ties and binding relationships between individuals, groups, and even nation-states. This framing includes both transnational relations and transnational identities. Tan et al. offer a definition of diaspora, which is useful for our purposes:

> The International Organization for Migration (IOM) and the Migration Policy Institute (MPI) (Agunias & Newland, 2012, p. 15) have defined diasporas as "[e]migrants and their descendants, who live outside the country of their birth or ancestry, either on a temporary or permanent basis, yet still maintain affective and material ties to their countries of origin."

This includes both the movement aspect as well as linkages with the country of origin, which is key, they point out (Tan et al., 2018, p. 3). Remittances, we suggest, are a key component of this linkage between individuals, families, and communities.

* * * * * *

Remittances for Development? The Case of India

As Saman Kelegama and Bilesha Weeraratne point out in their chapter "Migration and Economic Remittances: Impact on Development," the discourse of remittances for development has been prevalent since the late 19th century, with the work of Ravensterin pointing to the economic motives for migration (Ravensterin, 1885). The idea behind these theories was that migrants were pushed from their countries due to low economic development and the movement of migrants was seen as contributing to the development of the local economies (Kelegama & Weeraratne, 2016; de la Garza, 2013).

There are externalities associated with the flow of labor, with transfer of labor leading to transfer of technology as well as impacting the supply of skilled labor (de la Garza, 2013). There is either brain-drain, brain-grain, brain-waste, or brain-circulation in the country of destination and origin country, depending on the kind of signals that are sent, in the form of remittances. The scholars point to existing literature that the long-term impact depends on how the migrant children are able to benefit from the educational system and able to contribute to the local economy of the destination country or not.

In the case of India, the diaspora is seen as a 'model minority' in some respects in the U.S. with people of Indian origin enjoying quite high educational benefits and also being able to integrate into American society, while keeping their cultural and other traditions alive. Kelegama and Weeraratne call for "mainstreaming migration for development," meaning integrating the "implications of migration into all development efforts in the economy" (p. 212).

In a world that is constantly in flux, we are witnessing how remittances can play a key role in uplifting people. Certain countries have benefited enormously from remittances including Sri Lanka, Malaysia, the Philippines, and Indonesia. There are also both positive and negative implications of return migration back to India. Scholars have written about this from a theoretical perspective, pointing out the need to incorporate the rights of those who are returning to their country of origin (Bovenkerk, 1974; King, Strachan, & Mortimer, 1983). As Cassarino points out, the return experience of many migrants is varied—in terms of how they were received in the host country, their experiences there, and what their country of origin does to facilitate their return (Cassarino, 2016).

In the case of India, this return migration has been most recently seen in the case of information technology and other high-tech workers, who returned post the dot-com crash of 2000, in the early 2000s. Another wave of migrants seem to have returned to India, given the growing opportunities in cities such as Bangalore, Hyderabad, etc. that have established themselves as centers of technology and development. These 'U-turn candidates' are among the most recent migrants to return to India, given the growth of India's economy at about 7% and more opportunities. As a recent media report points out, the ability to be close to one's family, enjoy the benefits of being in one's home country, and participate in social life are some of the factors that are driving these migrants to return home (Little India desk, 2007). Despite taking cuts of about 20 to 25% in their salaries, many of these migrants are happy to return to India, the report says. The effect in terms of increase in skill transfers back to India, and also increases in technical know-how are undeniable.

However, with the push to hire more local workers and with policies such as 'Saudization' and 'Emiratization' that seek to replace foreign workers with local workers, the phenomenon of remittances may be in for a reconfiguration. There is a growing realization among oil-rich Gulf nations that they need to restrict the outflow of cash and resources out of the countries, given their decreasing revenues from oil and natural gas products. Saudi Arabia, the largest of the Gulf economies is also facing a 'youth bulge' with an increase in the number of Saudi youth entering the workforce and the subsequent pressure on the government to employ them (Crockett, 2014). There are fears that increased unemployment among locals will be a burden that the Saudi government will have to bear. This renewed anxiety is the reason why the government is taxing migrants, with newer forms of taxes and restrictions in employment. This is also seen as a way of replacing foreign workers with local workers (Kammer, 2013; Alrasheedy, 2017).

From Benign Neglect to Proactive Engagement?

From the beginning of the 20th century, when migration out of India started to be prominent, there has been a policy of 'benign neglect,' as far as remittances are concerned. By this, we mean a policy of indifference that did not consider the potential of remittances to shape development or shape relations among diaspora communities and country of origin. It is only with the recent changes in discourse of remittances at the global level, originating with the World Bank framing it as a tool for development that countries such as India have started adopting this discourse as well. An indicator of this newfound interest in the Indian diaspora is the active engagement that the government of India is seeking with its diaspora, through various initiatives including the Pravasi Bharatiya Divas (NRI Day), which is an occasion to celebrate the Indian diaspora throughout the world.

India's remittances story is a story of its migration to the rest of the world. With an estimated 1% of America's population being of Indian origin, the number and kind of migration to the U.S. over the decades has varied. However, with greater flows of money and political support to the government, perhaps the Indian government is seeking to cultivate this source of money and influence.

One of the issues at the heart of remittances is the cost: according to the World Bank, the cost of remittances is about 7.9% of the total value sent (Remittances Prices Worldwide, 2017). This is one of the reasons for informal transfer of money, through hawala and other means—an issue that we will deal with later in this paper. This informal mechanism of sending money has existed for centuries, in the Indian context. However, it remains understudied and criminalized, given the fervor for regulating and monitoring mechanisms of financial flows.

There are ongoing efforts both at the private sector, governmental and inter-governmental levels to address this issue of cost of sending remittances, which is seen as an inefficiency in the sector. There is also talk and some initial effort being made to use Bitcoin and other currencies towards remittances, but it will be a while before they are adopted for use widely (Does Bitcoin Make Sense for Remittances, 2019). This analysis points to the fraud and malpractices being at the crux of the transfer mechanism internationally and not necessarily the costs involved. They also talk about the slow adoption rates—moving from a cash-based to a digital platform. The slow tech adoption may be in part because many of the low-income workers may not have smartphones or be comfortable sending money through apps. This article also points to the fact that most of the senders are not 'unbanked,' given that they have bank accounts and often use them for their personal and business uses, but are reluctant adopters of digital platforms, given their lack of trust in the system.

Policy Implementation in India: A Snapshot of the Most Important Developments

There have been several landmark policies and programs in the past seven decades since India's independence. While a complete analysis of these measures and policy initiatives is beyond the scope of this project, we suggest that the timeline in Figure 7.1 offers a quick overview of some of these measures and can throw light on what these policy measures were about. The economic and global context under which these measures were formulated is also important, as they shaped the discourses around remittances.

The main agency regulating flow of money from India is the Reserve bank of India. The Indian Revenue Service (IRS) also has a role to play in the process, as it comes to determination of amount of money flow in and out of India, in terms of per capita flows. With an approximately 55% of remittances flowing in from the Persian Gulf and about 15% from North America, the flows of remittances from these two regions are significant.

The main regulatory framework that guides the flow of money in and out of India is the Foreign Exchange Management Act (FEMA). It is enforced by the RBI—the Reserve Bank of India. The RBI is India's central bank, responsible for issuing currency, managing foreign exchange, and regulating India's entire financial system.

FEMA does two things: a) it tries to ensure that money being sent out of the country doesn't come from crime or b) is used in illegal purposes, related to funding terrorism. Also, FEMA tries to ensure that the Indian rupee market remains stable and there is no excessive flow of money out

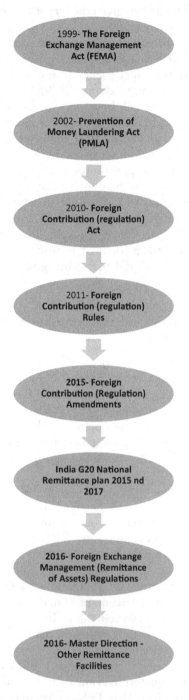

Figure 7.1 A timeline of key policies crafted and implemented in India that impact regulatory frameworks for remittances

of the country, which could have a potentially negative impact on India's economy (FEMA Guidelines & RBI, 2019).

The newly adopted Liberalized Remittance Scheme (LRS) aims to regulate the outflow of remittances from India for purposes of business, leisure, or education. While there were severe restrictions on the outflow of money from India, this barrier has been lifted and Indian citizens can remit out of India varying amounts of money, limits of which have been set for each category of use.

These regulations were put in place to ensure that the remittances being sent were used for development purposes, a stated purpose in many of the policy documents and discourse from the Indian government. We will turn to examine this, from a theoretical point, in the next section.

As Arun Kumar, an economist explains in his book *The Black Economy in India* (2017), there are various aspects of the 'Black' or 'undocumented' economy, which exists in parallel or alongside the mainstream economy. It is 'Black' because it is illegal and generates money from both illegal and legal activities. Pointing to clearly illegal activities like drug trafficking or smuggling of goods, Kumar points out that income from this market is often not declared by those individuals who gain from this income. Also, in conjunction with this income, there are millions of others who earn money from legitimate activities—such as their second jobs or businesses that are often not on the record. Incomes from such sources are also part of the 'Black economy' as they are undocumented and officially, this income is not accounted for in calculations of the Gross Domestic Product (GDP) of the country. This creates a dilemma for all sectors of the economy, including planners, who don't have a clear picture of what is really going on in the economy.

In 2014, this 'Black economy' amounts to about more than half of the economy. One of the main reasons this is the case is because the unorganized sector employs more than 93% of the workforce (p. 19).

Many of the policy changes and regulations that were passed were carried out to address this 'Black economy' and the unregulated sector, which continues to thrive, despite desperate efforts on part of government to address this gap. However, the other side of this story is that millions stand to gain from this system including the triad of business people, bureaucrats, and politicians. They each protect the other in their efforts to game the system and keep their incomes to themselves, without paying the requisite taxes. This is not only a demoralizing situation, as it harms the country, but also a highly contagious one, as those who are honest have no incentive to be honest.

Whether it is the hawala system or other forms of money laundering schemes that may facilitate drug trafficking or other illegal activities, this 'Black economy' is at the heart of the enterprise, Kumar argues (Kumar, 2017).

Sl. No	Act/regulation	Year passed	Key feature
1	FEMA	1999	Citizenship abolished and residentship introduced. • Greater importance to IT. • Realisation, repatriation and surrender of foreign exchange is now governed by FEMA. • Resident foreign currency account (RFC). • Posssession and retention of foreign currency.
2	PMLA	2002	• Foreign currency, foreign security or immovable property. • Punishment for money-laundering • Powers of attachment of tainted property • Adjudicating Authority • Presumption in inter-connected transactions • Presumption in inter-connected transactions • Appellate Tribunalis the body appointed by Govt of India. It is given the power to hear appeals against the orders of the Adjudicating Authority and any other authority under the Act.[16] Orders of the tribunal can be appealed in appropriate High Court (for that jurisdiction) and finally to the Supreme Court. • FIU-INDs the central national agency responsible for receiving, processing, analyzing and disseminating information relating to suspect financial transactions. FIU-IND is also responsible for coordinating and strengthening efforts of national and international intelligence, investigation and enforcement agencies in pursuing the global efforts against money laundering and related crimes.
3	Foreign Contribution (regulation) Act	2010	• Any association granted prior permission or registered with the Central Government under Section 6 or under the repealed FCRA, 1976, shall be deemed to have been granted prior permission or registered, as the case may be, under FCRA, 2010 and such registration shall be valid for a period of five years from the date on which the new Act has come into force. • While the provisions of the repealed FCRA, 1976 have generally been retained, the FCRA, 2010 is an improvement over the repealed Act as more stringent provisions have been made in order to prevent misutilisation of the foreign contribution received by the associations. • Any organisation of a political nature and any association or company engaged in the production and broadcast of audio or audio visual news or current affairs programme have been placed in the category prohibited to accept foreign contribution.

4	Foreign Contribution (regulation) Rules	2011	• The prime objective of the Act is to regulate the acceptance and utilization of foreign contribution and foreign hospitality by persons and associations working in the important areas of national life. The focus of the Act is to ensure that the foreign contribution and foreign hospitality is not utilized to affect or influence electoral politics, public servants, judges and other people working the important areas of national life like journalists, printers and publishers of newspapers, etc. The Act also seeks to regulate flow of foreign funds to voluntary organizations with the objective of preventing any possible diversion of such funds towards activities detrimental to the national interest and to ensure that individuals and organizations may function in a manner consistent with the values of the sovereign democratic republic.
5	Foreign Contribution (Regulation) Amendments	2015	The central government has the power to prohibit any persons or organizations from accepting foreign contribution or hospitality if it is determined that such acceptance would likely "affect prejudicially" (i) the sovereignty and integrity of India, (ii) public interest, (iii) freedom or fairness of election to any legislature, (iv) friendly relations with any foreign State, or (v) harmony between religious, racial, social, linguistic or regional groups, castes or communities. • The focus of the Act is to ensure that the foreign contribution and foreign hospitality is not utilized to affect or influence electoral politics, public servants, judges and other people working the important areas of national life like journalists, printers and publishers of newspapers, etc. The Act also seeks to regulate flow of foreign funds to voluntary organizations with the objective of preventing any possible diversion of such funds towards activities detrimental to the national interest and to ensure that individuals and organizations may function in a manner consistent with the values of the sovereign democratic republic. • Foreign funds received as fees for service, costs incurred for goods or services in the ordinary course of business, and trade or commerce are excluded from the definition of foreign contribution. • The Central Bureau of Investigation or any other Government investigating agency that conducts any investigation under the Act shall furnish reports to the Central Government, on a quarterly basis, indicating the status of each case that was entrusted to it, including information regarding the case number, date of registration, date of filing charge sheet, court before which it has been filed, progress of trial, date of judgment and the conclusion of each case.
6	India G20 National Remittance plan	2015 & 2017	Important aspects of this instrument and serves as a good starting point for further work on state-contingent debt instruments by interested sovereigns. We will continue to promote the incorporation of enhanced collective action and pari passu clauses in new issuances of sovereign bonds and explore options for incorporation into existing stock where feasible.

Figure 7.2 Key features of regulations/laws related to remittances/cash flow into India references

Sl. No	Act/regulation	Year passed	Key feature
7	Foreign Exchange Management (Remittance of Assets) Regulations	2016	Remittance of capital assets in India held by a person whether resident in or outside India would require the approval of the Reserve Bank except to the extent provided in the Act or Rules or Regulations made under the Act.

b) In terms of regulation 4(1) of the Remittance of Assets regulations, ADs may allow remittance of assets, up to USD one million per financial year, by a foreign national (not being a PIO or a citizen of Nepal or Bhutan), on submission of documentary evidence, in case:

(i) the person has retired from employment in India;
(ii) the person has inherited the assets from a person referred to in section 6(5) of the Act.
(iii) the person is a non-resident widow/ widower and has inherited assets from the person's deceased spouse who was an Indian citizen resident in India.

In case the remittance is made in more than one instalment, the remittance of all instalments should be made through the same AD.

c) In terms of regulation 4(1), ibid, ADs may allow remittance of balance amount, held by a foreign student in a bank account in India, after completion of his/her studies/training in India.

d) In terms of regulation 4(2), ibid, ADs may allow NRIs and PIOs, on submission of documentary evidence, to remit up to USD one million, per financial year:

(i) out of balances held in their Non-Resident (Ordinary) Accounts (NRO accounts)/ sale proceeds of assets/ assets acquired in India by way of inheritance/ legacy;
(ii) out of assets acquired under a deed of settlement made by either of his parents or a relative as defined in Companies Act, 2013. The settlement should take effect on the death of the settler.

In case the remittance is made in more than one instalment, the remittance of all instalments should be made through the same AD. Further, where the remittance is to be made from the balances held in the NRO account, the Authorised Dealer should obtain an undertaking from the account holder stating that "the said remittance is sought to be made out of the remitter's balances held in the account arising from his/ her legitimate receivables in India and not by borrowing from any other person or a transfer from any other NRO account and if such is found to be the case, the account holder will render himself/ herself liable for penal action under FEMA."

			e) In terms of regulation 4(3), ibid, ADs may allow remittances by Indian companies under liquidation on directions issued by a Court in India.
			f) In terms of regulation 5, ibid, ADs may also allow Indian entities to remit their contribution towards the provident fund/ superannuation/ pension fund in respect of their expatriate staff resident in India but "not permanently resident" in India.
			g) In terms of regulation 6, ibid, ADs may permit remittance of assets on closure or remittance of winding up proceeds of branch office/ liaison office (other than project office) as per Reserve Bank's directions from time to time.
			h) In terms of regulation 7, ibid, remittance of assets on hardship ground and remittances by NRIs and PIOs in excess of USD one million/financial year would require the prior approval of the Reserve Bank.
8	Master Direction - Other Remittance Facilities	2016	The Master Directions consolidate instructions on rules and regulations framed by the Reserve Bank under various Acts including banking issues and foreign exchange transactions. The process of issuing Master Directions involves issuing one Master Direction for each subject matter covering all instructions on that subject. Any change in the rules, regulation or policy is communicated during the year by way of circulars/press releases. The Master Directions will be updated suitably and simultaneously whenever there is a change in the rules/regulations or there is a change in the policy. All the changes will get reflected in the Master Directions available on the RBI website along with the dates on which changes are made. Explanations of rules and regulations will be issued by way of Frequently Asked Questions (FAQs) after issue of the Master Directions in easy to understand language wherever necessary. The existing set of Master Circulars issued on various subjects will stand withdrawn with the issue of the Master Direction on the subject.

Figure 7.2 (Continued)

References

Foreign Exchange Management (Remittance of Assets) Regulations, 2016. (2016, April 28), retrieved from https://www.rbi.org.in/Scripts/NotificationUser.aspx?Id=10371&Mode=0.

Foreign Contribution (Regulation) Rules, 2011, retrieved from https://taxguru.in/rbi/foreign-contribution-regulation-rules-2011.html.

Master Directions (2019), retrieved from https://www.rbi.org.in/Scripts/BS_ViewMasterDirections.aspx#.

Press Information Bureau Government of India Ministry of Home Affairs. (2011, May 01), retrieved from https://pib.gov.in/newsite/PrintRelease.aspx?relid=71995.

Slideshare.net. 2017. 04. The Foreign Exchange Management Act, 1999 (FEMA) from https://www.slideshare.net/PrakyathPalan/fema-1999-75314110.

Hawala, 'Black Money,' and Informal Remittance Flows

Informal mechanisms of sending money seem to be quite prevalent in the case of India. The World Bank estimates that this could be as high as 70% of the total transactions (Sirkeci & Tilbe, 2016). As they point out,

> Why informal channels are still very popular? For instance, in India, it is estimated that 70% of domestic remittances are sent through informal channels such as hawala system. Informal systems are not always the cheapest, but overall, they cost less than formal channels. Taxes and high transaction costs fuel the informal systems.
>
> (Sirkeci & Tilbe, 2016)

However, based on our own research and interviews with migrants sending remittances, trust, convenience, and cost all seem to be factors when it comes to the platform that users choose to send their money.

Savvy consumers who are aware of the options before them tend to do some research before choosing the best option for remittance. As one interviewee pointed out,

> Over last 7 years, I have moved away from using bank transfer services like ICICI bank remittance services, remit2india to using new online offerings like Xoom, TransferWise etc. Compareremit provides options offering best rates and transparency in regards to fees and spreads. I usually check this site before making transfers. So, access to information and explosion of more players in the market has been beneficial in terms of transfer rates, speed and ease of use.
>
> (Interview 12, 2019)

The same interviewee pointed out that the cap on the maximum amount of money that can be sent has been an issue for him. While he has not used remittances for sending money to nonprofits or other development projects, he has sent money towards disaster relief work, occasionally. The cost could be a barrier if it is perceived to be high by the sender. In many cases, there seems to be a factor of trust that plays into the equation, with senders wanting to make sure that the receivers receive money on time and in quantities that was agreed upon, when sending.

There has also been a discourse around 'Black money,' or money that has not been documented for tax purposes. This is estimated to be around 62% of the GDP of India, by some measures (Kumar, 2017). Kumar, a policy expert and economist, points out that despite the recent interest in this phenomenon, there cannot be any meaningful progress on cracking down on illegal transfer of funds as the 'triad' of bureaucracy, politicians, and business people are involved in perpetuating and propagating this phenomenon. With underreporting of incomes, stashing away of assets, and just plain dishonesty on the rise, it is impossible to control it without a significant change in how people think about their role in society, he argues.

Kumar makes a persuasive argument for why measures such as demonetization—where the Indian government recently scrapped the use of old currency notes of higher denomination and replaced them with newer currencies—is not an effective way to curb the use of ill-gotten wealth and 'Black money,' a term that is widely used in India and South Asia. He suggests that the changes needed to combat the flow of illicit money are more cultural and societal, involving this triad, rather than just technical or instrumental.

Business professionals can and often do manipulate existing laws to make extra money that they don't often declare, he suggests. What this means is that enormous amounts of money go undeclared and undetected, until it becomes an issue. "So, a teacher not declaring her income from tuition could continue to do so. A narcotics dealer would continue to peddle drugs, a businessman indulging in under, and over, invoicing could also continue her activities" (Kumar, 2017, p. xxv). Kumar's argument is that the Black economy is not parallel, but rather intertwined with the white (or mainstream) economy, and this makes cash move easily from one sector to another, without any problems.

Institutions such as hawala exist in this interstitial space, and those who use hawala also deploy similar strategies such as over or under invoicing, while maintaining dual books of account to evade taxes and other transaction costs that are part of a legitimate, over-the-board transaction.

While undocumented transactions of hawala and similar flows pose a threat, there is also the threat of banking secrecy laws that exist in many advanced economies. The dangers of drug trafficking, illegal fishing, terrorist financing are real, Kumar points out. Regulating financial transactions and looking for dirty money is like looking for a "needle in a haystack" (p. xxvi). Even if there is proof of illegal funds, many countries are reluctant to prosecute the culprits. Kumar points to the case of LGT Bank of Liechtenstein and HSBC in Switzerland in 2007. While this data included names of people who had accounts in these banks, the Indian government refused to take the names of these people and investigate them.

So, it seems that the problem of illicit money or extra-legal money is not just one confined to spaces and institutions that are not 'legitimate' but it also exists in institutions and venerable banks that maintain banking secrecy laws for the benefit of their clients, who may at times abuse this for stashing away their illegitimate wealth.

Diplomacy Through the Pravasi Bharatiya Divas?

Indian diaspora has been a source of pride for India. The policies towards engaging non-resident Indians (NRIs) have varied, from benign neglect in the early 1950s to proactive engagement in the present era. Here is an analysis of some speeches from the recent events involving the Pravasi Bharatiya Divas (NRI Day), a bi-annual event that is held in a different location in India every two years. This event has come to signify the ties between India and its diaspora and has become a tool for diplomacy on part of the Indian government.

The 2019 Pravasi Bharatiya Divas (NRI Day) was held in Varanasi, a Northern state in India, Sushma Swaraj (PIB, 2019). The NRI Day is held every two years to "strengthen the engagement of the overseas community with the Government of India" and to connect them with their roots (PBD India). The day includes sessions honoring Indians living abroad and are recognized with the 'Pravasi Bharatiya Samman Award.' The NRI Day was inaugurated in 2003 by the then Prime Minister, Atal Bihari Vajpayee (PIB, 2019).

The Chief Guest, PM of Mauritius Praveen Jugnauth, pointed out an aspect of migration and remittances that is insightful:

> This is a moment for all of us from Netherlands, France, U.K., South Africa, Mauritius and other countries, to be gathered as one roof, under one family; irrespective which part of which part of the world we come from and which language we speak and irrespective how many generations ago we left India.

He went on to point out the importance of the NRI Day, as an opportunity for the Indian diaspora to come together and engage with each other and with India.

Such gatherings show us a common-sense belonging and reinforces our identity, as sojourners, around the world, he went on to add. "In the process of nation-building, there was no important factor than human capital for us to grow, as a nation and we also learnt to respect all different religions and cultures," Mr. Jugnauth pointed out. He also said out that Mauritius hosts the World Hindi Secretariat, and this showcases the strong ties between India and Mauritius.

The use of Hindi as an international language is key, he argued. "If India is unique, Indianness is universal." Yoga is part of the global heritage and it is only right that we are able to celebrate it through the United Nations, he said out (PIB, 2019).

While focusing on the cultural exchanges, Jagannadh pointed out that an educated and self-reliant diaspora brings together investments, sources to markets that were untapped and networks that did not exist. These by nature are what make the diaspora networks crucial in the case of Mauritius and other countries.

India has been wooing its diaspora through the use of several incentives including an Overseas Citizens of India (OCI) card, a revision of the existing Person of Indian Origin (PIO) card that gave unlimited access to travel to India for those Indian citizens who had renounced their citizenship or others who wanted to claim this on the basis of their Indian ancestry, provided they could prove it.

Several Indian associations—both business and cultural—have maintained ties with India for cultural and business reasons. For example, the Asian American Hotel Owners Association (AAHOA), which was originally started by the Gujarati Motel owners, has continued to stay engaged with India through development projects and charitable contributions towards relief and development in India. The Malayalee Associations, which comprise of diaspora Indians from the state of Kerala donated over $32 million to help in post-disaster recovery after the flooding of 2018 (Interview 12, 2019).

Conclusion

With an estimated 232 million migrants around the world, the phenomenon of migration and remittances is robust, despite exclusionary rhetoric and closing of borders for the millions of poor around the world. With an estimated 300 million plus middle-class inhabitants and a diaspora that is truly the pride of the country, India has contributed much to the phenomenon of remittances, even if the policies that are in place seem to be evolving.

Many of the policies involved in regulating the flow of money are heavily security based. The primary lens to view these transactions is one of de-risking. In her concluding chapter of her book *Global Outlaws*, Caroline Nordstrom suggests that the idea of 'security' is an illusion. By this she means that we create regimes of control, security, and securitization that make us feel safer, but are in reality no safer than the most unguarded systems. Writing about the ports in Los Angeles and Long Beach, which are among the top three busiest ports in the U.S., she suggests that the containers coming in these ports hardly receive any inspection (Nordstrom, 2007). She writes that inspections, checks, and other controls that the shipping industry has in place actually are meant more to placate people and are not really a guarantee that no smuggling or illegal activity is taking place.

She talks about why inspections are rare in the world of shipping: delays of just one day on a ship can wreak havoc on the shipping industry and perhaps on the business of an entire economy. "Questions are impediments—they hold up the flow. Checkpoints, barriers and authorization points are bigger questions, bigger impediments to the whole world of ports" (p. 196). While this is true in the world of goods and commodities, the logic can be extrapolated to the flow of money as well. With billions of dollars flowing from one economy to the other, it is virtually impossible to enforce the 'know your customer' philosophy that is the backbone of the security architecture in place.

As Nordstrom further elaborates, the notion of flow is hard for modernist scholars and researchers to deal with, as they are obsessed with place. "The state is about the static. The defined and bounded. It has borders that are set and inhabitants that have sovereign identities that are equally set." She asks how might one analyze the idea of flows—whether of goods, commodities, or money—with this framing? She suggests that flows are critical to research and capture cultural realities shaped by the people who create them and flows are "political, economic, philosophical and poetic forces" (p. 207).

There has been much momentum to cooperate with other countries, in combating illicit financing and flow of money that is not regulated. At a recent meeting of BRICS countries in Rio De Janeiro,

> The Ministers also reaffirmed their commitment to support international cooperation in combating illicit financial flows from all types of criminal activity, including within the Financial Action Task Force (FATF) and the World Customs Organization. In this regard, they underscored the importance of improving mutual exchanges and data sharing. They emphasized the importance of upholding and supporting the objectives of FATF, as well of intensifying cooperation to implement and improve its Standards on Combating Money Laundering and the Financing of Terrorism and Proliferation.
>
> (MEA, 2019)

This level of government collaboration in combating illicit financial flows is also a part of how discourses around remittances are being shaped. On the other hand, there is an implicit understanding on the part of the governments that host Indian diaspora that one needs to engage this diaspora that is over 31 million strong (MEA 2, 2019).

However, there are big challenges to the Indian diaspora, the most significant one being the changes to migration policies in many countries that host Indians. It remains to be seen how the modernizing people of this ancient land deal with the changes before them. As migrants, the ties that bind them to their homeland remain forever tenuous. Yet, the connections to communities, families, and the nation-state that gave them the freedom to travel and become entrepreneurs, scientists, or doctors bring them back, in more ways than one.

References

Agunias, D., & Newland, K. (2012). Engaging the Asian Diaspora. Issue in brief. *International Organization for Migration*, Vienna. Issue 7.

AlRasheedy, A. (2017). Monetary Policies for Full Employment and Price Stability in Saudi Arabia: An Endogenous Money Approach. Thesis. University of Missouri-Kansas. KS.

Anand, P. (2003). *Hindu Diaspora and Religious Philanthropy in the U.S.* Conference paper, Toronto.

Bovenkerk, F. (1974). *The Sociology of Return Migration*. The Hague: Martinus Nijhoff.

Cassarino, J. P. (2016). Return migration and development. In *The Routledge Handbook of Immigration and Refugee Studies*. Abingdon, UK: Routledge Press. Pp. 216–222.

Crockett, T. (2014). Rethinking Arab employment: A systemic approach for resource-endowed economies. Geneva, Switzerland: World Economic Forum.

De la Garza, R. O. (2013). Impact of migration on development: Explicating the role of the state. In J. Cortina & E. Ochoa-Reza (Eds.), *New Perspectives on International Migration and Development*. New York: Columbia University Press. Pp. 43–66.

Does Bitcoin Make Sense for Remittances. (2019). Accessible at www.saveonsend.com/blog/bitcoin-blockchain-money-transfer/. Retrieved on Apr 20, 2019.

FEMA Guidelines and RBI. (2019). Accessible at https://transferwise.com/au/blog/rbi-fema-guidelines-remittances. Retrieved on Apr 18, 2019.

Foucault, M. (1973). The Order of things: an Archaeology of the Human Sciences. Vintage Press. New York.

Gmelch, G. (1980, October). Return Migration. Annual Review of Anthropology. Vol. 9, 135–159. Accessible at https://doi.org/10.1146/annurev.an.09.100180.001031

GPFI. (2017). *India's National Remittance Plan*. Report Submitted as Part of G20 Meeting, Hamburg, Germany. Accessible at www.gpfi.org/sites/default/files/GPFI%20National%20Remittance%20Plan%20Update%20Template_India.pdf

Interview 12. (2019). Interview with President of Malayalee Association. SF.

Kammer, A. (2013, June 24). Saudi Arabia: Selected issues: Assessing Saudi Arabia's systemic role in the oil market and global economy. In *IMF Country Report No. 13/230*. Washington, DC: The International Monetary Fund.

Kelegama, S., & Weeraratne, B. (2016). Migration and economic development. In *Handbook of Remittances and Immigration and Refugee Studies*. Abingdon, UK: Routledge Press. Pp. 209–215.

King, R., Strachan, A., & Mortimer, J. (1983). *Return Migration: A Review of Literature*. Discussion Papers in Geography Number 19. Oxford Polytechnic, Oxford.

Kumar, A. (2017). *The Black Economy in India*. New Delhi, India: Penguin Random House.

Levitt, P. (2015). *Social Remittances: How Migrating People Drive Migrating Culture*. Routledge Handbook of remittances. Abingdon, UK: Routledge Press.

Little India Desk. (2007). Indian diaspora returns. Retrieved from archives.

MEA. (2019). *Press Statement at Meeting of BRICS*. Accessible at https://mea.gov.in/Speeches-Statements.htm?dtl/31687/Press_Statement_at_Meeting_of_the_BRICS_Ministers_of_Foreign_Affairs__International_Relations

MEA 2. (2019). Remarks by the president of India. *Pravasi Bharatiya Divas*. Accessible at https://mea.gov.in/Speeches-Statements.htm?dtl/30950/Address_by_the_President_at_the_valedictory_session_of_the_15th_Pravasi_Bharatiya_Divas

Migration and Remittances Data. (2018). The World Bank. Washington D.C. Accessible at https://www.worldbank.org/en/topic/migrationremittancesdiasporaissues/brief/migration-remittances-data

Nordstrom, C. (2007). *Global Outlaws: Crime, Money and Power in the Contemporary World*. Berkeley: University of California Press.

Pande, A. (2018). 2018, India's experience with remittances: A critical analysis. *The Commonwealth Journal of International Affairs*, 1, 33–43.

PIB. (2019). *PM Narendra Modi Inaugurates 15th Pravasi Bharatiya Divas Convention 2019*. Accessible at www.youtube.com/watch?v=ZoepHIW9Vss

Ratha, D. (2014). *Dilip Ratha: The Hidden Force in Global Economics: Sending Money Home*. TED Talks. Accessible at https://www.ted.com/talks/dilip_ratha_the_hidden_force_in_global_economics_sending_money_home?language=en

Ravensterin, E. (1885). The laws of migration. *Journal of Statistical Society of London*, 48(2), 167–227.

Remittances Prices Worldwide. (2017). World Bank. Issue 21. Accessible at https://remittanceprices.worldbank.org/sites/default/files/rpw_report_march_2017.pdf

Sirkeci, I., & Tilbe, F. (2016). *The Migration Conference Proceedings*. London: Transnational Press. Accessible at www.researchgate.net/profile/Atakan_Durmaz3/publication/319490471_Diaspora_Bonds_as_a_New_Foreign_Capital_Tools_A_Research_on_the_Countries_Applying_and_Potential_of_the_Turkish_Diaspora/links/5a451e31a6fdcce1971a4fa2/Diaspora-Bonds-as-a-New-Foreign-Capital-Tools-A-Research-on-the-Countries-Applying-and-Potential-of-the-Turkish-Diaspora.pdf

Tan, Y., Liu, X., Rosser, A., Yeoh, B., & Guo, F. (2018). Transnationalism, diaspora and development: A purposive review of literature. *Geography Compass* (12).

Välikangas, A., & Seeck, H. (2011). Exploring the Foucauldian interpretation of power and subject in organizations. *Journal of Management and Organization*, 17(6), 812–827.

8 Remittances and the Persian Gulf Nations

With the rise of the oil- and natural gas-rich Persian states as magnets for migrant workers, the phenomenon of the guest worker has boomed since the late 1970s. With this, we have also seen the rise of remittances to South and South-East Asia, where a majority of the migrant workers are from. However, with the falling oil prices and shift in geopolitical significance, we are witnessing a realignment of the remittances landscape.

We offer an up-to-date analysis of how the changing economy in states such as Qatar and the Kingdom of Saudi Arabia with the ongoing political and economic upheavals might impact the remittances landscape and what it might mean for the recipient states. It is also worthwhile to examine how their own economies might change. As the resource-rich Gulf states shift their positioning in the global landscape from being a magnet for fortune seekers and seek to become hubs of innovation, we are interested in understanding how this shift may impact the millions of people working there who are the primary remittance senders. We also examine whether nation-states have a role to play in this phenomenon?

Modi's comments to the Indian diaspora in Qatar addressed workers at a health checkup. He pointed out that the work done by doctors at such camps is significant as it brings people together and reduces depression. "It is hard for people to live on their own and struggle. I was also told that there is a lot of diabetes among workers." He added that the image of India is created through the actions of Indians, the way in which Indians work and live. "You are the pride of India and your actions are an example. As a diaspora community, you have earned the love and respect of those who have been your hosts," he added.

The Indian diaspora continues to be a strong link between India and the Gulf Cooperation Council (GCC). The diaspora as it is imaged in popular literature and even in scholarly sources is not one monolith, with one set of viewpoints or attitudes towards India or its politics. It is a varied mix of opinions, desires, aspirations that sometimes coincide and conflict, but is often an object of government regulation (Luthra, 2017). The diaspora and the Indian state have had an on again, off again relationship for decades now, but of late, this relationship has warmed. Given the economic potential of what the diaspora can offer to the nation-state, the state machinery has created a new apparatus of communicating, managing, and regulating the diaspora.

A Brief History of Remittances From the Gulf: Oil Money and the Rise of Migration

Ever since the first Arab traders landed on the shores of India, relations between people of the Indian sub-continent and Arabs have been prevalent. The trade between the Arabian peninsula and Asia predates Islam, and excavations in Bahrain and other parts of the Gulf indicate similarities between irrigation systems used in India and those parts, showing mutual borrowing of technologies, etc. As Khalid Nizami points out, "In Bahrain and Kuwait numerous small tombs which belong to the second millennium BC, or to some even earlier period, have come to light and provide evidence of ancient links between south India and the regions bordering the Gulf" (Nizami, 1994, p. 52). Nizami points out the rich history of exchanges between the people of these regions and suggests that trade and commerce were at the heart of these exchanges that also spurred innovation and ingenuity on part of these people. He adds, "The Arab traders came to the sea coasts of India and carried Indian goods to European markets by way of Egypt and Syria" (p. 60). This also had an impact "first on language and literature and subsequently on other aspects of their life and thought." The development of a new language in the form of Urdu, which is the national language of Pakistan and was the court language of some of the Mughal rulers, is testament to this confluence of cultures and civilizations.

This vast network of traders also built a large network of flow of money between these regions. The trade between the regions is a centuries-old phenomenon that has led to innovations in financing, credit transfer, as well as in how money is transferred.

The rise of the idea of a nation-state led to greater regulation and norms of doing business. This rise in the ability and desire of the states to control what is going on across its borders is part of the reason that remittances have also been regulated (Thompson, 2011). Many scholars such as Carolyn Nordstrom and Barbara Harris-White have written about the regulation/non-regulation of economic worlds. Nordstrom's work on the 'shadow economy' throws light on how the state is missing in many of the conflict/post-conflict zones and in border areas.

Harris-White's insight is that these 'unregulated' networks that lie outside the state are not "haphazard collections of people in ad hoc groups circling like moths around the light of profit"; rather, they are "governed by the rules of exchange, codes of conduct, hierarchies of deference and power—in short, they are governed by social principles, not merely the jungle law of tooth and claw" (p. 37). This is an important insight to keep

in mind as we start to examine the growth and development of both formal and informal mechanisms of cash flow between these nation-states.
The 'unregulated' life in many parts of the Middle East and South Asia
is also 'regulated' by many norms, customs, traditions, she seems to be
saying. And this is important for us to remember, as we critique some of
the existing discourses of development, remittances, and aid as they come
together to describe these parts of the world.

* * * * * * * *

The rise in remittances to India is recent, as Muzaffar Chishti points
out. In a policy brief for the Migration Policy Institute written in 2007,
he points out that "The Reserve Bank of India (RBI) has reported that
Indian migrants transferred $24.1 billion to India in fiscal year 2005–
2006. India, thus, continues to retain its position as the leading recipient
of remittances in the world" (Chishti, 2007). He further adds that the
"World Bank estimates for 2005 put India in the lead at $23.5 billion,
with China and Mexico close behind at $22.4 billion and $21.7 billion,
respectively." This is all very new, he adds, pointing to India's liberalization process and how it accelerated migration out of India and the role of
Indian migrants in sending money back to India.

Chisthi points to the fact that in "1990–1991, for instance, RBI
reported that remittances from overseas Indians were a modest $2.1 bil-
lion. They have risen steadily in the last 15 years, and dramatically in the
last 10 years" (p. 2). This move on the part of the Indian government to
include its diaspora in development, through encouraging them to invest
in local development projects through remittances, has been met with
limited success.

The relative importance of remittances to the Indian economy has
been rising. In 2007, remittances represented over 3% of the total Gross
Domestic Product (GDP) and in 2005–2006, remittances were more than
the $23.6 billion in revenues that India earned from software exports
(p. 3). He further adds that the policy from Indian government towards
remittances has been minimal. There has been a push to increase NRI
deposits into India rather than have an increase in remittances, through a
combination of incentives that include higher interest rates, etc. Despite
this, the real success story has been that of remittances, he argues.

With economic liberalization and opening of the Indian economy, incentives for hawala were also reduced, Chisthi suggests. This was because
hawala networks in India were used because of the favorable exchange
rate and also to get around the tight controls on transfer and possession
of gold.

This factor, combined with the rise in migration of Indian workers to
the U.S.—as a result of the software boom and also increase in number of
workers to the Gulf—have led to an increase in flow of money back into
India, as Indians continue to send money back to their home country for

Country	% of total remittances into India
UAE	18%
Saudi Arabia	15%
Kuwait	7%
Qatar	6%
Oman	4%
USA	16%
UK	5%
Canada	4%
Nepal 4%	4%
Others	21%

Figure 8.1 Quoted in CNBC report (2016) citing World Bank statistics

a variety of reasons. For some, it is to build up savings; for others, it is a matter of building up post-retirement capital.

Migration to the Gulf-Cooperation Council (GCC) Countries From India and South Asia

The attitude of Indian government towards its diaspora has varied over the decades. As Luthra points out, in the 1940s and '50s, with the dawn of independence, India's first prime minister set the tone for how the government would conceptualize and think of its diaspora. He is reported to have argued that for those who choose to maintain their nationality as Indians, they must receive a favored alien treatment and for those who seek to receive nationality in their adopted countries, they must be given the same rights as any other citizen of that nation (Luthra, 2017).

The migration to the six GCC countries, Bahrain, Kuwait, Oman, Saudi Arabia, and the UAE, is the one driving remittances. As Naufal and Temor point out, the annual

> GCC gross domestic product (GDP) growth rate for the period between 2002 and 2006 ranges between 2.1 per cent to 9.4 percent with an average of 6.5 per cent (Ratha & Xu, 2008). A driving force behind this growth is an increasingly growing labor force that is mainly composed of expatriates from all over the world.

The GCC countries have pegged their currencies to the U.S. dollar, when the U.S. abolished the gold standard and the U.S. dollar was adopted as the official currency of oil trade.

The migrant population in each of the GCC countries is more than 50% of the total population with Qatar having the highest (78.3%) and Oman the lowest (at around 25%).

The total number of Indian diaspora is estimated to be around 20–25 million people, globally. As Binod Khadria points out, the emotive concern that existed in the earlier part of the 1950s and '60s, that highly educated Indians were 'deserting' India for greener pastures through large-scale migration, has transformed in perception. This has changed to a more nuanced understanding and perception of these migrants as a source of capital and remittances, which could help the country. "Both these perceptions need moderation as there are positive as well as negative implications for the countries of origin and destination to tackle together," he points out (Khadria, 2006).

Luthra argues that the three forces of "globalization, geo-politics and Diasporization," act in tandem, as an "international triad" that is impacting and being impacted by the diaspora. The size of international diaspora is on the rise, he points out. A new dataset from the United Nations, 'Trends in International Migrant Stock: The 2015 Revision,' shows that the total number of migrants globally has outpaced the world's population (World Bank, 2014). This is not a uniform growth, with Europe and North America witnessing the largest number of people migrating, while Asia and Africa have a smaller share of the migrant population. Luthra joins other scholars in pointing out that this diaspora of Indians is also very complex and plural—with people of different languages, cultures, and traditions all lumped into this one term called 'diaspora.' Singh put this succinctly when he says that "what possibly distinguishes the Indian diaspora from its counterparts is its extreme heterogeneity, diversity and in some cases, a persistent localism—a plurality" (Singh, 2003, p. 5).

Remittance Governance Regime: Some Basics

The regime that governs the 'legitimate' flow of money involves the following actors: the government of each country, international organizations such as the United Nations, nonprofit institutions, banks, money transfer companies, etc. The regime that governs has arrived at certain norms and regulations that are sometimes mutually agreeable, and at other times, not; creating a complex apparatus can be confusing at the best times. Given the rise of 'securitization' of flow of people and resources, there has been a marked shift in how careful the regime has become, in terms of framing the flow of money through this lens of security (Thompson, 2011; Nordstrom, 2004). In a post-September 11, 2001 world, where the (perceived) threat of terrorism is real and stringency about financial flows is also at an all-time high, the governance regime of remittances has become highly regulated (Harris, 2003).

Dodd-Frank Act (DFA) in 2010 came as another regulatory mechanism for money transfers. As Diane Katz points out in a brief for the Conservative think tank Heritage Foundation, the Dodd Frank Act granted the Consumer Financial Protection Bureau (CFPB) authority over remittances including the right to resolve errors, maintain recordkeeping rules, maintain standards for disclosure of fees, exchange rates, taxes, etc. (Katz, 2013). The DFA also assumes that agencies and service providers will have the kind of business relationships that allow them to document and monitor every aspect of all transfers. As Katz adds,

> Service providers do not necessarily have a standing business relationship with all the various transfer agents, and the remittance costs will vary depending on location, time, and other factors. Nor are monitoring services always available overseas, as they are in the United States.

What this means is that there are bound to be errors, slips, and inconsistencies in transactions, especially in areas that are not too developed or are conflict or post-conflict zones. The cost of sending remittances can also increase substantially with every additional layer of regulation or check that needs to be done. This cost has to be borne by the company as a compliance cost, but it is eventually passed onto the consumer, who has to bear it.

The World Bank quotes a figure of $600 billion as total size of remittances. These numbers are a combination of migrant stocks and balance of payments data that comes from the IMF and other sources. This methodology does not consider the undocumented workers and also money that is not accounted for (Khan, 2018). Faisal Khan, an expert on money transfer business, argues that the 'informal money transfer' methods exist in every part of the world. "It is possible to do a hawala type transaction, given the right amount of money." No one seems to have a sense of how much money is in the informal system; it could be trillions of dollars, he suggests. Khan says that with the addition of cryptocurrencies, this may have gone up.

The centuries-old trade between the Arabs and people of Asia led to the development of vast systems of credit, or letters of credit—colloquially called 'hawala'—that was used to facilitate trade, given the risk of carrying vast amounts of cash, in person. As Edwina Thompson points out, when the development aid sector came up with the linkage between 'good governance' and 'security,' these terms became intertwined in a big way. This linkage and the logic of building institutions that were democratic and fell into the gamut of 'liberal peace' agenda has shaped the flow of people and money. This liberal peace agenda is one that seeks to build democratic institutions, free trade, and strong government, all factors that are supposed to lead to 'positive peace' (Thompson, 2011). She points out that "The hard security priorities of the great powers have increasingly set the agenda for both security and development" (p. 48). This is evident in the funding priorities of funding 'good governance' over health or education programs in these regions, she says. When it comes to flow of money and remittances in many of the conflict, post-conflict, or autonomous zones that are 'ungovernable' such as Afghanistan, one needs to remember Thompson's advice about the lack of systems or democratic institutions. This also means that one cannot think of the flow of money and remittances the same way that one thinks of them in a technologically advanced society such as the U.S., or the U.K.

When these approaches of building more 'secure' 'democratic' and other institutions have failed, the response has been to build more of the same and to invest more aid and funding along the same (failed) approaches. The liberal peace approach is a pipe dream in contexts where there are no democratic institutions and local tribes set many of the rules and laws point out many critics such as Christopher Cramer and Jonathan Goodhand (Thompson, 2011, p. 49).

The present-day remittances that flow into India and other parts of South Asia are a modern manifestation of this centuries-old relationship of South Asia with the region. The remittances governance regime that is in place follows the model of money flow that emphasizes institutions and 'legitimate' people, as Thompson reminds us. This universalist way of thinking about the flow of money is what is problematic in these contexts, she argues.

Remittances by Numbers: A Brief Summary

In 2016, the media reported that the decrease in oil prices had not impacted remittances from the Gulf in a very big way. $68.9 billion were sent back from Indians from the Gulf in 2015 (CNBC, 2016). The numbers in 2013 and 2014 were respectively $69.9 billion and $70.3 billion. The report from CNBC pointed out that remittances to India were more than that for China, which has a greater number of people working abroad. "The Gulf manages to be the major source of remittances, accounting for more than half of the global remittances coming into India," the CNBC report points out.

The migration pattern from India is also changing, with states like Bihar growing while the traditional states such as Kerala, etc. have seen a slowdown. Twenty-five percent of total remittances to India come to Kerala.

Culture of Remittances

Prior to the liberalization of Indian economy, much of the flow of money was primarily through two channels: official ones such as banks, etc. and unofficial ones such as hawala, which was (and still is) unregulated.

However, with 1991 and the liberalization of the Indian economy, there was a move towards newer ways of transferring money, including through money transfer companies such as Western Union, MoneyGram, etc. that offered convenience and faster transfer of money, often in minutes between the country of origin and destination country. This has also led to not only faster but also more efficient remittances. With the rise of smartphones and apps for remittances, we are witnessing a new revolution which aims to change things dramatically.

While the newer forms of transfers rely on individuals, the older forms of transfers relied on groups and 'trust networks,' a term used by Charles Tilly, which he points out are distinct because they rely on both the competencies and incompetence of others in the network (Tilly, 2005). This 'ascribed trust' is key to the functioning of informal systems of remittances and can lead to 'process-based trust,' as John Humphrey and Hubert Schmitz point out (quoted in Thompson, 2011).

The growing ease of sending remittances and the reduced cost of doing it has not eliminated the informal networks such as hawala. As Khan and Thompson separately point out, these networks exist simply because of trust. There is implicit trust between the actors in this system and this cooperation has been built over decades, if not centuries of norms and practices of doing business across borders. While there is potential for abuse of the hawala and other networks, to think of them as purely illegal or 'evil' would be short-sighted, Thompson suggests (Thompson, 2011).

Remittances and Diplomacy Between India and the Gulf Nations

Naufal and Termos (2009) have looked at the responsiveness of remittances to oil prices and found that "oil price elasticity of remittances is around 0.4. While most studies have examined the impact of remittances on the real economic activities in the receiving countries, this study emphasizes the impact of remittances on the remitting countries," they add. We examine various policy implications with regard to macroeconomic shocks, monetary policy and fiscal policy of the GCC countries.

A Theory of 'Cultural Affinities' in Remittances

We propose that migration to the Gulf and remittances from the region are driven by economic incentives—following neoclassical theories of migration—and also wage differentials, given that Indians and other South Asians can earn much more for the same level of job in the GCC countries (Kurekowa, 2011). However, their movement is subject to migration policies in the Gulf countries and their own ability to travel and adapt to the new situation.

As scholars have pointed out, there hasn't been much theorizing in this space. We propose a mid-range theory, based on empirical data and observations and call it the theory of 'cultural affinities' for remittances. We suggest that remittances flow from countries to those where the migrants have cultural affinities. This is to suggest that once the cultural affinities or social capital between nations decreases, the amount of remittances are also likely to go down. This is being played out now, as Gulf countries are clamping down on migration. To illustrate this theory, consider that most of the GCC countries have large South Asian populations and as other scholars have pointed out earlier and demonstrated empirically, the pattern of chain migration is what sustains new migration (Arango, 2000; Massey, 1999).

Our theory is closely aligned to the migration network theory, which suggests that "migratory movements arise in response to prior existence of links between sending and receiving states, such as colonial ties, trade or investment flows" (Castles & Miller, 2009).

Kurekowa points out rightly that many of these theories are interesting but fail to point out why migration is declining in some contexts or also doesn't explain the change in context.

We argue that culture is at the heart of the remittance (and migration) phenomenon, as both are so strongly linked.

Rise of Nationalism, Change in Migration: Impacts of Saudization, Emiratization

The recent drop in oil prices has had a big impact in how the GCC countries are formulating policy when it comes to labor as well as remittances. The World Bank reported that there has been a slight increase in remittances in the year 2015; however, the growth has been slower than in previous years, indicating that there could be a further drop. The report added,

> Officially recorded remittances to developing countries amounted to $431.6 billion in 2015, an increase of 0.4 percent over $430 billion in 2014. The growth pace in 2015 was the slowest since the global financial crisis. Global remittances, including those to high-income countries, contracted by 1.7 percent to $581.6 billion in 2015, from $592 billion in 2014.
>
> (World Bank, 2016)

The report added that the oil price is already having an impact on the remittances to India, the world's largest recipient of remittances.

With the newly appointed Crown Prince in Saudi Arabia, the oil-rich kingdom, which is also the largest economy in the region, has adopted stronger policies to replace foreign workers with local Saudi talent. This has also led to thousands of foreign workers being laid off and sent back to their country of origin.

As Kirsten Schuettler at the World Bank points out, the Nitaqat program, a Saudization program intended to replace foreign workers with local ones, has been aggressively pushed since 2011. She adds that "Following the introduction of the program, the percentage of Saudis employed in the private sector increased from 10 to over 15 percent. But enterprises do not seem to diminish the number of foreign employees to achieve the required quotas." She points out that over 1.3 million work visas were issued for foreign workers. Even despite the requirements of the Saudi quota, these limits are not enforced in micro-enterprises, where many foreign nationals are employed, she suggests. What this means is that the remittances drop may not be immediate. However, her analysis doesn't include the new taxation regime that the Crown Prince has instituted and additional tax levy on foreign workers. All these measures are meant to encourage foreign workers to leave the kingdom.

An unintended consequence of the measure to allow women to drive is that this may also allow women to enter the workforce, which may further incentivize employers to hire Saudi nationals instead of foreign workers. All of this cumulatively have a strong impact on remittances, in the long term.

Here is a quick snapshot of how recent changes in immigration/labor practices in the leading three GCC countries have impacted workers and the phenomenon of remittances:

Saudi Arabia

Saudi Gazette reported a 17.6% drop in remittances in 2018 as hundreds and thousands of workers were laid off in the ongoing Saudization program.

The fall in employment in the retail sector and growing push to hire local Saudi workers has caused a drop of over 300,000 expat workers. As the Saudi Gazette reports adds, "In total, expat remittances for the first half of the year were also almost flat on the same period in 2017, increasing 0.1 per cent from SAR71.02bn ($18.93bn) to SAR71.06bn ($18.95bn)" (Gulf Business, 2019). This has also coincided with the slow in lending from leading banks including Al Rajhi Bank. The number of expat workers is going to be reduced in the coming years, as part of the Vision 2030, a bold, yet untested policy program instituted by the Crown Prince Mohammed Bin Salman (MBS), the new ruler of KSA. An earlier proposal by the Shura council to impose a 6% tax on remittances has yet to be implemented. In 2017, the council announced that it would not go ahead with the proposal.

However, the Kingdom has taken a hard stance on limiting the flow of money out of the country and is finding creative ways to ensure that expat workers do not displace local workers.

Kuwait

Kuwait is one of the countries with a large expat population. Kuwait is also one of the countries with a highly regulated and restrictive labor market. A lawmaker has floated the idea of a 5% tax on remittances for a few years now. While it has not been implemented yet, this issue has come up again as a possibility, early this year (McGinley, 2019). This proposal has been opposed by the Ministry of Finance in Kuwait.

As Arabian Business reports,

> Remittances sent home by expatriates in Kuwait rose 3.5 percent in the first quarter of 2018, to around $3.4 billion, according to figures from the Central Bank of Kuwait. In 2017, total expat remittances from Kuwait fell 9.2 percent to 4.14 billion Kuwait Dinars ($13.69 billion), down from KD 4.56 billion ($15.08 billion) in 2016.

While this debate is being resolved, technology seems to have made headway, with Kuwait Finance House offering a zero-fee instant international transaction—with blockchain tech using RippleNet (Cobb, 2019).

UAE

As one of the larger recipients sending countries, the UAE figures prominently in the remittances discussion when it comes to the Gulf countries.

Western Union, which has over 150 million customers globally and moves $300 billion around the world, has recently launched digital services that allow consumers to move money from their phones to the recipients' bank account (Haine, 2019). "The remittances phenomenon is more than just sending money, it is about connecting people," CEO of Western Union points out (Haine, 2019). The traditional Know Your Customer (KYC) paradigm that has existed in the traditional banking model has changed, and now banks and financial institutions are looking to transfer this into the digital landscape as well. With the UAE accepting digital identification and changing the landscape of regulation with respect to remittances, there may be more ease of transfer of funds, according to some sources.

The biggest factor impacting remittances from the UAE, similar to those from other countries, is the change in migration laws, which are changing to prefer local talent as compared to expat workers. While the recipient nations would like to keep the inflow of money coming, they are facilitating this flow through monetary policies as well as regulatory policies. As the Reserve Bank of India initiated reforms to lower the cost of transferring money from the UAE, the amount of remittances may change (Duttagupta, 2019).

Conclusion

The labor and migration landscape is changing around the world. While the U.S. and U.K. have both shown increasing reluctance to hire foreign workers under the influence of more right-wing governments that are in power, there is also growing resistance to foreign workers in the Gulf countries. Employment prospects for South Asians in the Gulf have reduced and continue to fall, as Saudization, Emiratization, and other forms of initiatives to hire locals catch steam.

Amidst this shift, there is also technological innovation that is driving changes in how people send money, for what purposes they send, etc. These shifts could be significant and can be a game changer in the years to come. While there is no doubt that remittances provide a much-needed boost to economic development, there is also no doubt that they often come with a huge cost to the migrants—in terms of lost social networks, less time with immediate family and other forms of hardships. There is also the added dimension of job insecurity, harassment, and other forms of potential hazards that meet people as they migrate to another country to earn more than they did at home.

With an estimated $19 billion sent to Pakistan alone, remittances from the UAE are a significant part of the economy of South Asia (Home Remittance, 2019). Millions of workers send money through hawala and also through banks. Hawala was the preferred method earlier, but banks are the preferred way now.

A question that has not been asked and one that needs greater focus and theorizing is the following: do nation-states have a role to play in remittances and how they are managed? Most of the analysis that is carried out is at the level of aggregate groups of senders or receivers—i.e., individuals and not necessarily that of countries. Even if there are some studies that examine how countries shape remittance policy and how it impacts the flow of money, these studies have not theorized the phenomenon of remittance. In this chapter, we have tried to offer a theory of nation-to-nation interactions, when it comes to remittances. This 'soft power' analysis can be very helpful in understanding how individuals make sense of their lives in relation to the nation-state that defines them.

"Hawala is just a transaction that is not documented. No one has a sense of how big the market is," Khan suggests. He considers even crypto markets similar to hawala, even though it is logged on a blockchain, but regulators are not documenting them. Transfer of money is a geography-dependent issue and no one seems to know. The global average was about 9.5% around the world and this is quite high.

There are as many negatives as there are positives to the remittance phenomenon: for instance, the disintegration of families facing abuse and other challenging situations as a result of not being in a position to negotiate their work situation (The Remittance Business, a Documentary, 2016).

However, for many, this sacrifice is the only way for them to provide for their families and also to better their condition. The tradeoff seems worth it, even if years of one's life is spent without family or friends. The migrant workers in the Gulf countries are trading their time for money and once they've had enough of the latter, there is little, if anything, they can do to gain the former.

References

Agunias, D. R., & Newland, K. (2012). Engaging the Asian Diaspora. Accessible at publications.iom.int/bookstore/free/ MPI_Issue_No7_20Nov2012.pdf

Arango, J. (2000). Explaining migration: A critical view. *International Social Science Journal*, 52(165), 283–296.

Castles, S., & Miller, M. J. (2009). *The age of migration: International population movements in the modern world*. Basingstoke, Hampshire: Palgrave Macmillan.

Chishti, M. (2007). The phenomenal rise of remittances to India. *MPI*. Accessible at www.migrationpolicy.org/research/phenomenal-rise-remittances-india-closer-look

CNBC. (2016). *Gulf Remains Remittance King*. Accessible at www.youtube.com/watch?v=leM6499CxF8

Cobb, A. (2019). *Kuwait House Launches Zero Remittances Using RippleNet*. Accessible at www.youtube.com/watch?v=KBoh0HscMhg

Duttagupta, I. (2019). *How the Remittances Landscape Is Changing for Indians*. Accessible at https://economictimes.indiatimes.com/nri/visa-and-immigration/how-the-matrix-of-remittances-is-changing-for-indians/articleshow/64809196.cms?from=mdr

Foucault, M. (1973). *Discipline and Punish and the Birth of Prison*. New York: Random House.

Gulf Business. (2019). Accessible at https://gulfbusiness.com/saudi-expat-remittances-drop-17-6-november/

Haine, A. (2019). *Western Union Rolls Out New Digital Services in UAE*. Accessible at www.thenational.ae/business/money/western-union-rolls-out-digital-services-in-the-uae-amid-improving-regulatory-landscape-1.854871

Harris, B. W. (2003). Unruly and Informal Globalization and Its Impact on Development: A Background Note. Lund University, Dissertation.

Home Remittance. (2019). *Wajahat S Kha Speaks to People Residing in Dubai*. Accessible at www.youtube.com/watch?v=p8UxAj8Gc9A

Humphrey, J., & Schmitz, H. (1996). Trust and economic development. *Institute of Development Studies*. Brighton, UK.

Katz, J. (2013). *The Big Truck That Went By: How the World Came to Save Haiti and Left Behind a Disaster*. St. Martin's Press. New York: Palgrave Macmillan.

Khadria, B. (2006). *India: Skilled Migration to Developed Countries, Labor Migration to the Gulf*. Migración y Desarrollo, núm. 7, segundo semestre, pp. 4–37. Red Internacional de Migración y Desarrollo Zacatecas, México.

Khan, R. (2018). Fintech podcast: Money on the move. *Around the Coin Podcast*. Accessible at https://aroundthecoin.com/podcast/fintech-podcast-money-on-the-move-episode-2-behind-the-figures/

Kurekowa, L. (2011, April). Theories of migration: Conceptual review and empirical testing in the context of the EU East-West flows. In interdisciplinary conference on migration. *Economic change, social challenge*, pp. 6–9. University College London, UK.

Luthra, S. (2017). Indian diaspora policy and the "international triad": Of voices and visions beyond pragmatism. *Alternation*, 24(1), 50–75. 50, Electronic ISSN: 2519-5476. https://doi.org/10.29086/2519-5476/2017/v24n1a4

Massey, D. S. (1999). Why does immigration occur? A theoretical synthesis. In C. Hirschman et al. (Eds.), *The Handbook of International Migration*. The American, pp. 34–52. Russell Sage Foundation.

McGinley, S. (2019). *Kuwait Revives Debate about Remittances*. Accessible at www.arabianbusiness.com/banking-finance/419756-kuwait-revives-debate-of-5-expat-tax-on-remittances

Naufal, G. S., & Termos, A. (2009). The responsiveness of remittances to price of oil: The case of the GCC. *OPEC Energy Review*, 33(3/4), 184–197. doi:10.1111/j.1753-0237.2009.00166.x

Nizami, K. A. (1994). Early Arab contacts with South Asia. *Journal of Islamic Sciences*, 5(1), 52–59.

Nordstrom, C. (2004). *Shadows of War: Violence, Power and International Profiteering in the Twenty-First Century*. Berkely, CA: UC Berkeley Press.

Ratha, D., & Xu, J. (2008). *Data and Remittances Handbook*. Washington, DC: World Bank.

The Remittances business, a Documentary. (2016). Accessible at www.youtube.com/watch?v=GgMyDtfUHv0

Schuettler, K. (2015). Will nationalization policies in Saudi Arabia reduce migrant remittances. *World Bank*. Accessible at https://blogs.worldbank.org/people move/will-nationalization-policies-saudi-arabia-impact-migrants-and-remit tance-flows

Singh, G. (2003). Introduction. In B. Parekh, G. Singh, & S. Vertovec (Eds.), *Culture and Economy in the Indian Diaspora*. London: Routledge.

Thompson, E. (2011). Trust Is the Coin of the Realm. Oxford, UK: Oxford University Press.

Tilly, C. (2005). *Trust and Rule*. Cambridge: Cambridge University Press. P. 12.

World Bank. (2014). *Remittances & Migration Report*. Washington, DC: World Bank. Accessible at https://data.worldbank.org/indicator/BX.TRF.PWKR.CD.DT

World Bank. (2016). *Remittances to Developing Countries Edge Up Slightly in 2015*. Accessible at www.worldbank.org/en/news/press-release/2016/04/13/remittances-to-developing-countries-edge-up-slightly-in-2015

World Bank. (2018). Remittances & Migration Report. Washington, DC: World Bank. Accessible at https://www.knomad.org/sites/default/files/2019-08/World%20Bank%20Board%20Briefing%20Paper-LEVERAGING%20ECO NOMIC%20MIGRATION%20FOR%20DEVELOPMENT_0.pdf

9 Remittances as Subaltern Giving
The Case of Mexico

Introduction

Ben Page, in his article titled "Why Do People Do Stuff," points out that remittances have been examined largely in the context of economic rationality, while not focusing on the fact that diasporas are "communities of practice" (Page, 2012). The current focus is on individual rationality and motivations, which are derived from an economic reading of the individual as a rational, economic entity. What this perspective does not take into account is the non-rational and socio-cultural motivations and actions that are part of the repertoire of actions that arise from each individual's belonging to a community—and more specifically, a community of practice, Page argues.

Page further points out that "Existing theorizations underpin, and thereby uncritically endorse, potentially unsustainable development policies based on remittances. The alternative approach presented here opens up new areas for policy and research based on medium to long-term changes in the socio-technical remittance regime" (Page, 2012, p. 2). What he is implying here is that the perspective of treating purely economic and rational motives have severe limitations both for policy and for practice.

Why do migrants, who are often separated from their immediate families, send money for years, sometimes decades to relatives—both close and distant—what motivates them to continue doing this, at the detriment of their own financial security? Cultural notions of obligation and duty may partially explain some of this action, but not all of it. As Katharine Rankin points out, and Ben Page quotes, "In the age-old structure agency debate, practice theory puts the emphasis on how the structure is produced, reproduced and transformed through human agency" (2012, p. 711). Page suggests that autonomy of the individual is embedded in the social structures. There needs to be less emphasis on individual choice as it "obscures the potential for simultaneous change in social structures and practices" (Page, p. 4). We agree with Page and point out that there needs to be a greater focus on the social structures and norms of communal solidarity and belonging that tie these individuals together. Page's call for examining the daily live of diaspora may be a useful one, as it helps examine how agency and structure play out in the diaspora.

We take this as a starting point for our own arguments and theorizing and point out that our research in Oaxaca, Mexico and Kochi, India points to notions of 'community of practice,' and goes beyond the purely economic rationale on which much of policy-making and current theorizing is based.

Page makes the point that policy makers often assume diaspora communities to be rational actors who are motivated just by good information on how to send money and to prioritize it in a manner that benefits the town/village where they originate from (Page, 2012). Page also points out that the list of options before the diaspora are many, including lobbying, protesting, use of economic and political leverage, etc. (Kleist, 2008; Sheffer, 2003). There are reasons to look beyond these 'rational choice' paradigms of how the diaspora behaves. As many scholars have documented, there are multiple uses of remittances and how return migrants use their money (Kleist, 2008; Sheffer, 2003; Fox & Rivera-Salgado, 2005; Cuevas-Mohr, 2019).

* * * * * * *

Here is something that one of the authors, Khan, wrote in his journal about meeting two Mexican workers who sent money to their home country regularly:

> I first met Eduardo and Alejandro at a local restaurant in Southern California (SoCal). They were introduced to me by a mutual connection and this facilitated our speedy meeting. The fact that they worked at this restaurant and my friend was their supervisor also helped. However, I was happy to learn that they were eager to meet me and share their experiences of remesas, the Spanish word for remittances.

They were quite clear about their obligation to send money 'home,' though they had not returned in 10 and 13 years, respectively. While Eduardo had become a citizen, through marriage, Alejandro's case was more precarious, given that he was an undocumented worker and saw that his only way of contributing to his family in Mexico was to send money.

"We feel guilty that we are not able to do more, and that our families are not able to live comfortably. It is my duty to send money," each one said, almost in unison.

Both are workers in a Mexican restaurant that pays them enough to save a bit and send the rest to their needy relatives.

What Is Subaltern Theory and Subaltern Giving?

We draw upon several theoretical foundations to analyze remittances between people. One is the *subaltern* framework, developed by thinkers such as Ranajit Guha, Gayatri Spivak, and Homi Bhabha, among others. Guha is considered the founding father of this theoretical school and founded it as a way to explain the evolution of India's freedom movement. Guha developed this framework as he felt that until then, India's national movement (freedom struggle) was one-sided and "blinkered" from the perspective of the ruling elite. There was no focus on the ordinary men and women who had contributed significantly to the development of the national movement which had earned India freedom. As Vinayak Chaturvedi, another Indian scholar, writes,

> He further explained that elitist historiography was narrow and partial as a direct consequence of a commitment by scholars to a particular "class outlook" which privileged the ideas, activities, and politics of the British colonizers and dominant groups in Indian society.
>
> (Chaturvedi, 2007)

The group of scholars that originally founded subaltern studies used it to describe any form of subalternism, whether it was due to class, race, religion, or other status that made them the subaltern.

There is a long and varied history of how scholars, both Indian and Western, have used this theoretical notion to further our understanding of various issues from Indian farmers struggles to feminist movements in the West (Spivak, 2010). One of the developments of interest to us and one we develop in this paper is that offered by Partha Chatterjee, who argued for the notion of 'community' to be relevant in the sphere of political organizing and to examine the notions of power contained therein, following Foucauldian analysis (Chatterjee, 1983b).

* * * * * * *

As pointed out earlier, we argue that remittances can be considered 'subaltern giving,' or help/solidarity that is given by other marginalized people to each other. This form of action can be framed as an in-between to *philanthropy* (voluntary action for the common good; Payton & Moody, 2008) and *development aid* (Sen, 1999). While philanthropy is all support and help given to strangers, or those who are not immediately related to one another, and development aid also falls into that category, with the general understanding that it is given between nations or organizations to one another, remittance falls into an interstitial space, which is from individuals (or in some cases nonprofits or civil society groups) and offered typically for other individuals, and in some cases, organizations in receiving countries.

Ben Page points out that there are three modes of theorizing diaspora action: diaspora as decision makers and diasporas as option setters and finally diasporas as 'communities of practice' (Page, 2012, p. 4). Page's definition of remittance also includes what is known as 'social remittances,' which includes ideas, skills, attitudes, and aspirations that move across borders as seamlessly—perhaps more so—as the actual money transfer (Sanchez-Ibarra, 2014). We focus on the third type of diaspora action and seek to examine them in developing our own theory of remittance action, but keeping in mind that there is a rich tradition of theorizing based on 'theories of practice,' following Pierre Bourdieu and Michel Foucault (Foucault, 1975; Bourdieu, 1995).

Diasporas as Subalterns?

Similar to Partha Chatterjee's analysis of Foucauldian capillary power, which permeates all forms of daily life, including one's bodies, we suggest that remittances are governed by many forces—both in the country of origin and the one where the migrant resides (Chatterjee, 1982; Foucault, 1975). A capillary force is one that "reaches into the very grain of individuals, touches their bodies and inserts itself into their actions and attitudes, their discourses, learning processes and everyday lives" (Chatterjee, 1983b, p. 384). The notion of disciplining the body, of controlling its regulation and making it behave in a manner that 'capillary forces' operate to regulate, is the premise of a Foucauldian analysis.

This sort of intervention is seen in the governance regime that exists when it comes to managing the flow of money and transfers—though it is being increasingly challenged by the rise of newer technologies that are making the flow of money less regulated and more outside of the purview of the nation-state.

The migration-remittance regime is a rather complex one and one that needs to be studied in combination. While migration is highly regulated task and one that has become increasingly complex and complicated by recent change in laws in the U.S. (vis-à-vis Mexico), there is a loosening of the regulatory space in the remittance sector, with more ease of sending money (Fox & Rivera-Salgado, 2005; Cuevas-Mohr, 2019).

This dichotomous factor may be one reason why despite the fall in migration to the U.S., the amount of remittances going into Mexico over the past few years have increased (CEMLA, 2019). While it is harder to move people across borders, it is becoming easier to move money or capital, a factor that is not lost on commentators of the current state of capitalism in our world (Harvey, 2001).

Framing Remittances as Subaltern Giving

We posit, based on the interviews and using a Grounded Theory approach, that there are three forces shaping the remittances behavior: government policies, family and friends, and finally, the diaspora community itself. This three-force vector is what shapes remittance praxis and is part of the 'habitus' that Bourdieu described.

Remittances can also be framed as part of the 'habitus,' of survival among migrants, to borrow a term from Bourdieu (Bourdieu, 1995). Migrants to a new country are vulnerable, and are away from their families and friends and often lack the social and cultural infrastructure that helped form them. Despite this, they send money—often a large portion of what they earn—to their families 'back home.' This is an unusual act of charity, if one were to consider it purely objectively.

> Why do Latinos, Asians and Africans send money and not Anglos. My friend from Ireland (whose father lives in Ireland) pointed out that his father would be horrified if he sent him money, as remittances. It is just not culturally appropriate, nor expected that I send money to my parents,

pointed out Hugo Cueva-Mohr, during a conversation (Cuevas-Mohr, 2019). This culturally predetermined reaction to remittances can also be seen as a class-related issue.

Of course, an upper-middle class family in Mexico would not expect remittance from their son or daughter who lives and works in the U.S. or Europe, but rather this is an expectation from the poorer sections of migrants, who often migrate for economic opportunities. Of relevance here is the fact that much of the recent migration to the U.S. took place in the context of NAFTA and other trade deals that decimated Mexican agriculture and laid the groundwork for massive migration, given that there were so few opportunities, other than agriculture—which was a dying occupation.

Community Solidarity Among the Subalterns: The Case of Los Angeles and Oaxaca

Oaxacan community has used remittances and solidarity building in the form of a) social networks of support, b) building cooperatives and supporting organizations/businesses in Oaxaca, and also c) supported institutions such as churches and local organizations.

There are several community-based organizations in the greater L.A. area, including in Oxnard (Ventura County) that support recent migrants to California from Oaxaca. One such example is the Mixteco (Mixteco, 2019).

The mission of Mixteco is:

> The Mixteco/Indígena Community Organizing Project (MICOP) unites indigenous leaders and allies to strengthen the Mixtec and

indigenous immigrant community in Ventura County, estimated at 20,000 people. Most are strawberry farmworkers, and many speak primarily their indigenous language. MICOP's majority-indigenous staff builds community leadership and self-sufficiency through education and training programs, language interpretation, health outreach, humanitarian support, and cultural promotion. We organize the community to advocate for shared concerns. MICOP reaches approximately 6,000 individuals each year. MICOP is also the founder and home of Radio Indigena, out of Oxnard, CA, a radio station with programming in indigenous languages such as Mixteco.

Many of the communities in Oaxaca come from an agricultural background. These, who are daily wage earners or those who rent out their farmland, have struggled to survive in a new economy of agriculture that emerged in the 1980s and '90s.

Data From Interviews: Gaining Access, Building Trust, and Gathering Data

We use a 'Grounded Theory' approach, which is very inductive, to place the context of giving among the migrants (Charmaz, 2014). Our data is gathered from interviews that the authors conducted in parts of Oaxaca. The source for this data were semi-structured interviews set up in assistance with a professor in Oaxaca. Visits to the field included visits to pueblos and meetings with representatives of the community, including elders, some recent return migrants, local businesses, etc. This data gathering took place in October 2019 and subsequently, the data was transcribed into Spanish and translated into English by the researchers.

Gaining access to interviewees can be challenging and we did experience some of this during our research process. However, with time and patience, we gained access to the gatekeepers and upon demonstrating that our project would ultimately help dispel some of the myths surrounding the phenomenon of remittances and the negative biases around migration to the U.S., many of them agreed. For many, it was a process of healing and the interview process itself seemed to be cathartic. The approach used in our ethnographic approach included focusing on the basic process—that of migrating and sending of remittances—and this illuminates much of the complete picture, as Charmaz points out. The recursive nature of the conversations helped enliven the topic and also helped bring about new perspectives and insights that may not have been obvious in the beginning. This approach is particularly useful in digging deep into a phenomenon (Charmaz, 2014).

The visits to the pueblos included San Pablo Huixtepec, Santa Catarina Quiane, Ayoquezqo de Aldama, and San Jeronima Tlacochahuaya, all villages in the vicinity of Oaxaca City in the state of Oaxaca, Mexico. Our local contacts in Oaxaca sought permissions and other logistical details for our visit to the villages and accompanied us to the interviews. Given their familiarity with the local norms and availability, they were able to follow up with people who were not available and helped us understand the context of their lives. This inscription of social discourse and the writing down of it turned it into an account, as Clifford Geertz informs us (Geertz, 1973). As Geertz reminds us, cultural analysis is about "guessing at meanings, assessing the guesses and drawing explanatory conclusions from the better guesses, not discovering the continent of meaning and mapping out its bodiless landscape." Towards this we turn in our analysis of what we observed and noted down in our field notes.

We are also cautious about the generalizability of this data. As Geertz again reminds us, when we study a little village in Morocco, we are studying that village and not the entirety of Morocco. This means that studying a village in Oaxaca should help us understand that village, not the entirety of Mexico, which has very different and unique patterns of migration and remittances. However, one can draw upon the notion of 'analytic generalization,' meaning generalization across various analytic categories.

Some Insights From Data: Diaspora and Remittances Behavior

We offer some insights into the patterns of remittance sending and its impact on local communities. These insights are gathered from data collected during interviews. As discussed above, these interviews were conducted in Oaxaca, Mexico between September and October 2019. Among the 15 interviews conducted, certain theoretical categories emerged, which are explained below. We offer a more substantive theory of remittance action in the section that follows.

1. Migration, Remittances as a Disciplining Behavior

Migration has been described in literature from the perspective of push and pull (Lee, 1966). Everett Lee's framework of understanding migration from the perspective of distance of migration, the personal motivations involved, etc. are quite useful for understanding how and why people migrate to a new place. However, an aspect of migration and subsequent behavior of the migrant that has not been delved into much detail is how migration leads to a new regime of management in the life of a migrant.

As one of our interviewees pointed out, migration can also be seen as a method of 'disciplining oneself' (Interview 4, 2019). He argued that when he migrated from Mexico, he was very young and not well organized in life.

> I didn't take care of my own self too well. I didn't dress too well, I would sleep late into the day and get up when I wanted to. Going to

California changed all that. To survive, I had to get up at five a.m., I had to work hard—sometimes up to 14 hours a day and six days a week. I saved diligently and sent as much money as I could, to my family in Mexico. This phase—lasting over 15 years—is what has shaped my life. I have a nice family now, kids who are in school and also a nice house, here in Mexico.

(Interview 4, 2019)

Photo 9.1 Director of MENA, a cooperative in Oaxaca, Mexico

Photo 9.2 A money transfer agent in San Pablo Huixtepec, Oaxaca, Mexico

In short, this interviewee, and a few others in Oaxaca, pointed out that migration can be seen as a disciplinary regime, one that could help form the habits and life rhythms that guide one's life in a new place. This notion of the 'habitus,' as Bourdieu described, is key to understanding how migrants themselves see migration (Bourdieu, 1995).

Photo 9.3 A modern-looking home in rural Oaxaca, likely built by money from remittances

Another interviewee pointed out that the process of migration has helped him form new habits and also learn new skills.

> I went to adult school in the evening to learn English school. There was a motivation to learn a new language. I realized that if I had to

live in the U.S., I had to learn English. It was very difficult, but something I had to get used to. I am glad I put myself through it, as I could do my job better. My boss promoted me after that and my customers loved me too,

he pointed out (Interview 5, 2019).

2. The Actual Cost of Sending Remittances: Discrimination, Family Break Down

Several interviewees pointed out that migration and the pattern of remittance sending has not been sustainable for their families. One of the female interviewees pointed out that her husband abandoned her for another woman, while in the U.S., others suggested that the amount of stress and the pressure to just survive has had major impacts on their families (Interview 6, 2019).

As another interviewee said, this 'grand adventure' was not all happy.

I was discriminated against, I had to put up with a lot of bad behavior from others. Some had evil intentions towards me and people of my nationality. It was not pleasant, but I worked hard and tried to improve my situation. The $3.50 I earned in the 1980s was a grand amount for me and my family. I helped many members of my family with the earnings and also met my wife while working at a restaurant.

(Interview 7, 2019)

In the case of this return migrant, the actual cost of remittance and his own migration seems to have been the amount of discrimination he has had to put up with. This factor, which is not lost on scholars, is often ignored. "The sacrifices made by migrants is not captured in the statistics and numbers that are calculated by educated people," he suggested (Interview 7, 2019). While the positive in his life was that he met his wife, started a family—with four children now, all U.S. citizens and living in Mexico—the negatives were the loss of time with family, the sense of belonging he had with the family and everything that he held dear. "You cannot replace that. We are only trying to make up for lost time now, now that we are back in our pueblo," he added.

3. Female Remittances and Migration—Creating More Space for Themselves

Some recent research from CEMLA points to the complicated picture when it comes to remittances from women. While it is assumed that male migration is more significant and the amount of remittances sent by men is greater, this narrative is only partial and not complete, a recent report argues (Cervantes, 2015). Jesus Cervantes argues that the amount of remittances received by the parents of migrants is larger than that of the wives and children; when it is the wives who are sending remittances, the amount is larger and more frequent (Cervantes, p. 1). He points out that "Millions of women have migrated to the U.S. and have sent thousands of millions of dollars to their family members in Mexico every year" (p. 1).

Some macro-indicators of migration from Latin America include the number and percentage of women who have migrated. This has gone up from 49.7% in 2007 to 51.2% in 2013, making them a larger number than even the men who have migrated. During the period of 2007–2013, there was a negative net migration to the U.S., as a result of slowing down of the economy, increase in performance of the Mexican economy, and better opportunities for Mexicans to work in their own country.

As one interviewee shared her experience,

> I had to deal with issues not only at work, but also with my husband. We constantly had arguments about everything and ultimately, he left me for another woman that he met at work. My life was a daily struggle, as I first worked in a cloth factory, where we were paid per piece and then, when I was looking for new work, I found work as a nanny. Even that didn't pay too well and I could not save much. After all that work, what did I have to show? Not much.
>
> (Interviewee 8, 2019)

This interviewee, who had returned to Santa Catarina Quiane had been frustrated that there were few opportunities for women to work and save.

This migrant shared her experience with several others who are not well educated and are at a relative disadvantage, compared to native-born women. The language barrier and lack of higher education limits their ability to break into better jobs that pay more.

It is worth noting that when statistics capture the total earnings of men and women, they do not capture the fact that many of the women work part time. This is one explanation for why women in total earn less than men from Mexico (Cervantes, 2015).

4. Culture Preservation Through Remittances

Based on this empirical data and theoretical insights, we propose the following framework to analyze how migration and remittances are tied rather intimately. The theory we propose has two components: the virtuous and vicious cycle of migration-remittance. The theory, built by focusing on some of the codes and using abductive reasoning—that is, focusing on both concrete data and also generalizing from it—yielded the results that we share here. One of the striking features of this process is that we found counter-intuitive results. While much of scholarship and commentary on remittances talks about the influence of U.S. and Western nations on the developing countries, the converse is not acknowledged—on how remittances and migration may in some cases lead to the preserving of traditional values, gender roles, etc. In the paragraphs that follow, we describe this process and offer our theoretical explanation on how this can occur.

****

The Virtuous and Vicious Cycles of Migration: Findings From Our Grounded Theory Data

Our theoretical framework is based on a Grounded Theory (G.T.) approach, where the data informs theory building (Charmaz, 2014). We use Charmaz's advice of following "flexible guidelines, not methodological rules, recipes and requirements" (p. 16) when designing and implementing the research project. The G.T. approach can be extensively used for analyzing processes and action, and we suggest that remittances sending and receiving are a 'process' in as much as there is action, actors, and processes involved. G.T. serves as a "way to learn about the world we study and a method for developing theories about them" (p. 17). As Charmaz points out, G.T. and especially constructivist G.T. can be aided by flashes of insights and analytic connections that occur during the research process and the researcher should make ample use of such insights.

As Charmaz suggests, a G.T. approach emphasizes a comparative method, comparing data at the beginning of the data collection process and comparing it with other data as it is happening, not after it is done. The comparison of data with emerging categories and drawing of conclusions is an iterative process that yields rich results. This means also that the researcher is completely involved and absorbed in the settings and in data collection. This dispels the notion of a researcher and the "positivist notion of passive observers who merely absorb their surrounding scenes." (p. 41).

We follow her advice in building on the pragmatist basis of G.T. and "Advancing interpretivist analyses that acknowledge these constructions" (p. 17). Interpretation is at the heart of theory building and we are conscious not to over-read or interpret the findings in a manner that goes beyond what the interviewees themselves meant.

Charmaz's advise is to adopt an approach and ask oneself some of the following questions: What is going on here and what are people doing and why? What is noteworthy and interesting, what hunches do you see when you observe the data? What are the human and non-human actors here? What is their significance? How does one become part of this group (of action), what is the criterion for membership or admission? What (if any) hierarchies exist, who has control and power? How do these shape behavior and action? What are the various groups trying to accomplish? What are they taking for granted? What do the participants' experiences mean to them? How do the participants use language? What words are key to them and what symbols do they use when they describe their experiences? What is the criterion for judging action and what is success in this context and who defines it? (Charmaz, 2014, p. 43).

We put in place a process of checking with the interviewees again, after our analysis, to ensure that we were interpreting the information shared accurately.

We posit that there are two sides to the migration-remittance cycle (Figures 9.1 and 9.2). For many, migration was the only option, given the decimation of Mexican agricultural sector, post NAFTA (Wright, 2005). As Wright argues in his book and shows quite clearly, the local norms of agriculture in most parts of the world, including Mexico, are at odds with the international norms and needs of production. This tension has resulted in massive changes in the way people farm, live, and also migrate.

Through our interviews with return migrants—people who have lived in the U.S. and Canada for many years and migrated back to Mexico— we have offered a theoretical perspective of how these changes are being incorporated into Mexican society and what it means to migrate and send remittances.

In terms of data gathering, we have also followed Charmaz's guidelines in terms of gathering rich data and placing it in the social context—of the return migrants. Given that we could not spend enormous amounts of time in the field, we did visit the interviewees in their own towns and

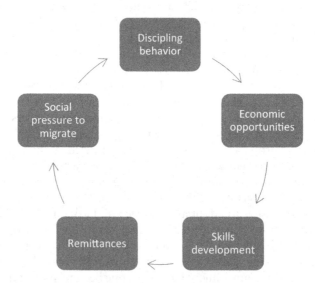

Figure 9.1 The virtuous cycle of remittances-migration

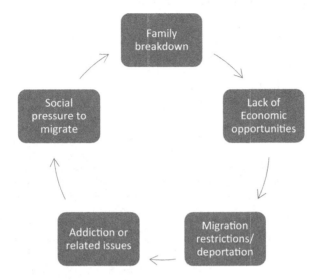

Figure 9.2 The vicious cycle of remittances-migration

villages, to place their words and descriptions in the context of their world. Words shape world views, and we were conscious of picking settings that would facilitate dialogue, open sharing, and also transparency, which would also reduce our influence on what they said. As researchers, both of us were foreigners to this context and despite the challenges, we believe we have managed to gather data that is both 'rich' and meaningful to the narratives that the narrators shared.

Some of the negatives: as one interviewee pointed out, the community in Ayoquezqo de Aldama was 100% migrant in the 1980s until mid-1995.

> Once we graduated secondary (high school), we would not even consider going to the local university, but rather talk amongst ourselves about which state in the U.S. we would go to. For instance, many people in this community have family in Washington state or in California—particularly Los Angeles and Southern California. This was just a normal part of growing up.

This interviewee pointed out that despite having universities close to their village such as the Autonoma Benito Juarez de Oaxaca University or the Universidad Regional del Sureste (URSE), many of the youth just did not consider education as an option (Interview 1, 2019).

"This trend has continued until today, and even today, we have 90% of the youth in schools thinking of going to the U.S. to earn the green money, rather than go to university," he added (Interview 1, 2019).

Tres por Uno: An Example of Subaltern Action, Legitimized by the State?

Sanchez-Ibarra's research focuses on a specific program titled Tres por Uno, or Three for one, which was a government initiative launched to match individual remittances with government funds from the federal and municipal levels, to ensure that the amount of assistance that

Photo 9.4 A bank, in rural Mexico

Photo 9.5 Fiesta in rural Oaxaca

reached the local level was three times what the individual giving would have been.

She argues, "My findings show that hometown social capital is positively related to Program participation." She points out that ethnic and socio-economic homogeneity are negatively associated with involvement in the program (Sanchez-Ibarra, 2014, p. 2). As other scholars have

Photo 9.6 Local church in Tepic, Nayarit, restored with savings from remittances
Photo credit: Samantha Lara

pointed out, the program faced challenges to its sustainability, including planning—on part of the government—and also financial sustainability and involvement of the diaspora communities (Zamora, 2005).

Conclusion

Growth of civil society in Mexico and adopted homes in the U.S. is an interesting phenomenon. Remittances offer us a lens, though a very personal one, to examine not only how migrants make decisions and determine how they spend their money, but also how they prioritize 'development,' that of their own as well as that of the communities to which they belong.

We base our theorizing on mid-range data, collected during interviews of return migrants to Mexico. What the data tells us is that there is a sense of obligation, solidarity towards one's pueblos even after a long time has elapsed, and the migrant has been in his/her adopted home for many years.

There are as many negative externalities from remittances as there are positives. In many cases, the positives are clearly visible: better homes for families, greater access to healthcare, education, and other amenities for the recipients (Interview 3, 2019).

For instance, in pueblos of Oaxaca, the price of land may go up substantially due to the newly acquired purchasing power of the remitters. In several interviews, this fact became apparent and there are instances where farmers are buying land to build houses or other structures, driving up the prices unintentionally (Interview 2, 2019).

As Angus Wright points out, the context of industrialization, work, and export promotion that exists has locked nations such as Mexico in a bind. This pattern of 'debt and dependency' makes it very difficult for such nations to change course, in spite of the disastrous social and environmental costs. His question is relevant to our discussion of remittances and economic opportunities. He asks, "Can the pursuit of economic prosperity be made consistent with ecological health and some reasonable degree of human equality?" (p. 245). This question becomes salient in the context of renewed actions by the American administration to regulate and restrict migration to the U.S. from Mexico. Assumptions about the amount of yield, the feasibility of agriculture and technologies that are used in agriculture have fueled policy debates in this field, he argues. Many of these assumptions are faulty at best, Wright writes. This debate is relevant to our discussion as many of the waves of migration are related to availability, or lack thereof, of opportunities to engage in agriculture and to live off of this as an occupation. Given the rural nature of Mexican society, this aspect of the discussion may become crucial for us.

As we point out, both the virtuous and vicious cycle operate almost simultaneously when it comes to migration to the U.S. and Canada from Mexico. External environmental conditions have a bearing on how these changes ebb and flow, however; the dynamics of flow of people and money are impacted more by the migrants' perceptions of the costs and benefits of migration.

Remittances are a form of solidarity action, and should be seen as a form of social action. While a majority of remittances may be used for consumption purposes, there is growing evidence that some of it is used towards investment and other long-term projects. As Zamora reminds us:

> It is estimated that the remittances also contribute major resources to development in communities with a history of international migration,

which has significant multiplier effects in terms of regional and local economic activity. It is calculated that at least 10% of the remittances are allocated to savings and productive investment.

(Zamora, 2005, p. 6)

Other scholars have also pointed to this pattern of consumption/investment, Zamora argues (Castro and Tuirán, 2000).

The subsequent stoppage of this program since 2005 points to the risks of assuming that remittances are a sustainable way to sponsor or continue a macro-economic development project. The Tres por Uno program and its limitations give us pause, to consider what the phenomenon of migration can do or cannot accomplish when it comes to achieving larger social objectives. Lozano (2004) is among the other researchers who have pointed out the limitations of relying on remittances to 'fix' issues such as those of development, creating economic opportunities, etc. These are essentially the responsibility of the state, he reminds us (Zamora, 2005).

We have argued in this paper that there needs to be a greater acknowledgment of the power as well as limitations of remittances as a phenomenon. While they can have positive externalities on a community and society at large, there are also negative externalities that are often not accounted for in academic and policy-related literature. We point out that it is key for us to acknowledge this persistent challenge and to see the gaps in this practice as a natural limitation on the kind of social activity it is.

We agree with Zamora (2005) that remittances can play the role of a catalyst when it comes to starting new ventures or projects but by themselves cannot be expected to spur economic development in a region. That would be an unrealistic expectation and one that has not borne fruit in the past. In the example of MENA, a women's cooperative in Ayoquezqo de Aldama, Oaxaca, Mexico; there has been a concerted effort by migrants (some of whom were involved in founding of the organization) to use their savings towards starting and running it. There is evidence that social remittances—through the transfer of skills and human capital—may have played a key role in its success. This aspect can and should be studied further in the context of Mexico and other countries. While the actual money transferred may dry up in the short run, the professional skills, personal contacts, etc. may endure, helping further the organizations that are started by the return migrants.

References

Bourdieu, P. (1995). *Outline of a Theory of Practice*. Cambridge: Cambridge University Press.

Castro, J., & Tuirán, R. (2000). Las remesas de los trabajadores emigrantes mexicanos a los Estados Unidos. *Comercio Exterior*, 50(4).

CEMLA. (2019, Nov). *Women's Migration to the U.S.* Presentation made at CEMLA, Mexico City.

Cervantes, J. (2015). *Female Migration and Remittance Flows to Mexico.* Mexico City, Mexico: CEMLA.

Charmaz, K. (2014). *Constructing Grounded Theory.* Thousand Oaks: Sage Publications.

Chatterjee, P. (1982). Agrarian relations and communalism in Bengal, 1926–1935. *Subaltern studies I: Writings on South Asian history and society,* 9–38. Oxford Press.

Chatterjee, P. (1983b). More on modes of power and the peasantry. In R. Guha (Ed.), *SS II.* New Delhi: Oxford University Press. Pp. 311–349.

Chaturvedi, V. (2007). *A Critical Theory of Subalternity: Rethinking Class in Indian Historiography: Left History.* Baltimore, MD: Alternative Press Center.

Cuevas-Mohr, H. (2019, Nov). *Comments Made during a Talk at the IMTC Conference.* Miami, USA.

Foucault, M. (1975). *Discipline and Punish and the Birth of Prison.* New York: Random House.

Fox, J., & Rivera-Salgado, G. (2005, Marzo). Building migrant civil society: Indigenous Mexicans in the US. *Iberoamericana (2001–) Nueva época,* 5(17), 101–115.

Geertz, C. (1973). *The Interpretation of Cultures.* New York: Basic Books.

Harvey, D. (2001). *Spaces of Capital: Towards a Critical Geography.* New York: Routledge Press.

Interview 1. (2019, Oct). Interview with return migrant from California in Ayoquezco de Aldama.

Interview 2. (2019, Oct). Interview with return migrant from California in Ayoquezco de Aldama.

Interview 3. (2019, Oct). Interview with return migrant from California in Ayoquezco de Aldama.

Interview 4. (2019, Oct). Interview with return migrant from California in Ayoquezco de Aldama.

Interview 5. (2019, Oct). Interview with return migrant from Washington State in Quiane.

Interview 6. (2019, Oct). Interview with return migration from New York in Santa Ana Del Valle.

Interview 7. (2019, Oct). Interview with return migration from New York in Santa Ana Del Valle.

Interview 8. (2019, Oct). Interview with return migration from NY in Santa Ana Del Valle.

Kleist, N. (2008). Mobilising 'the diaspora': Somali trans- national political engagement. *Journal of Ethnic and Migration Studies* 34, 307–323.

Lee, E. (1966). A theory of migration. *Demography,* 3(1), 47–57. Accessible at www.jstor.org/stable/2060063

Lozano, F (2004). "Efectos económicos de la migración México-Estados Unidos. Implicaciones y retos para ambos países. Seminario Migración México Estados-Unidos, Consejo Nacional de Población, Mexico City.

Mixteco. (2019). Accessible at http://mixteco.org/about-us/

Page, B. (2012). Why do people do stuff: Reconceptualizing remittance behaviour in diaspora-development research and policy. *Progress in Development Studies,* 12(1), 1–18.

Payton, R., & Moody, M. (2008). *Understanding Philanthropy: Its Meaning and Mission.* Indianapolis: IUPUI Press.

Sanchez-Ibarra, P. (2014). *Remesas colectivas y desarrollo local: Análisis de la participación de los municipios marginados en el Programa 3x1 para Migrantes en México.* Master's Thesis. Barcelona, Spain: Institut Barcelona.

Sen, A. (1999). *Development as Freedom.* New York: Random House.

Sheffer, G. (2003). *Diaspora Politics: At Home Abroad.* Cambridge: Cambridge University Press.

Spivak, G. (2010). *Can the Subaltern Speak?* New York: Columbia University Press.

Wright, A. (2005). *The Death of Ramon Gonzales.* Texas: University of Austin Press.

Zamora, R. G. (2005, Nov 4 and 5). *Collective Remittances and the 3x1 Program as a Transnational Social Learning Process.* Presentation made at a Conference Titled: "Mexican Migrant Social and Civic Participation in the United States." To be held at the Woodrow Wilson International Center for Scholars. Washington, DC.

10 Remittances as 'Soft Power'?

Examining the Power of Money-Flows Between Communities and Nation-States

Remittances are flows of money that migrants send to their country of origin from their country of residence. This phenomenon often is examined with the individual as the unit of analysis. In this paper, we take a different point of view—examining the countries of sending and receiving as the units of analysis. The objective of this exercise is twofold: to turn the focus on nation-states and to use concepts such as diplomacy and soft power and to examine whether this lens can be used to understand remittances and its manifestations as a tool of diplomacy (see Figure 10.1 for an overview of remittance channels).

Given the rise of nationalistic rhetoric and 'American first' and 'Saudization' policy, whereby expatriates are being replaced by local Saudi nationals, the idea of immigration itself has come under attack. We seek to understand how remittances play in this mix, and what impact—if any—they have on the way that national policies are impacted, as a result of remittances. We use the theoretical contributions of Joseph Nye (2010) and other international relations theorists to understand these concepts.

****

Prime Minister Modi, the head of state in India, is a frequent traveler to the Gulf nations. Indian media covers the visits of heads of state to each of the six Gulf nations—Kuwait, Oman, UAE, Saudi Arabia, Qatar, and Bahrain—quite extensively and in one such article, it pointed out that "With Modi visit India cements strategic connect with Gulf nations." This was an article about his visit in August 2019.

A media report by IANS news agency pointed out that "Though this August 24 visit is a first ever prime ministerial visit by India to Bahrain, the Modi government has been maintaining close ties with Manama since its first term" (IANS, 2019). The sheer number of Indian workers in the Gulf nations makes the region significant for India—both from an economic and strategic perspective. In addition, the support of these Gulf nations is seen as being crucial for India, which has a sizeable Muslim population, estimated to be about 12 to 15% of the entire population (Shariff, 2012).

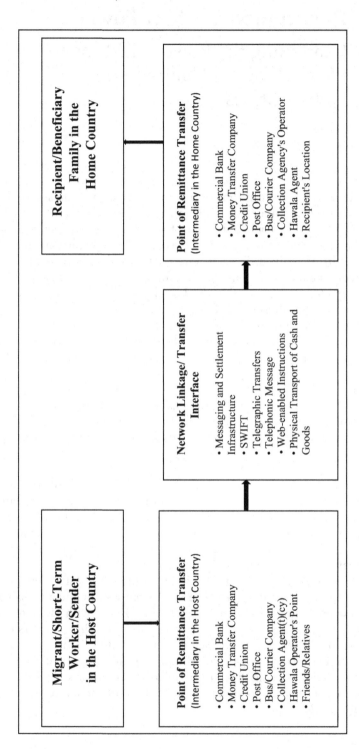

Figure 10.1 Overview of remittance channels

Source: International Monetary Fund (2009)

There is another geopolitical element to these visits, in addition to the geo-economics—that of reducing Pakistan's influence in the region. As the media article argues, rightly, with over 40% of its oil imports coming from the region, India's relationships with the 22-member Arab League and the 57-member Organization of Islamic Cooperation (OIC) is important for these very reasons. Indian leaders have, over the years, sought to use both geo-economics and geopolitics strategically to position themselves as leaders in South Asia.

The welcoming embrace from the GCC nations is due to the fact that India (and South Asia) in general is a supply of cheap labor for the oil-rich nations, which often have issues in recruiting people to work in its various industries.

* * * * * * * *

International relations is the study of how nations relate to each other. Whereas notions of how national discourse about sovereignty shapes relations between people, there has been a growing trend to look at the notion of 'citizens diplomacy' as a lens to examine how ordinary citizens can shape relations between nations and how they can act as a bridge between them (Nye, 2010; National Council for International Visitors, 2010). Joseph Nye argues in his book *The Future of Power* that economic power might be more important in the decades to come, with the rise of China and other actors that are emerging as being far more important in the global arena, due to their might in the economic sector. However, as Nye further elaborates, economic might can produce soft power, through attraction.

> The basic economic resources that underlie both hard and soft power are such things as the size and quality of gross domestic product (GDP), per capita incomes, the level of technology, natural and human resources, political and legal institutions for markets, as well as a variety of shaped resources for special domains, such as trade, finance and competition.
>
> (Nye, 2011, p. 52)

Relative gains are important to keep in mind as well, as joint gains are often not the most important factor, as he reminds us.

What this means is that some nations may gain more from an economic relationship than others and this may give them a stronger advantage than the other, even though the nations are on good terms with each other. Other observers have argued that economic power is not necessarily real power or influence, as it could be that a few businesses or individuals may be controlling the trade and not the nation-state (Kay, 2009). Nye counters that despite the state not having absolute power in these situations, given the influence of interest groups, lobbies, trans-national organizations, etc., there is definitely scope for the state to be influential. It all depends on the nature of the market and how the relationship of the state is with the other key power holders.

Oil economics has been central to our understanding of relations between countries and this fact has been made manifest in the recent past. The oil crisis of the 1970s made it clear that oil-rich Gulf countries can bring their agenda to the table in a forceful way that may not be to the liking of the U.S. and other European powers (Nye, 2011). Nye argues that symmetry in interdependence made oil a somewhat less effective tool, even though it worked for a while. Given the GCC countries' dependence on the U.S., they had to tone down and cooperate with the U.S., he suggests.

Using the same analogy with India, the GCC has other needs that India can supply—human labor and other goods and services that are essential for these economies to function. If they were cut off, for any reason, there is reason to believe that the economies of these regions would grind to a halt.

Understanding Soft Power and Social Capital

To get a better sense of what we mean by remittances as a tool for soft power, let us understand the basic concepts behind this idea. The key one being soft power itself. Nye defines soft power as the ability of a country

Photo 10.1 Money transfer agents in Singapore

Photo 10.2 Money transfer agents in Singapore

to do what it wants others to do—without coercion (Nye, 2004). The United States is an exemplary example of soft power in action, though in the past few years, scholars have argued that it is diminishing (Nye, 2004; Walt, 2018a).

In more recent times, scholars have called for examining the impacts of reduced American soft power on America's primary as a superpower

Photo 10.3 A bracero in rural Oaxaca

(Datta, 2009; Walt, 2018b; Muenning, 2018; Putnam, 2015). This decline is reflected in healthcare, education access, general well-being, and a host of other factors.

The factors that Putnam and Muenning and other scholars point to are all too easily noticeable: growing economic inequality, lack of access to quality early-childhood education, lack of social networks that help the poor grow out of poverty and also flourish as adults.

Putnam defines social capital as any group of informal neighborhood watch groups, a group of Hassidic Jews trading diamonds without having to test each item for its genuineness, or barn-raising on the frontier, as well as exchanges among groups of cancer patients, etc. He points out that social capital is found in families, friendship networks, churches, schools, civic associations, and various forms of social networks. Internet-based groups can also have social capital; however their negative impact is also significant, so he doesn't give any definitive account of what their role is in building or reducing social capital. Declining social capital and economic prosperity has also given rise to extreme politics—the politics of exclusion, racism, anti-Semitism, and Islamophobia, according to some researchers and social commentators (Reich, 2010; Putnam, 2000).

Putnam, among other scholars, has argued that there has been a decline in social capital in the U.S. in the past few decades due to many factors, including the rise of technology (Putnam, 2000). All of this is important because social networks provide people with access to advice, job leads, strategic information, and other networks that can help people advance (Putnam, 2000, p. 318). With a lack of these intangibles, people find it hard to advance in life and break out of the cycle of poverty they are born into. What is also relevant here is the discussion around how a general rise of economic inequality in the U.S. has had a cascade effect on how Americans view themselves, their life chances, and the role of 'outsiders' in the U.S. What this implies is that there is often a direct rise of xenophobia, hatred and suspicion of those not deemed American or belonging to the 'community.' Putnam and other scholars show how this happens in their discussion of the negative side of social capital.

There are many different kinds of social capital, but broadly defined one can think of two kinds: bridging and bonding. While bridging is the kind of social capital that brings people together regardless of one's relation or shared heritage, bonding social capital bonds or brings together people on the basis of shared heritage, race, religion, or other factors. There can be bridging and bonding at the same time and often these two categories are not as exclusive as they seem, Putnam reminds us.

> Most groups are bridging in some ways and bonding in others: the Knights of Columbus is bonding in terms of religion and gender but bridges across class and income. In America religious communities constitute a particularly abundant form of social capital, both bonding and bridging.
>
> (Putnam, 2017)

This key insight is crucial for us to understand as we examine the role of remittances and other forms of giving across the border. Of course, there are many significant faith-based NGOs that are working on issues of education, healthcare, migrant rights, etc. across the border. For them, the partnerships they forge are crucial.

As we have discussed before, there has been a serious decline in social capital in the U.S., and the consequent impact on individuals and communities has been disastrous. The impact has been felt at various levels, both at the household level and the individual levels. For instance, there

Photo 10.4 A bracero in rural Oaxaca

Photo 10.5 A representative of a firm that manufactures a machine that operates as an ATM, money transfer device, and much more

has been a decline in life expectancy in the U.S. that has also coincided with the decline in its power around the world (Muenning, Reynolds, Fink, Zafari, & Geronimus, 2018). This decline in health and well-being reflects the amount of investment that is being made in these areas, by policy makers. As these authors write, "The United States has experienced what amounts to a social crisis that dates back to at least the 1980s. This crisis is reflected not only in various measures of worsening despair but also in declining relative life expectancy" (Muenning et al., 2018, p. 1626). They echo what others such as Putnam have argued for, saying that the U.S. must invest more in various policies that target the poor and disadvantaged, rather than take that support away.

Soft power in international relations can be also seen as a reflection of 'social capital' that Americans have within their communities, at the local level. As Robert Putnam, the sociologist who is well known for his work on social capital explains, "A growing body of hard-nosed literature over the last several years shows that social capital helps provide many important individual and social goods. Individuals who are better connected socially are healthier and happier, find better jobs, live longer" (Putnam, 2017). This means that the effort to increase soft power within American society is well worth the effort and can yield positive results.

Remittances as Soft Power?

Do remittances have the ability to define relations between nation-states? Just to remind ourselves of the definition of soft power, here is what we wrote earlier: Nye defines soft power as the ability of a country to do what it wants others to do—without coercion (Nye, 2004).

By this means, that remittances have—and we will show how—the ability to shape one country's actions, though the extent of this is arguable. We argue that remittances have helped shape the relations between Mexico and the U.S. as well as Saudi Arabia (and the larger GCC) with India and the sub-continent in many subtle and not-so-subtle ways. This is a case of the individual shaping the destiny of the nation-state. When there is smooth flow of money, both sides win, and each time there has been some hindrance or policy change to make the flow of money harder, both countries have suffered the consequences of this decreased soft power.

As some economists have argued, remittances have benefits for the U.S. too. Justin Sandefur argues that the loss of money to Mexico is not a real loss, rather that this exchange of labor for money brings far more benefits (Sandefur, 2016). As he points out,

> Figuratively, we trade pieces of paper with green ink for real stuff. If families in Mexico use those dollars to buy things made in Mexico or elsewhere, then America has essentially gotten immigrants' services without paying anything tangible in return. If, on the other hand, families in Mexico use their remittances to buy things made in the United States, then American exports increase. Either way, the American economy wins.

> (Sandefur, 2016)

The other reason that remittances are good for the U.S. is that through exchange rate appreciation of the peso through remittances, American goods become cheaper as the cost of manufacturing increases, he reminds us. So, in any case, there is a win for America. We suggest that this phenomenon is a win for Mexico as millions of people get much desired remittances, which are the lifeline for many millions more.

There was, at least in early 2017, some news that Trump would tax remittances, in an effort to raise money for the border wall with Mexico. This contentious announcement—which eventually didn't amount to anything more than a threat—did raise some eyebrows.

Observers who have followed this issue point out that the reaction from the Mexican side has been quite swift and direct. Also, there is no way really for Mexicans to pay for the wall (Ordonez & Kumar, 2018). As a direct response to Mr. Trump's announcement in early 2017, President of Mexico Pena Nieto made a public announcement that the Mexican government would protect the interests of its citizens. "Our 50 consulates in the U.S. are there for the protection of Mexicans and we will not let our people down. Our communities are not alone." President Pena Nieto reinforced the country's position that Mexico would not pay for any wall that would divide the two countries.

CATO's Alex Nowrasteh points out that a remittance tax would not work in the case of Mexico.

> A remittances tax would have to be very high to raise enough revenue to pay for a wall, even assuming there is no fall off in revenue at higher rates. The state of Oklahoma has a wire transmitter fee equal to about one percent of the funds transmitted.
>
> (Nowrosteh, 2017)

He points out that this is an impractical solution to the problem at hand, as such a tax, if implemented nationally, will drive a lot of the remittances underground. With technologies such as Bitcoin and other newer forms of sending money, the manner in which money is sent will just change.

There are also hawala-like systems that are off the books that could be used to transfer money to Mexico (Interview 13, 2019). There could be a shift towards using those mechanisms for sending money, as well. This mechanism of the black market is available to many of the undocumented workers and they will start using it, if there is a need.

With the change in strategy on how the border wall is to be funded, there seems to be lesser focus on remittances as the mechanism for this funding.

Mexican-American Citizens and the Mexican State

The relationship of the Mexican state with its diaspora is a complicated one. While there are significant public diplomacy initiatives between

Mexico and the U.S., the two countries have also had a rather tense relationship when it comes to diaspora relations. As Tigau, Pande, and Yan point out, "Public diplomacy is based on the use of the public opinion to communicate a state's or nation's interest on an international sphere, be it through cultural educational or scientific messages" (Tigau, et al. 2017, p. 87). Cultural diplomacy refers to creating a better understanding of culture, films, and literature of the country of origin of the diaspora, so that people across borders can have better relations with each other, they point out. Other scholars such as Van Ham have also pointed out that citizens' work has become important in building understanding between nation-states (Van Ham, 2001). The manner in which diaspora policies have been used to shape relations between nations can have significant impact on how the nation-states relate to each other, Tigua et al. argue (Tigau, Pande, & Yuan, 2017). They further point out that the Mexicans who immigrated to the U.S. prior to the 1990s were considered traitors and not reliable people. This changed only after several policy initiatives such as the Program for Student Mobility in North America (PROMESAN) in 1995, with the involvement of over 348 academic institutions that helped mitigate some of this ill feeling and built an infrastructure for a healthier exchange of Mexican diaspora with the Mexicans in Mexico. As Delano points out, it was President Ernesto Zedillo who admitted that the Mexican nation existed beyond its present borders and later President Vicente Fox who considered himself the president of 120 million Mexicans, many of whom lived abroad (Delano, 2011, quoted in Tigau, Pande, & Yuan, 2017).

Remittances and also social remittances have been one of the main reasons for this exchange to become important and the Mexican government realizes that this exchange can benefit its citizens, in more ways than one (Delano, 2011; Tigau, 2009). There have been several networks such as the Mexican Talent Network, the Association of Former Students of the Monterrey Technological Institute, etc. that have played a key role in keeping up the networking and exchanges across the border.

One classic example of how diaspora remittances have been factored into the development discourse is one of 'Tres por Uno,' or 'three for one' program. This program launched in the 1990s. Zamora, in his article, talks about how this policy was part of a new set of public policies initiated to attract remittances to Mexico and was meant to provide support for regional development, specifically.

He points out that between 1993 and 2005, the program helped finance over 1,500 projects in the Zacatecas region with over $62 million in remittances (Zamora, 2007, p. 166). The program was managed and run in conjunction with the Secretary of Social Development. Zamora also points out that between 2003–2006, the program helped finance over 6,250 projects with the involvement of federal government contribution of $15 million, on an average. Zamoras points to a few positives from the program: a) it helped organize the transnational community, b) it created a positive space for negotiating with the government, c) it helped finance over 6,000 projects, d) it taught aspects of social development to all the actors, e) it helped the diaspora community to contribute to their community of origin, f) it offered a way for people to contribute and engage—and a way to measure performance of social programs. An evaluation carried out by Instituto Technologico Autonomo de Mexico and The Universidad Autonoma de Zacatecas showcased some basic problems in both design and implementation of the Tres por Uno program.

One of the issues they found, Zamora adds, is that this was a federal program implemented without much analysis of the local needs, at the grass roots levels. One of the bigger problems was the low level of the involvement of the beneficiary communities. The federal budget was also limited and did not support enough of the work that was needed, he points out. There was also contradiction or conflict between what the local authorities thought was important and what the federal agencies and the migrant group representatives felt was key for development. They could not agree on certain projects as worthy of investment, he points out. There was also politicization of the Tres por Uno, with some politicians touting it as a success of the particular party, rather than claiming credit for it as a program in general. These problems are all part of the challenges when it comes to measuring social change, as scholars such as Alnoor Ebrahim have pointed out (Ebrahim, 2019). His insights that accountability mechanisms must be clear when it comes to social problems, are key. Ebrahim points out that accountability should be spelled out clearly and the actors must know 'who' they are accountable to and 'for what' (p. 30). This is crucial for all actors involved. There is also the role of leadership, and one of its key tasks is to make sure that the various stakeholders are clear and know what mechanisms exist, to hold them accountable.

As the Zamoras article points out, this seems to have been the case with Tres por Uno, where the most powerful stakeholders, rather than the most vulnerable ones, were calling the shots, and the priorities of the powerful were being implemented. Ebrahim points out that the most powerful tend to be donors or investors, rather than beneficiaries—and they can threaten to withdraw or withhold funds (Ebrahim, 2019; Najam, 1996). Tres Por Uno seemed to have suffered a similar fate, in which case the diaspora remittances were the carrot, which turned into a stick and were used to regulate or dictate terms to the local groups. Ebrahim's insight that the organization's upward mobility—to funders—must align with the downward accountability towards clients is key in programs such as Tres por Uno or similar programs where the donors are quite powerful, not only because they give money, but also because they wield outsized influence in the process.

While the complex and multi-layered relationship of the Mexican state with its citizens and diaspora begins to play out, in many ways it is crucial to remember that for any such process input from all parties is key. One cannot ignore the input of local communities, the recipients of donations/ remittances, as they are a crucial part of the chain and ones that are at the heart of the whole enterprise. Without their meaningful input, the entire exercise can be quite a big failure.

Indian Diaspora and the Politics of Remittances: The Rise of Populism

Indian diaspora is key to the success of politics back home. With over 2.4 million Indians in the U.S. with a median household income of about $107,000 per year—which is twice that of the average American house-hold, Indians in the U.S. are a powerhouse. As Betigere of the Lowy Insti-tute points out, Indians are more likely to be enrolled in higher education, to participate in labor force, and "twice likely to be employed in man-agement, business, science and arts as the general population" (Betigere, 2019). She points to the rise of several prominent politicians, businessmen and women as well as even presidential hopefuls such as Kamala Harris and Nikki Haley. The amount of Political Action Committees (PACs) that have been established by people of Indian origin is also noteworthy.

One can argue that the soft power of India, as a rising economic power and also with its talented migrants to the U.S., has shaped U.S.-India rela-tions over the past three decades or so. This growing economic might and influence is changing how mainstream American politicians are viewing the community in the 2020 U.S. elections. This is a long journey for a community that has been reviled and excluded from American society (Ghaneabassiri, 2010).

The long history of exclusion of Indians in the American mainstream has also led to lobbying efforts by Indian groups, for greater rights, includ-ing the right to property, etc. It was only with the passage of the Hart-Cellar Act in 1965 that immigration from India and other parts of Asia become regularized (Janardhan, 2013). This background is important as we understand the role of current diaspora, which often uses 'victim nar-ratives' to shape its discourses around its sense of belonging in the U.S.

The support of the Indian diaspora for American politicians has been crucial to their soft power both in the U.S. and back home in India. As Janardhan points out,

> Indian Americans, along with the larger Asian American community, emerged a significant political constituency by the 2008 presidential elections (Fennerty, 2008, pp. 56–57) and consolidated their posi-tion in 2012 elections. According to a survey conducted by the Asian American Legal Defense and Education Fund (2008), 2008 polls revealed that 69% of Indian Americans were enrolled in the Demo-cratic Party compared to 7% in the Republican Party. Out of those

surveyed, 91% Indian Americans said they voted for Barack Obama, while 8% voted for John McCain.

(p. 25)

The diaspora has also supported Indian politicians—both financially and in terms of lobbying for them in the U.S., given their influence and financial clout. This has been a recurring theme for Indians in the U.S.

The outreach of right-wing Hindus towards Mr. Trump has gained some attention, as Trump spoke at a big rally in 2016 and declared, "I am a big fan of Hindu and a big fan of India." However, as observers have pointed out, a majority of Indians—well over 65%—are Democrats who are not as vocal as the right-wing minority (Betigere, 2019). During the same rally, Trump vowed to work closely with the Indian Prime Minister Mr. Modi (Schrekinger, 2016).

Eviane Cheng Leidig points out in his analysis of social media discourses of Trump and Brexit that communication technologies have played an outsized role in shaping opinions (Leidig, 2019). Leidig's analysis points to how the Indian diaspora imagines itself as a collective that is non-Muslim, as individuals who support Trump and right-wing issues and seek to create boundaries of inclusion/exclusion. This insight is also key as we analyze how soft power is manifest, as Indians back home look to these Indians in the U.S. who have 'made it' and are model professionals for those back home.

In the case of Indian diaspora, which is complex and comprises of people of various religious identities, the Hindu majority shows marked learnings towards Hindutva or the politics of right-wing Hinduism. Leidig argues that the diasporas tend to organize themselves around religious identities and in the recent past, there has been a rise in anti-Muslim sentiment among the Indian diaspora, that defines itself as non-Muslim and also as victims of Islamic aggression—a trope that is used by their Western counterparts to 'other' the Muslims in these societies (Leidig, 2019; Kurien, 2016).

As Leidig adds, "Diasporic Hindutva becomes a mediator of transnational ideological manifestations of anti-Muslim anxiety, albeit adapted to local contexts. It is thus the outcome of a highly politicized agenda that combines transnational and multicultural identity politics" (Leidig, 2019). Leidig's point is particularly poignant as it relates to how the diaspora seeks to mobilize support for Mr. Modi and the amount of political and financial support he has received over the past decade or so. Scholars have pointed out that the Indian diaspora played a key and instrumental role in Mr. Modi's rise and also helped exonerate him after he was banned from visiting the U.S., following the massacre of Muslims in Godhra, Gujarat in 2002, for which he was held responsible.

The U.K. had barred Modi from visiting the country for ten years, from 2002–2012 and it is only by the active lobbying of Indian diaspora in the U.K. that he has been welcomed back with open arms (BBC News-night, 2015).

Growing Nationalism, Rise of Anti-migrant Sentiment and Impact on Remittances

Based on our interviews in Oaxaca, Mexico, there definitely is a growing sense of anxiety among migrants from Mexico living in the U.S. There is also a growing sense and need for sending greater remittances to Mexico—as a safety net—as many of the migrants feel that stronger and stricter immigration laws may lead to their deportation back to Mexico. In that scenario, the remittances could potentially help them restart their lives or at least form a basis for their retirement (Interviews 8, 12, 13).

The growing sense of xenophobia has increased since the emergence of Donald Trump as a candidate for political office and eventually having been elected as the President of the United States (Ramos, 2018).

Stephen Walt points out that the wars on Afghanistan and Iraq cost us a lot. "American intervention has created failed states—Libya and Yemen and even in Syria" (Walt, 2018b). He argues in his new book that our commitment to liberal hegemony has brought us here—democracy, markets, human rights have alienated us from the world and this is one reason our 'soft power' is no longer working. In the web of institutions that the U.S. built, liberal hegemony sought to change the world and remake it in its image. "Liberal values are not good exports and it was a failed strategy," Walt points out. The world we are witnessing today is a result of the policies and programs that have been in place for the past 60 plus years, since World War II, when the U.S. emerged as the undisputed global power. Today, it is no longer the only superpower, with several other nations competing with the U.S. for global or at least regional hegemony, Walt seems to be saying. However, the allure of the U.S. remains, even if it is slightly diminished.

"Primacy meant that this campaign wasn't necessary—then why did we do it? There was strong bipartisan support among foreign policy elite, not the public . . . the Chicago Council on Global Affairs, AEI, think tanks and many others."

Walt argues that there are no formal requirements—no medical license, no degrees. The American foreign policy elite have defined norms that guide American conduct around the world. How that plays out in the context of remittances is also key to our understanding. There seems to be a growing inwardness in how Americans tend to see their role in the world.

"In 2016, 64% of Americans said that Americans should stop being the police of the world." He further points out that more and more public opinion seems to be aligning with this view. The past four presidents have won on doing less in the global state, Walt reminds us.

This perspective that Walt brings can be seen through the lens of soft power, and American hegemony tells us that soft power has its limitations too. Nye acknowledges it and says that "soft power can tend to have diffuse effects on the outside world and is not easily wielded to achieve specific outcomes" (Nye, 2004).

Walt points out that main challenge in Asia is diplomatic, not military. The distances in Asia are enormous and to hold those countries as a coalition is hard—for if something happens in Taiwan, why would India intervene? he asks. This means that there are diplomatic challenges in Asia for the U.S. "We need really smart people engaged in this part of the world."

China's role is being curbed and there is consensus in Washington that the country needs to be reined in.

With the rise in nationalism, restrictions on migration to the West from Asia and Africa, we may see a decline in remittances in the coming years. As a result, there is potential to believe that there could be a decline in its role and impact as a 'soft power' tool. However, the numbers that are being compiled and the stories of remittances that we have documented in this book remind us time and again that the impact and relevance of remittances remains. There is no doubt that recipients think highly of the sending countries, even if they disagree with the policies of the country in question.

For instance, Mexican interviewees that took part in our research admire and want to emulate American freedoms as much as they want to retain their Mexicanness. They also have great respect for American work ethic, discipline, and values. This is similar to the way that many Indians feel about the Gulf nations. Given the geographic proximity of those nations, there is a shared history and culture in that part of the world that political and business leaders have used to build on their narratives to succeed.

References

BBC Newsnight. (2015). *Survivors Speak Out*. Accessible at www.youtube.com/watch?v=wJrrJYEJKYs. Retrieved on Dec 15, 2019.

Betigere, A. (2019). The remarkable influence of the Indian diaspora. *Lowy Institute*. Accessible at www.lowyinstitute.org/the-interpreter/remarkable-political-influence-indian-diaspora-us. Retrieved on Dec 15, 2019.

Datta, M. N. (2009). The decline of America's soft power in the United Nations. *International Studies Perspectives*, 10(3), 265–284.

Delano, A. (2011). *Mexico and Its Diaspora in the United States: Policies of Emigration since 1848*. Cambridge, MA, USA: Cambridge University Press.

Ebrahim, A. (2019). *Measuring Social Change: Performance and Accountability in a Complex World*. Palo Alto, CA: Stanford University Press.

Ghaneabassiri, K. (2010). *A History of Islam in America: From the New World to a New World Order*. Cambridge, MA: Cambridge University Press.

IANS. (2019). *With Modi Visit India Cements Strategic Connect with Gulf Nations.* Accessible at www.indiatoday.in/india/story/with-modi-visit-india-cements-strategic-connect-with-gulf-nations-1590239-2019-08-22

International Monetary Fund. (2009). International transactions in remittances: Guide for compilers and users. Washington, D.C.: International Monetary Fund.

Interview 8. (2019, Oct). San Pablo Huixtepec. Oaxaca, Mexico.

Interview 12. (2019, Oct). Ayoquezco de Aldama. Oaxaca, Mexico.

Interview 13. (2019, Oct). Ayoquezco de Aldama. Oaxaca, Mexico.

Janardhan, V. (2013). Political participation of Indian diaspora in the U.S. *Journal of International and Global Studies*, 5(1), 16–33.

Kay, J. (2009, Mar 25). The fallacy of equating economic power with influence. *Financial Times.*

Kurien, P. A. (2016). Majority versus minority religious status and diasporic nationalism: Indian American advocacy organizations. *Nations and Nationalism*, 23(1), 109–128.

Leidig, E. C. (2019). *Immigrant, Nationalist and Proud: A Twitter Analysis of Diaspora Supporters of Trump and Brexit.* Accessible at http://dx.doi.org.ezproxy.lib.vt.edu/10.17645/mac.v7i1.1629

McClatchyDC. Accessible at www.mcclatchydc.com/news/politics-government/white-house/article198740894.html

Muenning, P., Reynolds, M., Fink, D., Zafari, Z., & Geronimus, A. (2018). America's declining well-being, not just a white problem. *American Journal of Public Health*, 108(12).

Najam, A. (1996). NGO accountability: A conceptual framework. *Development Policy Review*, 14, 339–353.

National Council for International Visitors. (2010). *A Salute to Citizens Diplomacy.* Washington, DC: The National Council for International Visitors.

Nawrosteh, A. (2017). A Tax on remittances wont pay for a border wall. *CATO Institute.* Accessible at www.cato.org/blog/tax-remittances-wont-pay-border-wall. Retrieved on Dec 14, 2019.

Nye, J. (2004). Soft-power: The means to success in the real world. *Foreign Affairs.* Accessible at www.foreignaffairs.com/reviews/capsule-review/2004-05-01/soft-power-means-success-world-politics

Nye, J. (2010). *The Powers to Lead.* Oxford: Oxford University Press.

Nye, J. (2011). *The Future of Power.* New York: Perseus Books.

Ordonez, F., & Kumar, A. (2018). *How Trump Plans to Make Mexico Pay for the Wall.* Impact 2020. Mcclathy DC. Accessible at https://www.mcclatchydc.com/news/politics-government/white-house/article198740894.html

Putnam, R. (2000). *Bowling Alone: The Collapse and Revival of American Community.* New York: Simon & Schuster.

Putnam, R. (2015). *Our Kids: The American Dream in Crisis.* New York: Simon & Schuster.

Putnam, R. (2017). *The State of Social Capital in the U.S. Congressional Testimony.* Accessible at www.jec.senate.gov/public/_cache/files/222a1636-e668-4893-b082-418a100fd93d/robert-putnam-testimony.pdf

Ramos, J. (2018). *Stranger: The Challenge of a Latino Immigrant in the Trump Era.* New York: Vintage Books.

Reich, R. (2010). Xenophobia and the economy. *Christian Science Monitor.* Accessible at www.csmonitor.com/Business/Robert-Reich/2010/1011/Xenophobia-and-the-economy

Sandefur, J. (2016). Why remittances are good for America. *CNN.* Accessible at www.cnn.com/2016/04/08/opinions/remittances-good-for-america-sandefur/index.html. Retrieved on Dec 14, 2019.

Schrekinger, B. (2016). Trump goes Bollywood. *Politico.* Accessible at www.politico.com/story/2016/10/donald-trump-bollywood-india-hindus-new-jersey-229848. Retrieved on Dec 15, 2019.

Shariff, A. (2012). *India: Social Development Report 2012.* Oxford: Oxford University Press.

Tigau, C. (2009). *Diplomacia en la era digital: la ayuda alimentaria como maniobra neoliberal.* Universidad Nacional Autónoma de México (UNAM), Centro de Investigaciones sobre América del Norte and Ed, Cenzontle.

Tigau, C., Pande, A., & Yuan, Y. (2017). Diaspora policies and co-development: A comparison between India, China and Mexico. *Migration Letters*, 14(2), 189–203.

Van Ham, P. (2001). The rise of the brand state: The postmodern politics of image and reputation. *Foreign Affairs*, 2–6.

Walt, S. (2018a). *The Hell of Good Intentions: America's Foreign Policy Elite and the Decline of U.S. Primacy.* Farrar, Straus and Giroux: Just World Books.

Walt, S. (2018b). *You Tube: Realism and Restraint: American's New Foreign Policy.* Accessible at www.youtube.com/watch?v=MmRhdYXgh3U

Zamora, R. G. (2007). El Programa Tres por Uno de remesas colectivas en Mexico: Lecciones y desafios. *Migraciones internacionales.* 4(1), 165–172.

11 Conclusion
Forces Shaping the Future

This book has been an attempt at synthesizing some of the existing research on remittances and also offering a new *lens* to look at remittances. This new perspective that uses both the individual, *micro level perspective* with that of the community or national level, *macro perspective*, can be particularly helpful as one seeks to understand how remittances impact communities, nation-states, and relationship between them.

Indeed, we have argued that remittances have the power to shape relations between communities and potentially nation-states, even if indirectly. President Trump's mention of remittances in the context of the border wall with Mexico showcases how important remittances have become when it comes to U.S.-Mexico relations. Prime Minister Modi's constant invoking of the Indian diaspora in the Gulf countries and in the U.S. during his visits speak to the crucial role that the diaspora (and their money) plays in the local politics in the receiving countries.

In the field of diplomacy, there has been much talk of 'citizen diplomacy,' and in the field of philanthropy, much has been written about strategic giving. Both these perspectives are useful as one seeks to understand how civil society groups, governments, and nonprofits seek to engage with these disparate entities, to bring them together, to solve problems of the commons. Issues such as the relationship between the two countries, development, education, etc.

In Chapter 1, we have argued that there is a need for crafting and sharing better *narratives* of remittances. While policy narratives have mostly focused on the securitization discourse—on how to make sure that the remittances are not being used for money laundering and financial terrorism—politicians have used remittances as a bogeyman to be taxed. In the most recent case, Mr. Trump has even proposed taxing remittances going out of the U.S. to Mexico, for the explicit purposes of using these taxes to build a border wall with Mexico.

The narratives of remittances can and should include perspectives of how migrants, return migrants, and policy makers see the role of remittances. Presently, the voices of the remitters are missing. We have made a modest attempt to incorporate their perspectives through interviews, participant observation, and by constructing theories of remittances using data from the ground, or in other words, creating 'mid-range' theories, as advocated by Robert Merton (Merton, 2007). We have sought to use an inductive approach to theorizing, going with minimal biases and perspectives of the phenomenon and iteratively using whatever data we gathered, to start the process of explanation building. Mid-range theories are used in sociological theorizing to guide empirical inquiry, Merton reminds us. "They lie between the day-to-day necessary hypotheses that evolve in abundance during the regular research and all-inclusive systematic efforts to develop a unified theory that explains all observed uniformities" (p. 448).

As we have pointed out, in the past, there have been regulations in place to prevent fraud and illegal activities and this has been the dominant model of governing remittances. The future may look different, as peer-to-peer transfer mechanisms are being explored and crypto remittances are becoming a reality. This means greater acceptance of cryptocurrencies and also more trust in these systems. This could mean friendlier regulations and more ease of doing business for both businesses as well as consumers, who would find these platforms cheaper and safer to transfer remittances.

We propose that with increased use of cryptocurrencies, there could be two alternate scenarios: governments around the world will work to develop protocols and regulations that will be friendly towards these new and emerging mechanisms of remittances or alternatively, adapt more restrictive means to control the use of cryptocurrencies. Examples from countries such as Venezuela, which is dealing with a financial crisis in the context of U.S. sanctions, is a good one, as it may show how governments try to adapt these technologies for their own good. Greater desire for control of this sector on behalf of governments may actually bring out more freedom and creative flourishing in how cryptocurrencies are used.

With remittances from the U.S. to Mexico increasing despite a drop in the number of migrants from Mexico, there are a few surprising findings in this space. India, a relatively young country, may continue to send migrants around the world. With this trend, there is likely to be a continued rise in the amount of remittances. Even with travel restrictions and fewer job opportunities for migrant workers from India and Mexico, we can anticipate a steady growth. As a recent report by the KNOMAD group at the World Bank points out,

> Remittance flows grew in all six regions, particularly in South Asia (12.3 percent) and Europe and Central Asia (11.2 percent). Growth was driven by a stronger economy and employment situation in the United States and a rebound in outward flows from some Gulf Cooperation Council (GCC) countries and the Russian Federation.
>
> (KNOMAD, 2019, brief 1, p. vii)

Globally, the costs of sending remittances remain high—at about 7% of the total cost—while for sub-Saharan Africa, it could be as high as 9%, the report points out. This may likely change with greater adoption of cryptocurrencies, etc. which will bring it down to almost zero.

Several macro-changes in the migration policies of various countries could impact how much remittances are being sent. For instance, there is likely to be a reduction in the number of South Asian workers in the GCC in the years to come, the KNOMAD report points out. The increased number of workers from South East Asia in Japan is another interesting development.

In Chapter 2 we pointed out the need for reexamining and synthesizing the various theories of remittances—with regards to motivations to send. While theories of decay point to the quantity of decrease of remittances over a period of time, there are not too many theoretical explanations of how remittances behavior is shaped. Our analysis of data and interviews conducted during this project point to the important role of 'communities of practice' and also the role of identities of individuals—as part of a collective. For instance, in the case of return migrants from Oaxaca, we saw the role of fiestas or community festivals and how key they are in the early socialization of these individuals in their pueblos. These fiestas remain important for these migrants and their families as they navigate their new lives as migrants.

For many of the migrants in the U.S. and North America, the fiestas remain a way of staying connected to their pueblos and also offer a way of maintaining their social relevance. Hence, their remittances play a key role in maintaining their ties. These are the 'ties that bind' the Oaxacans, even as they seek to build their lives thousands of miles away from their homeland.

Our interviews also revealed a similar dynamic with respect to many of the migrants from Kerala, who felt that their sense of belonging and group identity was kept intact with participation in the Onam festivities in the U.S. For others, it was also very important to be involved in mentoring and grooming young professionals, especially in the field of information technology, an area that many of them worked in. There are many migrants who may stop remitting after some time, as it "doesn't make sense to send money," as one interviewee pointed out (Interviewee 10). He pointed to the economic self-sufficiency of his immediate family and friends as reason not to remit money. There was an uptick in remittances to Kerala from the U.S. following the devastating flooding in 2018; this disaster-giving phenomenon has been well studied by scholars of philanthropy and the fact that remittances have gone towards the reconstruction and rebuilding of infrastructure is not too surprising. However, as some of the interviewees pointed out, there seems to be a lack of trust in how the government agencies spent the money, among many of the diaspora community members.

We are not sure if the money we sent last year was utilized properly. For instance, when I visited my home town earlier this year, I noticed that there was a lot of trash floating in the local river. I know from experience and also from reading about these issues that this can cause flooding.

(Interviewee 11)

In short, whereas there is a willingness to engage with the government and policy makers in India, among the diaspora there seems to be also some skepticism, as far as proper and 'strategic' use of money that is sent by the diaspora.

With the change in rules on H-1B visas, the most used category of visas by Indian professionals, and a preference to hire American workers, there could be a slowdown in remittances in the years to come. But for now, the phenomenon of remittances remains robust.

In Chapter 3, we saw the changing role of technology in remittances. One of the more significant changes has been the rise of mobile-based money transfer mechanisms as well as the move towards the use of cryptocurrency in remittances. The question of regulation is also on the minds of scholars, policy makers, and practitioners, in this context. To address this, George Harrap, the co-founder of Bitspark, one of the pioneers in crypto remittances, points out that even though remittances transfer via Bitcoin may take place using existing (meaning traditional) money transfer agents, who are regulated, the actual transfer between one agent and the other agent may not be regulated. So, there are parts of the process that are currently regulated, whereas some parts of it are not (Harrap, 2019). To remind us of the potential for use of technology, we must keep in mind that over 90% of the remittances transactions take place in cash. In addition, less than 30% of the global population has a bank account. Harrap points out that most of the innovation in this space is being driven by demand from countries such as India, China, the Philippines, Nigeria, and Vietnam. He advises others about the fallacy of assuming that a smart app is the solution to many for accessing money transfer agencies. Cash is still king, and remittance-sending firms are wise to remember that, he suggests.

Similarly, Hugo Cuevas-Mohr, one of the pioneers in the money transfer business, points to the tensions that this shift offers: the tension between the money transfer agents, who have been in the business for decades and have earned the trust of consumers, who remit billions of dollars around the world and the newer entrants such as Xoom, Transferwise, etc. and dozens of other phone-based apps. Cuevas-Mohr points out that this tension can cause some mis-information, some exaggerations, and some turf battles, which are not easy to overcome. He does point to a future that will include cryptocurrencies. As someone who is optimistic about the role of technology in remittances, he suggests that consumers and money transfer agents need to embrace new developments. While practitioners are leading the changes, governments around the world are struggling to catch up. This needs to change, he suggests, pointing to the need for greater collaboration between policy makers and implementers of technology.

When it comes to remittances and development, the match between the needs of remittance senders and the policies and programs seem to be limited. As we discuss in this chapter, there have been several initiatives, both in India and in Mexico, to incorporate remittances in national development. However, these measures have met with limited success. Whether it is Tres por Uno in Mexico or the Chief Minister's Fund for Development in Kerala, India, the devil seems to be in the details (Zamora, 2007; Interview 11). The focus on macro-economic development seems to not have worked; however, success in initiatives at the local level, for instance in Oaxaca, Mexico, seem to point to the need for more localized and customized campaigns, where migrants may feel more connected and are likely to contribute. This seems to work better at the local level.

In Chapter 4 we offered a quantitative approach of remittances, seeking to paint a vivid picture using numbers of the expanse of remittance giving and receiving. Using an objective, concrete, hard-numbers approach to recognizing the magnitude of remittances globally is a needed component to crafting a complete narrative to the remittance landscape.

Data draws heavily from World Bank reports and open-access data. These numbers are presented in a funnel style descriptive to first offer the worldwide view of low- to middle-income countries, aggregating all the countries' remittance data into a single number: $500 billion USD. This number represents the total amount of documented monies moving in the world for the impacts, influences, and perhaps even potential power of remittances. Note that this is the reported amount of remittances; we have discussed at length that there are numerous methods of money transfers that are not documented or reported. Though many countries (our focus nations of Mexico and India as well) have taken it upon themselves to create policies that require documentation by financial service organizations, there still exist multiple avenues that have no or next to no reporting mechanisms or oversights. The first, and potentially largest, of these being the hawala system of giving that offers a faith-based, tradition-steeped, and near anonymous way to give monies. It is estimated that through the Indian hawala system, there are at times upwards of 30% more remittances being transacted that are undocumented. And for a nation as vast as India, where total remittances are upwards of $78 billion USD, hawala is a huge number that may not be accounted for.

Within Chapter 4 we moved from the worldwide viewpoint to a regional lens, focusing the information on Latin America and the Caribbean and South Asia. We look primarily at these regions, as both Mexico and India are incorporated within these two categories. And as our book presents the combined micro and macro lensing into a continual discussion, it made sense to continue that narrowing of focus within this chapter. The quantitative data brings to light that there may be more reasons for increases and decreases in the flow of remittances. Although the numbers data cannot offer the answers to why or even at times how, we can surmise and postulate that are there economic, social, humanitarian, and political reasons that the inflow and outflow of remittances are at times higher or lower. For example, when migrants hear reports of natural disasters in their country of origin, and these reports make headline news, private money transfers for those years seem to have a spike. This can be gleaned through the quantitative data in the large upturn of inflow monies to India in 2018. However, combine that data with qualitative data from interviews conducted of persons in the southern India state of Kerala and we learn that the floods of 2018 brought about the need for more monetary assistance, requests for donations, and further opportunities for migrants to support their country of origin. These combined data points then lead us to further hypothesize that there are multiple reasons for the ebbs and flows of monies. All this is to say that remittances can be viewed by way of multiple lenses; however, the type of the data is also important to notate as well.

Looking further into the regions, it was found that South Asia has seen an increase of 12.3% in 2018 and Latin American and the Caribbean a 10% growth in 2018. Through forecasting measures from the World Bank, remittances are expected to continue to grow, though not at such a high level as in 2018.

Continuing on in this chapter we delve into an individual country or micro level, offering a richer way to interpret the information and more depth to our remittance narrative. First, we explored Mexico and then moved into our discussion surrounding India.

Mexico has internally taken it upon themselves to devote resources for tracking the inflows and outflows of remittances. Through the Center for Latin America Monetary Studies (CEMLA) we have been able to conduct interviews, read white papers, and have a fruitful discussion about remittances particular to Mexico. It was through these connections where we gained solid insight into the extent that Mexico uses its resources for understanding where monies are headed and where they originate. The U.S. is the largest contributor to Mexico.

In India, we learn and discuss that the country is experiencing huge turns in its economic growth and introducing areas of innovation to their markets. Although we do not link the quantitative data directly to these situational aspects of the country, we can surmise that the growths experienced in the Indian economy are also being seen in the growths of remittances.

Overall, this chapter is specific in its focus to offer a quantitative view of where the money is going and where it is coming from. We sought to specifically offer a worldwide, then regional, and finally specific country progression of information to assist the discussion of remittances globally.

Chapter 5 is a chapter built around policy, the determination of policy, and the public good that shaped or shapes policy. Public policy is simply defined as "government policies that affect the whole population" (Webster). And remittances are "a transmittal of money (as to a distant place)" (Webster). In this chapter, we combine these seemingly simple and straight-forward definitions to bring to light the multifaceted arena that is remittances. We explored the policy around remittances and giving, delving into humanitarian aid and its relationship to remittance giving, further looking at the modes available to remit monies in the context of Mexico and India. And then we discussed the multi-player environment that increases competition, offers variety, and further stimulates the need for governmental oversights. These oversights lead to the drafting, crafting, and passing of policies relating to remittances.

This chapter also lent the lens of what makes policy and how the public is impacted by policies. In the opening to this chapter, we sought to ground the discussion in the notion that at times there is an overlap between philanthropy and remittances, but we try to focus the discussion around motivation and identification surrounding remittances.

Looking at the case of Mexico, we offered a timeline approach of the major impact to remittances from a policy angle. And we sought to provide an understanding of the actors within the Mexican money transfer market. A major impact that we discussed was the relationship between the U.S. and Mexico and the joint policy ventures that were initiated during the second Bush's presidency. Primarily in 2001, Partnership for Prosperity, a private-public alliance, aimed to leverage the power of the private sector to develop and sustain an economically favorable environment in Mexico, whereby the goal was for Mexican citizens to not want to or have the need to migrate to the U.S. for better opportunities. As this was an example of a specific endeavor to change the migration rate of Mexican to the U.S., the impact on remittances was also taken into consideration as there would be a lowering of money transfers given the potential success of the program. Although there is no further data to support a link to success and lowering of remittance outflow from the U.S. to Mexico, this would be an interesting avenue for further research, given access to both U.S. and Mexican data. Additionally, in this chapter, we brought to light the discussion currently under President Trump's administration and briefly discussed the potential implications that the 2017 executive orders regarding border security have on remittances in Mexico.

This chapter also offered an understanding and appraisal of policies from India, again using a timeline approach to reviewing the policy. It is interesting to note that India as a whole does not have a standardized policy framework dealing with remittances. Although there have been numerous laws that impact and affect remittance giving, there is not a coherent remittance policy. However, given the large amounts of money flowing into India, if there was a remittance policy established, then used efficiently and effectively, it could yield many opportunities for alternative livelihoods and further economic development in India. In India there are multiple state-level policies that impact remittances with numerous actors playing a role in soliciting, collecting, processing, and distributing of remittances. All these actors have different roles and different levels of oversight. Banks are the typical place that one uses for remittances in India, followed by Money Transfer Operators such as Western Union. In India, it is the Ministry of Home Affairs that issues many regulations and acts as a clearinghouse for multiple organizations, especially related to nonprofits, at times dictating which international organizations are not allowed to be used as donors to Indian organizations.

Overall, in this chapter, we aimed to offer policy lensing that covered the actors, gave situational awareness to the environment, and delved into the multiple pushes and pulls from government oversight to the remittance landscape.

Chapter 6 looked at the discourse of remittances in policy as well as among migrants. We examine—through a purposive sampling—some of the major discourses around remittances in India and Mexico and categorized them into four distinct categories. Whereas mostly the receiving countries have a positive narrative around remittances and also policies that encourage and facilitate the reception of remittances, the sending countries seem to have some barriers built in the process. Whether it is the need for more documentation and specific identification requirements, or the call for taxing of remittances—such as Mr. Trump has done for building the border wall with Mexico—there is some aversion to the remittance phenomenon. Certain countries in the Gulf Cooperation Council (GCC) have called for taxing remittances at the point of sending them to create more revenues for the local governments. These proposals have not been implemented across the six GCC countries, though Kuwait came close with a draft bill. But the bill was scrapped earlier in 2019, with fears that this move could lead to an exodus of workers and the country could face a potential crisis with a shortage of workers (Goncalves, 2019).

Oman did consider a 2% tax on remittances and that was also scrapped in 2014 for similar reasons. The significant number of expats in the region—mostly from South Asia and South East Asia—have created a dependency on foreign labor that is not easy to replace. As Indian newspaper Economic Times reported recently, the Saudi Government is considering scrapping the newly imposed residency tax on foreigners, which it instituted about a year ago (Nereim, Algethami, & Shahine, 2019). As the article goes on to say,

> Announced in 2016 as part of a drive to increase non-oil government revenue—a key goal of Crown Prince Mohammed bin Salman's

economic transformation plan—the fees have been unpopular with business owners in a country accustomed to cheaper foreign labour.

The authors also point out that despite the commotion over the supposed benefits, the Saudi unemployment rate has not increased. The drop in oil revenues is one of the worries of the Saudi state, which has also gone on a rebranding campaign and has opened up its tourism sector, as part of its Vision 2030.

Even the local business communities have shown some resistance to these tax measures: the "Jeddah Chamber of Commerce and Industry (JCCI) has requested the Ministry of Labor and Social Development to cancel expat levy for firms that have an equal number of Saudis and expat workers on their rosters," according to Gulf News (Al Maeena, 2018).

The proposal on taxing expats was simple: for every expat employee, there would be a 400 SAR tax or 300 SAR depending on the size of the firm and number of expat workers that the firm has. The 100 SAR (about $25) per month per family member was initially set up as a mechanism to generate revenue for the Saudi state and was estimated to generate at least 1 billion SAR per year (Al Arabiya, 2017). This discourse that emanated from the government was part of its efforts to frame the Saudi narrative of remittances and flow of money.

Similarly in India, the government has been proactive in engaging the expat community, with an eye towards increasing its participation in nation-building.

Appeals for donations are sometimes very specific and originate for a specific purpose. For instance, during the flooding in Kerala, India in 2018, the Malayalee Associations in the U.S. went on overdrive to contribute funds and other forms of support to the Chief Minister's Distress Relief Fund. This fund, created by the state government of Kerala, brings together several entities—both government and private—to ensure that there is adequate communication and supply of life-saving aid as well as long-term development aid to the affected people. About 230 million rupees (about 3.23 million USD) have been collected through this fund as of December 2019. Several NGOs from India were also active in collecting funds during this process, stressing the need for help.

As we saw in this specific chapter and throughout the book, the securitization discourse has been prevalent and has negatively impacted remittances. While a halo of illegality is cast over hawala and other traditional forms of sending remittances, a similar perspective exists with regards to cryptocurrencies. With growing popularity and use, these newer forms of sending money may gain more legitimacy. However, this could turn out to be a long-term challenge.

In Chapter 7, we looked at India as a specific case—perhaps a paradigmatic case—of a receiving country. We have sought to place the examination of social remittances in India as a consequence of some of the policy decisions made by the decision makers. Whether it was the liberalization of Indian economy in the 1990s or the fluctuation of India's currency exchange, there have been multiple reasons for the ebb and flow of remittances to India. Regardless of the cause of fluctuations, what has remained constant is the desire among migrants to seek out opportunities in the U.S. and the GCC countries, primarily as a source of economic migration. The recent trends in 'Hire American,' 'Saudization,' and 'Emiratization' policies in the Gulf countries, which seek to replace foreign labor with a local labor force, is causing a rethink among Indian migrants in these countries. This is an ongoing situation in Saudi Arabia that has caused many thousands of Indians to leave the country. With a recent slew of laws targeting foreign workers, the Saudi government has imposed taxes and sought to make it difficult for companies to hire foreign workers. These measures have, both explicitly and implicitly, sought to replace Indian and other South Asian workers. We are already seeing the negative impact of these measures in India, with thousands of migrant workers returning home. What they do once they return to their home countries is anybody's guess. With a slowing economy in India and a historic level of unemployment, the situation in India is not all too welcoming.

The recent crackdown on non-governmental organizations in India and the shutdown of hundreds of them was done using the Foreign Contributions Regulation Act (FCRA). As media outlets in India point out, well-known international NGOs such as Greenpeace have had to drastically cut programming or even shut down altogether due to the government's crackdown on NGOs that work in the space of human rights or environmental justice (Dhara, 2019). The space for civil society action in India seems to be shrinking with the prime minister's initiatives in Kashmir and other parts of India receiving wide criticism both in India and abroad. The Indian diaspora is also protesting the National Registry of Citizens (NRC), a measure that they claim is set to discriminate and alienate the minorities in India. All these measures are likely to have a cumulative impact on remittances to India. How exactly this will play out remains to be seen.

Chapter 8 dealt with remittances from the Gulf nations. As one of the most significant sources of money flow, any change in the region is likely to have a domino effect on Indian diaspora. And there is plenty of change that is taking place. As we analyzed, there is a growing feeling in the region that expatriates working in host countries must pay more, by way of taxes. These calls for taxation have emerged in the context of falling oil prices, greater fear among Saudi, Kuwaiti, and Omani governments that more needs to be done to shore up revenues from non-oil sources. Millions of expatriates and their remittances are being seen as a reliable source of revenue. Narratives of migrant lives are being documented, such as the one by Jason LeParle's "A Good Provider Is One Who Leaves" that chronicles the life of a Filipino migrant to Saudi Arabia and then eventually to the U.S. (Munoz, 2019). The story of this one particular matriarch and her life exemplifies that of many such lives. Migrants leaving—legally—to work in countries where they are needed, are not always welcome. The details may vary, but the pattern remains the same: a migrant from a poor South Asian/South East Asian country, who has the necessary skill or education to do a job in a host country where there are not sufficient workers, fulfills a role. The pattern is of leaving one's family behind, for economic reasons but always providing what is needed for them. There are multiple contradictions in this story, as we have also pointed out. Although migrants leave to support their families, this move can also cause family breakdown at times.

The relationship of the Gulf nations with the rest of the world is complicated. None of the six GCC nations offer citizenship to migrant workers. While this dynamic creates a 'temporary worker' mindset, it also creates opportunities for many migrants to plan their next move—either to the U.S. or Canada.

Chapter 9 dealt with the notion of remittances as 'subaltern giving,' in which we argued that *remittances for development* can occupy a space in between pure philanthropy and pure consumption. The general understanding (and empirical evidence) points to a majority of remittances going towards consumption: food, shelter, education, or other immediate needs. However, when remittances are deployed for developing community-based organizations, such as MENA in Oaxaca, Mexico or towards community-based projects through churches or other faith-based organizations, there can be the possibility of this 'self-help' behaving more like 'philanthropy,' or acts of voluntary help towards others.

We argue in this conceptual chapter that there is a need for viewing remittances beyond the existing frameworks and this is an urgent need, as much of our existing theorizing is done through existing (and limited understanding of) remittances.

As we write about the decline of American soft power across the world, especially in Chapter 10, we must be cautious in our claims. Although this is not a book that relies on an empirical analysis of American power using data on American power, we have used an interdisciplinary lens to argue that remittances can be a lens to view and examine American power. While skeptics may point to American *hard power* and say this is unnecessary and irrelevant, we suggest that our line of reasoning is not entirely implausible. While money flows are a crucial part of U.S.-Mexico relations, the fact that Mexico receives about 2% of its GDP from remittances is not insignificant.

As Datta (2009) has pointed out, and scholars and pundits remind us almost on a daily basis, the cost of U.S. intervention in the world—on its own—is prohibitively expensive. The recently released 'Afghanistan papers' exposed a series of interviews totaling over 2,000 pages, with over 400 senior leaders of the U.S. military and diplomatic core. This stash of documents titled 'Lessons Learned' demonstrate that the U.S. had no clear strategy nor a direction in the war in Afghanistan (Whitlock, Shapiro, & Emamdjomeh, 2019). As the authors of the Afghanistan Papers point out, "Together, the interviews and the Rumsfeld memos reveal a secret, unvarnished history of the conflict and offer new insights into how three presidential administrations have failed for nearly two decades to deliver on their promises to end the war." Although this is a report on the state of American 'hard power,' it is also a commentary on how the 'soft power,' or the diplomatic and development arm of the U.S., worked (or didn't) in the country. While not entirely reflective of the dimensions of how American diplomacy works around the world, this set of documents and set of actions about them detail how the U.S. has failed to capitalize on its promise of building a safer world.

The war in Afghanistan, which continues as part of the 'war on terror,' is one of the costliest exercises of its kind and one that has not yielded any concrete results, the authors point out. And one is inclined to agree, just looking at the cost—both to the U.S. taxpayers as well as the cost of life, in terms of those service men and women and civilians who have laid their lives for this cause.

More painfully, both for the American public and policy makers, this new set of revelations point to the fact that the American officials made

> rosy pronouncements they knew to be false and hid unmistakable evidence the war had become unwinnable. Several of those interviewed described explicit efforts by the U.S. government to deliberately mislead the public and a culture of willful ignorance, where bad news and critiques were unwelcome.
>
> (Whitlock et al., 2019)

This searing critique of the U.S. efforts in Afghanistan to win the hearts and minds calls into question several strategies, not all related to 'hard power,' but to the nature of American 'soft power' as well. One is left to wonder how, if at all, the U.S. can build its credibility as a global power after such fiascos. With the presidency of Mr. Trump, which many analysts have argued is causing lasting damage to American credibility and legitimacy as a force for good, both American hard and soft power are being compromised. This new era is likely to be unlike another, and one can only imagine the important role that citizen diplomacy or exchanges between civil society groups are likely to play in this mix.

The Approach Taken in This Book, Limitations

The methodology used in this book has been largely iterative, given that much of this approach avoids the "pre definition of hypothesis but allows the researcher to construct an emerging story as the data is compiled" (p. 151) as Megan Stange explains when talking about the application of inductive approaches in policy work. We believe that this book is a first step towards synthesizing many of the approaches taken in studying remittances and can offer us both theoretical and conceptual guidelines on approaching this complex topic.

There are obvious limitations to what we have argued. The first being that we have used limited empirical data, mainly using what is relevant from the World Bank and interviews that we conducted in the four countries.

We have approached the question of 'Why study remittances?' and taken it in a slightly different direction than what most existing approaches do. We have problematized the notion of solidarity among diaspora communities, looked briefly at some of the policy contexts in each of the countries, and tried to offer a more nuanced perspective of the forces shaping this important phenomenon.

What the Future Holds for Remittances: A Quick Look at the Policy and Technological Developments

There have been some attempts at incorporating or involving remittances in the 'development' of a nation-state. Whether it is initiatives such as the Pravasi Bharatiya Divas in India or the Tres por Uno program in Mexico, there has been an attempt to tie these individual acts of giving towards one's kin to the nation-state. The merger of individual remittance with philanthropy is interesting. Even though most of these measures have met with limited success, there is reason to believe that cultural, political, and civil society organizations are heavily invested in these efforts, given the strong influence of the diaspora communities on the countries of origin. The rise of the Hindu right wing in India has been directly attributed to the financial and other forms of support of the diaspora. The success of their project points to this project progressing ahead.

What is going on in the field of remittances, both in praxis and in its regulation, is a moving away from individual action to a *collectivization* or *institutionalization* of this practice. While the individual act of remitting has been prevalent for centuries now, institutionalizing it and organizing it through community efforts—as in the case of diaspora groups—is the new phase of this collective action. The tensions lie in the way in which the institutions in charge—both governmental and private—deal with the various issues involving the transfer and monitoring of money.

As Philip Selznick points out in his book *The Moral Commonwealth*, individual actions should be seen in the context of institutions that shape them. Elaborating on the notion of values in institutions and the role of individual action in shaping the values of the whole institution, Selznick offers some insights that are relevant to our discussion. "Institutions endure because persons, groups or communities have a stake in their continued existence," he points out, offering examples of the Catholic church or any social practice that has endured (1992, p. 233). We can see how remittances have become an institutional form in many parts of the world, bringing together notions of family and communal, and, at times, national obligation.

As we have seen throughout the book, the Mexican or Indian diasporas are shaping the norms and values of remittance and building bridges between the sending and receiving nations. The formal 'organizations' such as diaspora associations seem to be defining how 'institutions' such as self-help groups and other collectives are to be run and what their objectives ought to be. One can see that gradual turn towards institutionalization of the space, with greater rational objectives being infused in the activity we call 'remittances.' These tensions are similar to what Peter Frumkin has pointed out, in discussing the 'expressive' elements of philanthropy versus the 'instrumental' purposes (Frumkin, 2006). A similar ideal lies at the heart of remittances as well, where civil society groups would like to help or assist in a specific manner, with certain desires or goals, while more organized entities such as governments may seek to influence the remittance process with a specific instrumental goal in mind—whether it is building of a school or repairing a damaged bridge after a flood.

Where This Book Can Lead: Next Steps or Future Research

One area where remittances have been utilized—but not much evaluation research exists on its effectiveness—is that of routing remittances towards development. We have touched upon this topic, using the lens of 'community development' at the local level, to argue for how it has worked, although at a limited extent.

At a scale, this idea of incorporating individual remittances for national level projects doesn't seem to have worked either in India or Mexico. One suggestion would be to look into the 'philanthropic prism' that Peter Frumkin has offered to design programs that meet the needs of the givers (Frumkin, 2006). Frumkin's model involves examining the five key elements that go into people's giving. As he says, "The prism could lurk behind the scenes and simply guide the structuring of fund-raising appeals" (p. 138). The prism can help to begin to compare, contrast, and better articulate the range of choices that donors confront. The five elements that form his prism include: logic model supporting giving, identity and style of giver, value produced through giving, vehicle or institution for giving, and timeframe guiding giving. While 'strategic giving' is an idea that has become prevalent in the West, this idea is only slowly taking hold in other parts of the world.

We believe there are areas of overlap between philanthropic studies and diaspora studies. How each discipline conceptualizes pro-social action has implications on how the other can be studied. We suggest that these overlaps be studied more carefully. We have taken a step in this direction and hope to continue our work in this space.

References

Al arabiya. (2017). *Saudi Arabia Introduces New Taxes for Expats*. Accessible at http://english.alarabiya.net/en/business/economy/2017/07/03/Saudi-Arabia-introduces-new-tax-for-expatriates.html. Retrieved on Dec 25, 2019.

Al Maeena, T. (2018). Saudi Arabia's expat tax conundrum. *Gulf News*. Accessible at https://gulfnews.com/opinion/op-eds/saudi-arabias-expat-tax-conundrum-1.2193754. Retrieved on Dec 25, 2019.

Datta, M. R. (2009). The decline of U.S. soft-power in the U.N. *International Studies Perspectives*, 10, 265–284.

Dhara, T. (2019). *Greenpeace to Halve Its Staff Amidst Crackdown from the Government*. Accessible at https://caravanmagazine.in/government/greenpeace-crackdown-halve-staff-operations. Retrieved on Dec 25, 2019.

Frumkin, P. (2006). *Strategic Giving*. Chicago: University of Chicago Press.

Goncalves, P. (2019). Kuwait to scrap 5% remittance tax. *International Investment News*. Accessible at www.internationalinvestment.net/news/4002040/kuwait-axes-expat-tax-remittance. Retrieved on Dec 24, 2019.

Interviewee 10. (2019). Kerala Malayalee Association. Washington, DC.

Interviewee 11. (2019). Kerala Malayalee Association. San Francisco, CA.

Harrap, G. (November 2019). Interview at IMTV. Miami.

KNOMAD. (2019). *Migration and Development, Brief 1*. Washington, DC: The World Bank.

Merton, R. (2007). *On Sociological Theories of the Mid-Range: Classical Sociological Theories*. Hoboken, MA: Blackwell Press.

Munoz, L. W. (2019). When providing for your family means leaving it behind. *The New York Times*. Accessible at www.nytimes.com/2019/08/20/books/review/a-good-provider-is-one-who-leaves-jason-deparle.html?searchResultPosition=5. Retrieved on Dec 25, 2019.

Nereim, V., Algethami, S., & Shahine, A. (2018). Saudi Arabia could revive the expat fee as the economy feels the sting. *Economic Times*. Accessible at //economictimes.indiatimes.com/articleshow/67015106.cms?utm_source=contentofinterest&utm_medium=text&utm_campaign=cppst. Retrieved on Dec 25, 2019.

Selznick, P. (1992). *The Moral Commonwealth: Social Theory and the Promise of Community*. Berkeley, CA: UC Berkeley Press.

Stange, M. T. (2016). *Policy Patrons: Philanthropy, Education Reform and the Politics of Influence*. Cambridge, MA: Harvard Education Press.

Whitlock, C., Shapiro, L., & Emamdjomeh, A. (2019). Afghanistan papers: A secret history of the war. *Washington Post*. Accessible at www.washingtonpost.com/graphics/2019/investigations/afghanistan-papers/documents-database/. Retrieved on Dec 24, 2019.

Zamora. (2007, Enero–Junio). El Programa Tres por Uno de remesas colectivas en Mexico. Lecciones y desafios. *Migraciones Internacionales*, 4(1).

Index

Note: Numbers in bold indicate a table. Numbers in italics indicate a figure or photograph.

Printed in the United States
by Baker & Taylor Publisher Services